Motorbooks International Illustrated Buyer's Guide Series

Illustrated

CLASSIC 4x4s

BUYER'S ★ GUIDE™

Jim Allen

First published in 1997 by Motorbooks International Publishers & Wholesalers, 729 Prospect Avenue, PO Box 1, Osceola, WI 54020-0001USA

Motorbooks International is a certified trademark, registered with the United States Patent Office

The information in this book is true and complete to the best of our knowledge. All recommendations are made without any guarantee on the part of the author or Publisher, who also disclaim any liability incurred in connection with the use of this data or specific details

We recognize that some words, model names and designations, for example, mentioned herein are the property of the trademark holder. We use them for identification purposes only. This is not an official publication

Motorbooks International books are also available at discounts in bulk quantity for industrial or sales-promotional use. For details write to Special Sales Manager at the Publisher's address

Library of Congress Cataloging-in-Publication Data Available

Allen, Jim.
    Illustrated classic 4x4 buyer's guide/ Jim Allen.
        p. cm. -- (Motorbooks
    International illustrated buyer's guide series)
    Includes bibliographical references and index.
     ISBN 0-7603-0340-1 (pbk. : alk. paper)
1. Four-wheel drive vehicles--Purchasing. I. Title. II. Series.
TL162. A45   1997
629.222--dc21   97-41447

On the front cover: With the success of the military trucks behind them, Dodge sought to capitalize on the reputation by building a postwar commercial 4x4. The name chosen for this rig was Power Wagon. This was not an entirely new name, having been used previously by Grabowsky in the early 1900s, but 50 years later, "Power Wagon" still inspires confidence born of many years of legendary service both on and off road.

On the back cover: The Stroppe is the Bronco collectors dream find. Jim Wright's is probably one of the best around and is very accurate. The exact production records are long gone, but it's likely that only several hundred Baja Broncos were built. *Jim Wright*

Printed in the United States of America

Contents

Acknowledgments

First and foremost, to my dearest Linda. She has made my dreams possible. This is only one.

To my brother, Ken, whose computer help saved my sanity and whose hard work and intelligence has been an inspiration.

To Lee Klancher of Motorbooks International. A chance phone meeting led to this book. His confidence in a magazine freelancer's idea and his help along the way contributed greatly to whatever good there is in this book.

To John Stewart, editor of *Four Wheeler* magazine, who opened the magazine archives to me and provided a great deal of encouragement.

To the enthusiasts along the way who shared their knowledge, photo collections, and valuable time. These are the real experts.

All Makes—Fred Crismon, John Monteville
American—Wayne Coffman
Chevrolet—Larry Kinsal (GM Media Archives)
Coleman—Glen Victor, Lyle Van Wert,
Dodge—Steve Arndt (Vintage Power Wagons), Dave Butler (Vintage Power Wagons), Bob Cherveney, Fred Coldwell, Steve Greenberg, Fred Potter, Brandt Rosenbush (Chrysler Historical)
Duplex—Bruce Rice, Jim Swinderman (Simon Duplex)
Ford—Colin Hutto, Fred Scharff, George Wright
FWD—Rick Goodell (FWD/Seagrave), Roy Thurston
IHC—Phil Coonrod (Coonrods), Mark Drake (Scout Madness), Kathy Kocinski (Navistar International), Greg Lennes (Navistar International), Chris Willsey, Cecil Winders
Jeep—George Baxter (Army Jeep Parts), Craig Brockhaus (FC Connection) , Art Carey, Don Chaffin, Fred Coldwell, Sam Denison (S&J Salvage), Ken Hart, Reg Hodgeson (Army Motors), Todd Paisley, Derek Redmond, Tony Standefer, Ron Szymanski (Jeep House Museum), John Vogelsang, Fred Williams, Randy Withrow (Alabama Center for Military History)
Marmon-Herrington—Don Chew, Frank Mantiglia (Chuck's Trucks), Bud Prouty, Fred Scharff
Mighty Mite—Daryl Bensinger (D&L Bensinger)
NAPCO—Lee Eidem, Butch Gehrig, David Paasch, Ken Reed
Nash Quad—Jim Dunn, Vincent McLaughlin, Bruce Rice
Nissan—Bill Garland (Nissan)
Oshkosh—Jean Anderson (Oshkosh)
Studebaker—Dennis Lambert (Newman & Altman), Lee Eidem, Richard Quinn
Toyota—Jeremy Barnes (Toyota), Marv Spector (Spector Off Road)
Unimog—Seth Kerzner
Walter—Phil Raeder (Walter)

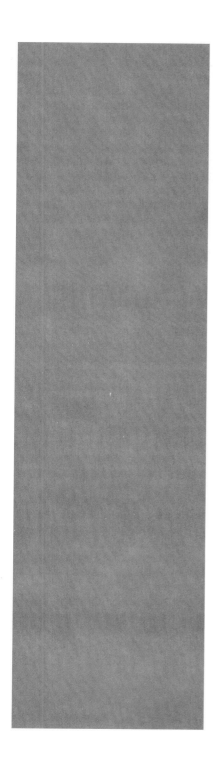

Introduction

The vintage 4x4 hobby is growing in popularity. Not so long ago, four-wheelers of the past were often used as the basis for built-up trail machines, with little regard for their historical significance. The growing trend is to lovingly restore them to original condition, or at least as close as possible, while adding a few modern features or conveniences. Being what they are, functional in the extreme, these old-timers can still be used on the trail as designed. What they lack in comfort, they make up for in raw ability.

At this writing, prices are still reasonable for most vintage 4x4s. Some vehicles, most notably older Land Rovers and early Ford Broncos, have already had a meteoric jump in price. Oddly enough, some of the oldest and rarest 4x4s are still very reasonable, though parts may be very difficult to obtain for some.

All in all, right now would appear to be the ideal time to jump into the collectable 4x4 arena. If you do, you'll want your eyes open and your brain firmly engaged in gear. That's where this book comes in.

The primary goal of this book is to educate. When you're through here, you'll have a basic understanding of the origins, history, technical details, and current status of the many 4x4s covered. The scope of the book is to illustrate the four-wheel drive vehicles, 1-ton capacity and smaller, that were built in, or imported to, the United States from about 1902 to about 1972. I'm not hedging when I say "about." In some cases, a model started production well inside these dates but continued well past. The International Harvester Scout, the Toyota Land Cruiser, and the Ford Bronco are three examples that I'll illustrate to the end of their production. The occasional 1 1/2 ton may be shown in a few cases also, usually to make a historical point.

Since the origins of four-wheel drive are rooted firmly in military history, you will note that many of the vintage rigs are of GI origin. These are among the most reasonable to buy and easiest to restore. NOS parts are often available and military vehicle clubs offer lots of help to the first-time restorer. Later rigs like Scouts, Jeeps, Broncos, trucks, etc. are also fairly easy to restore with lots of resources available.

When you get into more uncommon marques, like Marmon-Herrington/Fords, Colemans, and to a lesser extent NAPCO/Chevrolets, you may find them better suited to advanced restorers. Double ditto for the antique 4x4s. If you have experience restoring other types of very obscure vehicles, you may be well versed in the art of scrounging rare parts or rehabilitating a piece that can't be replaced.

Where possible, a complete listing of parts and information sources is included in the Appendix for each vehicle type. These will be up to date at the time of publication. Club listings are also included, as clubs can be the single most important resource to a vintage 4x4 restorer.

Specifications and evaluations are included for almost every type. The evaluations are based on current and period information and interviews with current owners, with the author's 20-plus years of 4x4 experience thrown in. Much of the older information was researched from sources listed in the bibliography. Some of the evaluations are admittedly subjective, but I'll stand by them until you prove me wrong. I'll welcome your opinions and corrections on any of the facts in this book.

Many of the photos in this volume illustrate vehicles in less than pristine condition. This is deliberate, and there are many reasons for it. The first is that there is something in the derelict vehicle that draws the eye to look and the mind to think, "What if?" So, instead of using only factory photos or restored rigs, I've thrown in a selection of real world trucks that have survived the years and abuse. In some cases, the trucks shown have aged gracefully. In others, they hang on by a thread but in every case you get to see the truck with all its battle scars. The 4x4 of old was built for work. Usually, this led to their demise at a young age. To have survived is, in itself, a badge of honor.

Finally, remember that the vast majority of restorations never leave the initial stages. In the heat of the moment, we bring home a needy truck and try to ignore our meager budget, home maintenance chores, overtime at work, the need for rest, and the obligations to our families. This is a death sentence to the project. There is more to life than old 4x4s. When you can balance the real part of your life with the restoration of an old 4x4 and get your family actively involved in the process, the project will be more fulfilling and enjoyable than you could ever have dreamed.

Jim Allen

Chapter 1

The Pioneers

The question of who was first with four-wheel drive in America is a hotly debated topic because the records conflict. It appears to be the Couple-Gear truck that was built as early as 1902 in some reports, or 1904 in others. Since the Couple-Gear was electric, with a motor at each wheel, and was designed for city use, it hardly qualifies as a *true* 4x4 by our current definition.

Next, we have the Cotta Four Wheel Drive, also in 1902. This chain-drive 4x4 system was designed by Charles Cotta, who later became a well-known transmission manufacturer, and was sold to a group of investors that began building four-wheel drive, four-wheel steer delivery wagons, and later a few touring cars. It is unclear just how many vehicles Cotta built under his own name.

A one-off 4x4 touring car was built in 1905 by one Charles Van Winkle in California. Apparently, a variation of his four-wheel drive system was eventually used in the Golden West trucks of 1913–1922 that were built in Sacramento. The American Motor Truck Company built a chain-drive, four-wheel drive, four-wheel steer truck starting in 1906, but it didn't have a steerable axle. Instead of pivoting at the ends, the entire axle pivoted in the center like a wagon. This design was similar in many respects to Cotta's.

The nod for the first viable 4x4 in America is a near tie between Duplex and the Badger Four Wheel Drive Auto Company (which later became the Four Wheel Drive Auto Company, or simply FWD). Both companies developed a four-wheel drive just a year apart. Most of Duplex's records were destroyed in a flood, but they get the nod with a working prototype at least as early as 1907, perhaps as early as 1906. It was 1908 before Badger got theirs up and running; Badger's four-wheel drive system, however, was most like the system we use today. Duplex started with a 3/4-ton 4x4 truck and Badger with a 4x4 Touring Car. Amazingly, both Duplex and FWD are still in business.

While some may argue who was first with what, history has recorded that many other 4x4 builders had viable ideas. In 1907 alone, some 700 patents were on file for a variety of four-wheel drive systems. While the efforts of the other companies must be acknowledged, to the most enduring go the spoils. Of the pioneers, this leaves Duplex, FWD, Oshkosh, and Walter. There is also a tenuous corporate connection between the Jefferey (later Nash) Quad and Jeep.

You may never have seen a truly vintage 4x4 but there are more around than you think and they are a collectable option. By today's

The first practical 4x4 was probably Charles Cotta's steam-powered, chain-drive 4x4 car of 1902. Few records exist about Cotta's 4x4 efforts, save this ad from a September 1, 1902, edition of the *Cycle and Automobile Trade Journal*. At least two ads appeared in 1902, but it is unknown how many cars were actually built. The line, "Secure the agency for the only four-wheel drive in the country," is noteworthy from a historical "who was first" standpoint.

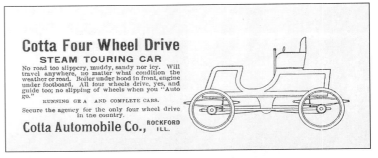

If you covet a Nash Quad but are intimidated by the scope of the restoration, Bruce Rice's 1919 is more than enough incentive to keep at it. It took about 2,000 man-hours to complete this ground-up resto, but Bruce reports that almost every minute was pure joy. Purchased in 1986, it took two years to put the truck into this show-winning condition. The truck was running and fairly complete when purchased. *Bruce Rice*

standards, they were pretty anemic performers, but in their era, they were regarded as nothing short of miraculous. In the early part of the century, less than one percent of our nation's roads were paved. This made for very tough traveling, and it provided the motivation for the development of four-wheel drive. In 1908, a trip by car to the in-laws in the next county could equal your most harrowing 4x4 trip of today.

Along the way, you will notice that the military also provided a great deal of incentive for the development of four-wheel drive technology. The U.S. Army bought their first 4x4 in 1912 and immediately recognized the benefits. The four-wheel drive truck was used in battle the first time by Americans in 1916, when the U.S. Army chased Pancho Villa around the Mexican desert. By the time the United States entered World War I, 4x4s were a common sight in army green and have stayed that way ever since.

This chapter will cover the most common of the early 4x4s. Many makes have sadly passed into oblivion but a goodly number remain to be discovered, restored, and given TLC from an admiring owner. Next time you see a really old truck, don't pass it by until you've looked underneath for a powered axle and a transfer case.

These antique 4x4s are definitely an advanced restoration. Many parts are unavailable and will have to be fabricated. Manuals and literature may be hard to locate. The enthusiast networks that can sustain the restorer of a more common rig are virtually nonexistent for the old-timers. Despite this, there is a small but growing movement in the antique 4x4s.

You will note that in this chapter we stray a bit from our light-duty guidelines. This is mostly because the light-duty 4x4 was an almost unheard of commodity in those early days. The market for such vehicles did not begin to expand until the late 1930s and World War II.

The Quad used a Buda Model HU four-cylinder. It displaced 312 ci with a 4.25x5.5-inch bore and stroke and produced 37 horsepower at 1,191 rpm. While some parts are still available, most early Buda parts must be fabricated.

Duplex

The Duplex Power Car Company of Charlotte, Michigan, started as early 1907 working on a prototype 3/4-ton 4x4 truck that looked more like the quintessential western "Buckboard" wagon than anything else. The standard Model B of 1909, powered by a 14-horsepower, two-cylinder engine, remained in production until 1915. Sometime between 1910 and 1913, Duplex had financial troubles and ceased production. A note in a May 1, 1913, *Motor World* business column noted that, "the manufacture of the trucks be taken up where it was broken off."

In 1915, a 3 1/2-ton truck was offered for sale. Shortly after, the company changed its name to the Duplex Truck Company and moved to Lansing, Michigan. This 1915 truck was apparently the first American 4x4 to use a dual range transfer case. The two-speed box had a direct speed and a 2-to-1 reduction. The Duplex truck also used locking differentials for extra traction. Early on, Duplex favored the style of four-wheel drive system later used by Jefferey and Walter, which featured a ring gear inside each wheel with a spur gear driving it. Later units used a more conventional differential and axle.

Duplex supplied a number of 4x4 trucks to the army in World War I, and right after the war announced their new two-ton "Limited." In 1920, a Duplex Limited set an endurance record at the Indianapolis Speedway. The stake-bed truck was loaded with 55 gallon barrels of fuel and ran 934 continuous miles at an average 38.96 miles per hour.

Through the 1920s, Duplex built a variety of trucks, from the 1-ton Model G, 1 1/2-ton GH, 2 1/2-ton AC, and the 3 1/2-ton Model E. In the 1930s, Duplex moved up in capacity, and gradually evolved into building extremely heavy-duty, large-capacity trucks and specialty chassis. This continued though the 1970s, when truck manufacturing tapered off. Duplex now builds fire apparatus for its parent company, Simon, as well as a variety of specialty truck chassis.

Early Duplex trucks are uncommon, but there are a handful of restored units. Diligent research, however, could not turn up an existing truck built before 1920.

Evolution of the U.S. Army's first 4x4. On the top, nicknamed the Scout Car, is the stripped down Touring Car as it left the FWD factory for the army late in 1911. Purchase price was a hair over $1,900. In the middle is the same vehicle after the addition of 42-inch tires, a cargo box, and 1,500 miles of mud. FWD driver Frank Dorn is behind the wheel, Capt A. E. Williams, the OIC (officer-in-charge) of the Army test, is to his right, and mechanic Jimmie Gaughan on the far right. Despite being built as a car, the FWD functioned as a 1 1/2-ton truck and carried 2,000 pounds of gear on the six-week expedition. On the bottom is the Scout Car at its final posting, with an Army Signal Corps unit near San Diego, California. *FWD-Seagrave, U.S. Army*

FWD

The FWD dynasty began in 1906 inside the fertile minds of two Wisconsin machinists. Otto Zachow and William Besserdich were partners in a machine shop operation in Clintonville and decided to branch out from steam engine, boiler, and sawmill repairs into the fledgling car industry. Their first goals were modest. They simply wanted to become the area's first car dealers and mechanics. In order to "learn the ropes," they purchased a 1906 Reo.

The fall, winter, and spring of 1906 and 1907 gave Zachow and Besserdich a big lesson in car ownership. Even in good weather, the poor roads could make a trip out of town an expedition. As fall descended and the ground got soft, the Reo was even more often stranded axle-deep in Wisconsin goo. As time progressed, the pair got pretty good at recovering the Reo but neither of them were happy about it.

Built from 1917-1922, the Twin Cities Four-Wheel Drive trucks were based on designs executed earlier by J.L. Ware. Versions of these trucks were marketed from 1912-1915 under the Ware badge. This 3-ton Twin Cities model used a 45hp L-head engine and a 3-speed transmission What was most unusual about the Twin Cities trucks was Ware's unique drive system. The transmission fed power to a single differential mounted in the rear. Two auxiliary gears took power from the single ring gear and ran power up to a pair of spur and ring gears, one on each side. A double yoke universal joint allowed the wheel to steer. Axle ratios were 8.5-1 and allowed the Twin Cities a 15 mph top speed. The trucks used 36x7 Artillery wheels. They wieghed in at 5,500 pounds and had a 120 inch wheelbase.

They learned right off that it was always the rear driving wheels that spun and mired. One of the easiest methods of recovery they learned was to apply torque to the unmired front wheels by using the spokes as levers. By the time the legendary Wisconsin snowfall came, it was all to no avail. The poor Reo and its fledgling drivers were totally outmatched. The trials and tribulations finally prompted Zachow to comment, "Who is it who ever heard of a mule walkin' on just two legs?"

Zachow was an inquisitive man and one whose curiosity was not satisfied by a few random thoughts on a problem. Once he read an issue of *Scientific American* that detailed European tries at harnessing four-wheel drive, he and Besserdich devoted every waking moment to the idea. In less than a year, they had designed a four-wheel drive system and by 1908, the patents had been approved. Soon after, the Zachow/Besserdich Machine Shop rang with the sounds of Otto and Bill building their first car.

On October 2, 1908, the car emerged for tests. It was steam powered with full-time four-wheel drive and a steerable front driving axle. The front axle was the major technical difficulty that had plagued all inventors. Variations of Zachow's ball and socket idea had been tried before without success. The difference was the 1/32-inch clearance Zachow allowed for movement.

Early on, FWD offered a 3-ton model B and a 1-1/2 ton Model G. An early Model B is shown on the left and two Model Gs on the right. Only one early Model G is known to have survived and it's housed in the FWD museum. The early trucks, from 1912 to the later part of 1916, used these one-piece radiators. The later trucks, starting with the military models, used a three-piece, bolted radiator. *FWD-Seagrave*

If you want to send the author into a fit of jealousy, find one of the standard production FWD Touring Cars like this one, built for August Matuzsak in 1911. Of the known sales, four stayed in Wisconsin, one was shipped to Colorado, two went to Chicago—one to Lincoln Park and another to the Pinkerton Detective Agency. One, of course, became the U.S. Army's first 4x4. *FWD-Seagrave*

The 4x4 tasted combat the first time in American hands in the 1916–1917 Punitive Expedition into Mexico. A Model B water truck is shown with two grizzled desert rats. Since the Army was almost devoid of motor vehicle experience, the manufacturers supplied drivers and mechanics for the duration of the hostilities. The cigar-smoking driver was no doubt hired by FWD to drive the truck for considerably more pay than the 1903 Springfield-toting GI. FWDs and Jefferey Quads comprised the vast majority of the 4x4s used in this conflict. *FWD-Seagrave*

Good numbers of FWD Model Bs have survived, like this 1918 ex-army rig built under license by Premier and now owned by Ralph and Chester Hicks of Evergreen, Colorado. This was a choice find, as the truck had been in storage for 30 years, and was complete, when the brothers purchased it in 1986. A coat of paint, a little magneto work, some upholstery and the truck was fully operational. The Hicks boys removed its flatbed to show off the unique four-wheel drive hardware.

"Car" may be stretching the term a bit for this first 4x4. It was a powered chassis with a dry goods box for a seat. Still, the machine later proved that the concept was sound. It could drive places where horses and people were barely able to walk. The four-wheel drive worked as well as predicted, but the steam engine proved to be a problem. A gasoline engine was ordered, and the pair set to work repowering the machine.

Sometime early in 1909, the new car was completed with a Continental engine and a stunning, maroon colored touring car body. After a few vigorous test drives, it earned the name "Battleship" because nothing could stop it. With financial backing from local businessmen, leadership from attorney W. A. Olen (later to become the longtime CEO and largely responsible for FWD's success) and technical savvy from the two machinists, the Badger Four Wheel Drive Auto Company was formed. In 1910, it was reorganized into the Four Wheel Drive Auto Company, later simply FWD.

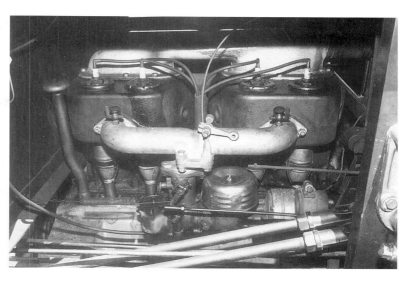

The Battleship became a sales tool for a line of FWD touring cars. It was driven to fairs and demonstrated all over Wisconsin. A standing $1,000 prize was offered to any car that could follow the Battleship for 15 minutes across rough ground. In 1910 alone, 116 cars tried—none collected. In more than three years and 12,000 miles, hundreds of the best automobiles of the era tried—and failed. The Battleship never lost and never had to be towed.

In 1912, after less than a dozen cars were built, FWD's focus turned to trucks. After learning of a U.S. Army-sponsored cross-country competition, one of FWD's touring cars was hastily modified into a 1 1/2-ton truck and sold to the army for $1,900. Known as the Scout Car, this "truck" successfully outperformed three of the best 1 1/2-ton trucks of the day in a 1,500-mile, six-week marathon from Washington, D.C., to Fort Benjamin Harrison, Indiana. Eventually, FWD's focus shifted completely to the more lucrative 4x4 truck market.

At the time of the 1912 army tests, there were 25,000 trucks in the United States. The army owned a total of 12. Later in 1912, a bigger army test was announced and this time FWD was ready with "real" trucks, their 1 1/2-ton Model G and 3-ton Model B. The new test pitted trucks against mules in a 250-mile march from Dubuque, Iowa, to Sparta, Wisconsin. In addition to the new Model B and Model G, the army used the old Scout Car, the 1 1/2-ton White, and the Sampson from the previous test, and rented eight other trucks, a Kelley-Springfield, a Mack, a Kato four-wheel drive, a 3-ton White, a Packard, a Saurer, a Graham, and a Velie.

Ultimately, the FWD, the White, and the Mack earned high marks. The Sampson (again) and the Kelley-Springfield were withdrawn due to mechanical failures and, oddly, the Kato 4x4 earned the comment, "The Kato, though four-wheel drive, did not prove satisfactory because the power was not properly applied."

The Model B 386-cid Wisconsin four-cylinder makes about 55 brake horsepower at 1,300 rpm. Oddly enough, this powerful engine with its cross-flow T-head and dual cams was also fitted to the Stutz Bearcat and the Mercer Runabout. Before long, Model B engines became popular for the olden day hotrodders to scavenge, and many FWDs are found sans engine.

Pioneers That Passed Into History

Most of the 4x4 pioneers have passed on. Many built only a few vehicles or stayed in business for just a short time. Their names deserve to be remembered. Besides, you never know what you might find out in a barn somewhere.

American Motor Truck Company—1906–1912
Detroit, Michigan

Avery Company—1910–1923 (4x4 1910)
Peoria, Illinois

Beech Creek Truck and Auto Company—
1915–1917
Beech Creek, Pennsylvania

Biederman Motors Corporation—1920–1955
Cincinnati, Ohio

James Boyd & Brother, Inc.—1908–1916
(1916 4x4)
Philadelphia, Pennsylvania

Bull Dog Motor Truck Company—1924–1925
Galena, Illinois

Clyde Motor Truck Company—1916–1938
Clyde, Ohio

American Coleman Company—1925–1986
Littleton, Colorado

Bollstrom Motors Inc.—1920–1921
St Louis, Michigan

Columbia Automobile Company—1899–1907
(1906 4x4)
Hartford, Connecticut

Couple Gear Freight Wheel Company—
1904–1922
Grand Rapids, Michigan

Double Drive Truck Company—
Chicago, Illinois 1918–1921
Benton Harbor, Michigan 1922–1930

Four Traction Auto Company ("Kato")—
1908–1913
Mankato, Minnesota

Four Wheel Drive Wagon Company—
1904–1907 (not FWD)
Milwaukee, Wisconsin

Freeman Motor Car Company—1928–1931
Detroit, Michigan

Golden West Motors Company—1913–1922
Sacramento, California

Hoadly Brothers—1915–1916
Gosport, Indiana

Jackson Motor Car Company—1907–1923
(1921 4x4)
Jackson, Michigan

Jarrett Motor & Finance Company—
1917–1934 (1934 4x4)
Colorado Springs, Colorado

Livingood Motor Truck Company—
1916–1920
Des Moines, Iowa

Markey Manufacturing Company—1912
Mt. Clemens, Michigan

Militor Corporation—1917–1918
Jersey City, New Jersey

Morton Truck and Tractor Company—
1912–1916
Harrisburg, Pennsylvania

Murty Brothers—1952–1965
Portland, Oregon

Nevada Truck & Tractor Company—
1914–1915
Nevada, Iowa

Quadru—1911
Michigan

Rogers Una-Drive Motor Truck Corporation—
1919–1922
Sunnyvale, California

Twin Cities Four Wheel Drive Company—
1917–1922
St. Paul, Minnesota

Ware Motor Vehicle Company—1912–1915
St. Paul, Minnesota

Weier-Smith Truck Company—1914–1919
Birmingham, Michigan

Winther Motor Truck Company (Winther-Mar
win)—1918–1927
Kenosha, Wisconsin

The Model B became FWD's mainstay, and during World War I, more than 16,000 were built. Some were manufactured under license by the Kissel Motor Corporation, Premier Motor Corporation, and the Mitchell Motor Car Company. The license-built trucks are easily identified by an extra data plate. The Model B was such a success that they were built into the 1930s and a wide variety of kits were made available, such as pneumatic tires, electric start, enclosed cabs, and higher gearing, to bring the old units into modern times.

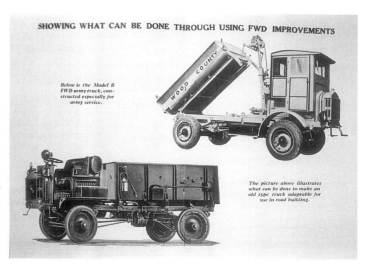

SHOWING WHAT CAN BE DONE THROUGH USING FWD IMPROVEMENTS

Below is the Model B FWD army truck, constructed especially for army service.

The picture above illustrates what can be done to make an old type truck adaptable for use in road building.

Of FWD's earliest vehicles, only two of FWD's touring cars have survived, but several hundred Models Bs exist, making them the most easily found and restored antique 4x4. With a long production run, parts are still fairly easily found. Until just 15 years ago, Model B parts were still in FWD's inventory. NOS parts can still be located on dusty shelves and a small network of owners exists to help each other over the tough times.

FWD remains in business in Clintonville, Wisconsin, though their focus has turned to building the Seagrave fire truck.

Jefferey/Nash Quad

The Jefferey Quad 4x4 appeared in 1913, when a pilot model was built for the army to test. The Thomas B. Jefferey Company had been building trucks and cars (the cars formerly under the Rambler nameplate) to that time but no 4x4s. The prototype 4x4 truck was a success and in 1914, Jefferey went into full production with the Quad and built between 3,096 and 5,500 units between 1913 and the end of 1914. Many of these trucks went into military service all over the world. Some were used to set an altitude record in the Andes, hauling ore 75 miles from 15,000 feet to sea level. Some participated in the 1916–1917 Punitive Expedition into Mexico alongside FWDs.

As World War I fireballed, the French and Russians bought large numbers of Jefferey Quads. The demand was great enough that a deal was worked so three other factories, Hudson, National, and Paige-Detroit, built Quads under license through the end of the war. These trucks can be identified by plaques attached to the dash and are virtually identical to the Jefferey units.

In 1916, after surviving the sinking of the Lusitania, Charles Jefferey had a change of life direction and sold his interests in the Jefferey company to Charles Nash. In late 1916, the Quad became a Nash. Nash continued with the Quad through the war and debuted a two-wheel steer model. Sales were brisk. After the war, sales slowed to a more modest pace until they trickled to an average of about a hundred per year by the time Nash stopped producing Quads in 1928.

A maximum of 14,000 Quads were built under the Jefferey nameplate and most of these went overseas. About 23,000 Quads were built under the Nash badge. The Jefferey Quads are the rarest. The earliest Quads had a small Jefferey emblem on the radiator shell, through about 1915. The earliest Nash models, 1916 to early or middle 1917, can be identified by the name cast in the radiator, which says simply "Quad." The later units say "Nash-Quad."

Don't be surprised or dismayed to find a Model B, or any other antique truck, with a lot of upgrades. Immediately after the war, the federal government gave away large numbers of military trucks to state agencies and local municipalities. Often, these rigs were their first motorized equipment. It also took a big bite out of motor truck sales. In those lean years of the 1920s, FWD concentrated on building and selling upgrades for the Model B and was able to make the basic design last well into the 1940s. This illustration comes from a booklet entitled, "List of Improvements for Your FWD Trucks," dated 1929 and identified as the third edition. Inside is a variety of equipment from pneumatic tires to downdraft carbs and manifolds for increased horsepower. None of the improvements, you may find, detract at all from the value or enjoyment of an antique 4x4.

Three Nash models were commonly seen, the Model 4017A, 4017L, and the 4017F. The A and L models are very similar four-wheel steer models, differing only in that the L has acetylene lamps and an impulse starter and the A has electric lamps, a battery, and generator. The F variant is similar to the L except it is front-wheel steer only. In many situations, such as pulling away from a curb, the four-wheel steer units were regarded as a problem. Many drivers, however, overlooked the fact that the rear steering could be disabled with a few adjustments. A long wheelbase variant was also offered.

There are about 20–25 Quads in the hands of U.S. restorers who are networking. If you count all the Quads lying in the weeds, there may easily be more than double that. Certain engine parts for the four-cylinder Buda engine are still available and a small supply of NOS parts can occasionally be found. For the most part, though, you're on your own. Most of the known remaining Quads are Nash models, and many of them ex-military or post-war models. The very late Quads—1920–1928—are extremely rare.

Oshkosh

The history of Oshkosh is tied very closely to FWD. Besides sharing the state of Wisconsin, they each share a founder. William Besserdich's contribution to the development of FWD was pivotal, but in the early lean years, he had grown increasingly restless. In 1913, he left with another FWD stockholder, Bernard Mosling, after disputes over patent rights and decided to set up his own company. Initially, it was called the Wisconsin Duplex Company and the first steps were taken in Besserdich's home in Clintonville.

After getting patents for various pieces of hardware, the first truck, later nicknamed "Old Betsy," was built in a Milwaukee machine shop. Later the company was moved to Oshkosh, Wisconsin. Late in 1917, the name was changed to Oshkosh Motor Truck Manufacturing in honor of the town that gave them a home.

Besserdich and Mosling put their FWD experience to good use by building the Oshkosh Model A in 1918. The 1-ton Model A, featuring some advanced items like pneumatic tires and an automatic-locking center differential, showed its "FWD-like" roots. In the post-World War I era, with the government giving away surplus military trucks to state and local agencies, sales were slow for Oshkosh and other truck companies. Oshkosh persevered and found a niche in the really big truck market that it still holds today. Their first truck, Old Betsy, survives in running condition.

Only a few, perhaps as few as 50 of the earliest trucks, are under 1-ton capacity. This author could find no existing Oshkosh trucks prior to 1925, other than Old Betsy.

Walter

Walter is truly one of the earliest pioneers in the automo-

We strayed a bit from our light-duty focus in the early years, but here's a rare light-duty FWD Model LD that was built from 1949–1954. The truck could be ordered in 1 and 1 1/2-ton capacities and with a variety of configurations that included this pickup. The LD was the first FWD that was not built almost completely out of FWD-built components. The engine was a 236-cid, 97-horsepower six. The four-pinion axles were Timken and four- or five-speed transmissions were available. The LD is a heavy-duty truck wearing a light-duty disguise. *FWD Corporation*

Model	Years Built	Units Produced
FWD Model B	1912–1925	26–30,000†
Jefferey/Nash Quad	1913–1928	11–20,000††

†Extrapolated from available 1912–1923 figures
††Estimates from 1917–1920 serial numbers, 1920–1928 total Nash truck production figures, and unconfirmed Jefferey truck production figures 1913–1917.

SPECIFICATIONS

FWD MODEL B (TYPICAL)

Engine:
Type- 4-cyl, T-head Wisconsin
Displacement- 389.841cid
Power- 55bhp @ 1,300rpm
B&S- 4.75x5.5in

Transmission:
Type- 3-speed constant mesh, Cotta
Ratios- 1=4:1, 2=2:1, 3=1:1, R=4.13:1

Transfer Case:
Type- Single-speed, Morse chain drive, full-time
4wd, lockable center diff.
Ratio- 2:1 reduction

Axles:
Rear type- Full-floating, spur and pinion differential
Front type- Full-floating, spur and pinion differential
Ratios- 4.31:1

Tires:
Type- Solid rubber
Size- 36x6

Dimensions & Capacities:
LxWxH- 213x70.5x92in (without body or top)
Wheelbase- 124in
Curb weight- 7,308lbs
Fuel capacity- 30gal

NASH QUAD (TYPICAL)

Engine:
Type- 4-cyl, L-Head, Buda H-U
Displacement- 312.3cid
Power- 37bhp @ 1,191rpm
B&S- 4.25x5.5in

Transmission:
Type- 4-speed constant mesh
Ratios- 1=6.10:1, 2=3.55:1, 3=2.02:1, 4= 1.22:1
R=6. 46:1

Transfer Case:
Type- Single-speed, Morse chain drive,
Ratio- 1:1

Axles:
Rear type- Solid axle w/spiral gear, M&S locking differential
Front type- Solid axle w/spiral gear, M&S locking differential
Ratios- 6.95:1:1

Tires:
Type- Solid rubber
Size- 36x6

Dimensions & Capacities:
LxWxH- 205.5x78.5x91in (without body or top)
Wheelbase- 124in
Curb weight- 6,700lbs
Fuel capacity- 27gal

The American was one of the earliest four-wheelers. American started in business in about 1906, and by 1911 advertised 1, 2, 3, 5, and 10-ton models. This vehicle, a 1 ton, is quite unlike any of the production vehicles and was probably a prototype. It was owned by the chief designer and company founder, Charles Hider. The vehicle is currently owned by Wayne Coffman of Tiffin, Ohio, and is in running condition.
Wayne Coffman

The Freeman four-wheel drive truck debuted in 1928 and died in 1931. Though Frank Freeman built his first truck in 1923, the articles of incorporation were not filed until 1924 and the company's first trucks were built in 1928. These were very advanced trucks for the day, coming standard with pneumatic tires, powerful six-cylinder Buda engines and air suspension up front. Bevel-gear differentials were used front and rear. A four-speed Fuller main transmission was coupled to a Freeman two-speed transfer case with a 2.65-to-1 low-range. Six models were offered, including these 3-yard dump trucks, but the stock market crash took the wind out of Freeman's sails after only a small number of trucks were built.

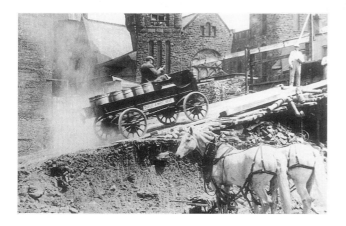

In an obviously staged shot, a Duplex Model B hauls a load up a ramp into what looks like a castle, much to the chagrin (or relief) of the team of horses in the foreground. No captions exist for this photo, but the area looks suspiciously European. *Simon-Duplex*

The Duplex Model B of 1909 was most likely the first viable American 4x4. The Model B was built until 1915. It featured a 14-horsepower, two-cylinder engine that mounted under the seat, a spur and ring gear drive system at the wheels, and a differential mounted above a solid beam axle. It is unclear whether the vehicle depicted is the prototype or a production Model B. *Simon-Duplex*

This is Oshkosh's first 4x4 truck, known today as "Old Betsy." The 1-ton prototype stakebed was built in Milwaukee, while the company was still operating under the Wisconsin Duplex nameplate. One of the most important aspects of the Oshkosh trucks was that they were an early advocate of pneumatic tires. Betsy was shod with 32x4 Firestones, and the trend followed with later trucks. Betsy was fitted with a four-cylinder LeRoi engine that made about 35 horsepower. It used a three-speed transmission with a single speed transfer case that had the first version of the Oshkosh patented automatic locking center differential. Old Betsy is maintained by Oshkosh in running condition.

bile and truck industries. Founded by William Walter, a Swiss immigrant, the company began as the Walter Automobile Company, which had its first cars built at the American Chocolate Company factory in Manhattan. Walter's first car was built around 1898, but sales did not begin until about 1902, in the form of the "Waltmobile." The next year the first Walter car appeared, and by 1905, 300 cars a year were rolling off the line. Most of them were sold in the New York metropolitan area.

By 1909, the Walter Automobile Company had gone belly-up. Realizing the burgeoning truck market offered great opportunity, Walter branched out and formed the Walter Auto Truck Manufacturing Company in New York City. By 1911, the company was offering a four-wheel drive truck that was based loosely on the French Latil 4x4, using a spur and ring gear drive similar to the Nash Quad and other period rigs.

Walter 4x4 trucks served in World War I in small numbers but earned a good reputation there. After 1919, Walter ceased building its own 50-horsepower, four-cylinder engines and began using Waukesha powerplants. By 1923, the factory had moved from "the city" to Long Island. Walker prospered building highway tractors as big as 15-ton capacity. While their earliest 4x4 trucks had been as small as 1 1/2 tons, by the 1920s, Walter's smallest was a 3 ton.

Walter stayed a heavy hitter in the truck business and built its famous "Snow Fighter" snowplow special in 1929. The company also branched out into building fire appliances. World War II brought more prosperity, and Walter built large numbers of snowplows and huge artillery prime movers. After the war, Walter focused on the development of airport fire trucks and has made itself a fine reputation to this day building crash trucks and airport snowplows, as well as a variety of specialty chassis.

Walter trucks prior to 1920 are almost impossible to find. Only a couple of examples have surfaced, in whole or part. Virtually everything you'll see wearing the proud Walter name will be big stuff.

The Oshkosh Model A, debuted in 1918, was the company's first production truck. Rated as a 2-ton truck, it was powered by the innovative Herschell-Spillman engine. This four-cylinder made a respectable 72 horsepower by preheating the gasoline three times before combustion. This apparently got the most out of the low-octane fuel of the period. The engine was backed up by a Model 35 Brown-Lipe four-speed and the Oshkosh transfer case with automatic locking center differential. Goodyear 36x5 Diamond Tread tires were fitted as well as electric start, electric lights and a speedometer. This truck sold for about $3,500.

Chapter 2

The Four-Wheel Drive Conversions

In the early days, the commercial market for four-wheel drive trucks was small. Most of the demand, with just a couple of exceptions, was for larger capacity trucks and from companies that could afford the extra cost and complexity. Some of that limited market was serviced by companies that converted 4x2 trucks into 4x4s.

Into the mid-1930s, the light-duty 4x4 essentially did not exist. The average Joe who needed a light-duty truck generally made do with a conventional 4x2. There had always been a small market for light-duty 4x4s with construction outfits, surveyors and, of course, the military, but the expense of building (and buying) them had deterred any major development.

The cost breakthrough came in the mid-30s with the advent of the light-duty 4x4 conversion, and the market grew until the beginning of World War II. After the war, the market showed signs that it would continue to grow, and companies like Dodge and Jeep built light-duty rigs in-house. For about a decade, the conversion companies profitably filled the gaps between the factory-built offerings and needs of the market, but gradually the mainline light-duty truck manufacturers found enough business incentive to start building 4x4s in-house. By the late 1950s, the heyday of the light-duty conversion companies was over. After a frenzy of cost-cutting and back room deals, most of them faded into obscurity.

American Coleman Company

G. L. Coleman started in the truck business in 1922, but didn't start manufacturing trucks until 1925. Located in Littleton, Colorado, Coleman based its all-wheel drive truck on a steerable front axle design by the company's design engineer, Harley Holmes. Through the 1920s, 1930s, and most of the 1940s, Coleman built a business in the big truck lines, 2 ton and larger.

After World War II, Coleman began dabbling in the conversion market and put together light-duty 4x4 conversions of Chevrolet, Ford, GMC, and Dodge trucks. A massive labor dispute from 1949–1950 nearly put the company out of business, but they bounced back and continued converting a variety of light, medium, and heavy-duty trucks. By 1956, however, the prospects in this market began to dim, and they discontinued any large-scale conversion efforts. The latest Coleman light-duty conversions to be found are 1956 model trucks.

An essential part of the conversion was the Holmes-designed Coleman front axle. The Coleman axle was probably a bit overbuilt for light-

This 1953 Chevy 3/4-ton Coleman conversion is one of just a few survivors from that era. Built and used during the uranium boom of the 1950s, this truck was used as a seismograph carrying vehicle around Moab, Utah. Glenn Victor has owned the truck since the mid-1960s. The truck is powered by its original 235 six and sports a 125-inch wheelbase. The Coleman transfer case failed many years ago and the truck was converted to a 4x2, awaiting a replacement.

duty applications, and it was also a complicated design. Repairs on these axles is not particularly easy for the unenlightened. A variation of a Spicer transfer case, called the T-32, was used for the smaller trucks. Coleman essentially went out of the truck business in the late 1960s and shut the doors completely in 1986, complicating the acquisition of repair parts.

The Colemans are an interesting truck with historical significance but because they are not well-known, they are far from being on the "hot" list for 4x4 collectors. In some cases, ailing Coleman front axles have been swapped out and once this is done, there is very little to mark them from any other early truck. The very earliest conversions (mid-1940s) used Coleman badging, though one expert who has reproduced these badges has found evidence that only the first 50 trucks were so equipped. The only real way to identify a Coleman quickly is by the distinctive "half-moon" front hub. The conversion also raised the truck significantly higher than stock.

It's doubtful that the Coleman conversions will ever reach "classic" 4x4 status, but the right truck at the right price could be an interesting and unique collectable. The collector/enthusiast network essentially does not exist for these trucks so this is not a first-timer's ideal choice.

This 1956 Dodge is a Coleman conversion and is among the last light-duty Colemans built. Parts failure caused the original owner to swap out the Coleman front axle for a Dodge 44F. The new owner, Lyle VanWert of Freeland, Michigan, managed to get the old axle along with the truck, and he plans to rebuild and reinstall it. This C3-B8-108 1/2 ton is powered by the original 259-cid V8.

J. L. Livingood Company

Probably the earliest convertor was the J. L. Livingood Company, of New Virginia, Iowa. Jesse Livingood started fooling around with four-wheel drive in about 1914 and developed a four-wheel drive conversion for Ford Model Ts and Chevrolets. In 1916, Livingood started the Livingood Motor Truck Company in Oceola, Iowa, and built an undetermined number of chain-drive, four-wheel drive, four-wheel steer trucks of about 1 1/2-ton capacity. That company lasted for about two years.

In 1936, Marmon-Herrington lit the fires of the light-duty 4x4 revolution when they converted this 1/2-ton Ford for the Belgian government. Tested at the King Ranch in Texas, it was quickly learned that this truck had no equal in the dirt. About 100 units based on this conversion were sold to the Belgian government, and a similar stripped-down truck, the B5-4 SQC, was sold to the U.S. Army in small numbers through the late 1930s. This conversion was dubbed the "Grandaddy" of the Jeep in a 1943 news broadcast by Earl Godwin. *Marmon-Herrington via the Don Chew collection*

Livingood moved to New Virginia, Iowa, and began producing Model-T conversions again. The records are sketchy but according to Jesse Livingood Jr., he built about 50 conversions there until he stopped manufacturing them in 1928. The conversion cost about $250, but you also had to buy a two-speed Warford auxiliary transmission at about $75 to make it work.

The heart of the conversion was a steerable front axle that used Spicer joints on the axle shafts. The axle mounted in the standard Model-T location and matched the Ford's 3.60:1 gear ratio. The conversion utilized a Warford two-speed auxiliary transmission (high and low range) to which a transfer case was attached to split the power front and rear. Even with the Model T's 176-cid, 20-horsepower engine, the lightweight vehicle did very well in the dirt.

Somehow a converted Model T found its way into an a U.S. Army testing program in 1923. The unit was tested at the Aberdeen Proving Grounds in Maryland. There is no known connection to the Livingood conversion but one of Livingood's sons is highly suspicious that the army test vehicle is a unit that was stolen earlier and submitted for tests by an

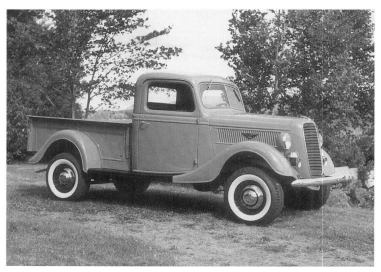

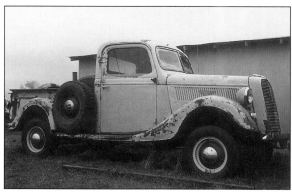

These two 1937 Marmon-Herrington/Ford Model LD1-4 1/2-ton pickups are the only ones known to still exist. The one on the left belongs to noted Marmon-Herrington expert and collector Don Chew and awaits restoration at his shop. On the right is the restored unit owned by Prouty Ford, in Dover-Foxcroft, Maine, and displayed in their showroom. Both trucks are still very original and powered by 221-cid, 85-horsepower flathead V-8s. In addition to the driving front axle, 4.44 gears and single-speed transfer case, the conversion used a heavy-duty four-speed, an 11-inch clutch, and hydraulic brakes. Marmon-Herrington usually converted the Ford's mechanical brakes during the job. Ford trucks did not come from the factory with hydraulic brakes until 1939. *Prouty Ford (right)*

Almost all the Ford cars could be ordered in four-wheel drive. This 1939 ad shows the range of models available that year. Few were actually built and only a handful remain. According to Chuck Mantiglia, a noted Marmon-Herrington collector, five are still known to exist, two 1947 Woody Station Wagons, a 1947 four-door sedan, and a 1948 Coupe. *Marmon-Herrington via the Don Chew collection*

What! A monster truck in a classic 4x4 book? This may be the grandfather of all monsters. It was built by Marmon-Herrington in 1937 and called the "Super Swamp Buggy." Built for oil exploration in tundra, the 1 1/2-ton truck was fitted with reduction gears in the axles and 10 tractor tires. No doubt the truck used some sort of power steering. It's a real "classic" monster truck. *Marmon-Herrington via the Don Chew collection*

unknown person. In any case, though the unit performed very well, nothing more was done. Apparently budget constraints put a damper on the project, but this Ford, whoever built it, was directly in line as a predecessor to the jeep concept.

Marmon-Herrington

Marmon-Herrington deserves a special place in history because they essentially began the light-duty 4x4 era. The story begins in 1931, when Walter C. Marmon and Col. Arthur W. Herrington partnered up to build all-wheel drive trucks. Marmon brought copious amounts of cash and business savvy into the deal, and Herrington brought many years of experience in military all-terrain transportation.

Among many other accomplishments, Herrington was a major mover in the development of military all-wheel drive vehicles during and after World War I. When the army tried to standardize its truck fleet in the 1920s, Herrington was actively involved in the development of the Quartermaster Corps Standard Fleet. Built from 1 1/4-ton up to 12-ton capacity, these trucks were actually assembled by army personnel at Camp Holabird, Maryland, from the best existing parts of the day.

Based in Indianapolis, the new Marmon-Herrington Company started off building 1 1/2-ton and larger trucks of its own design. There was no attempt to hide the similarities of these rigs to the QMC trucks. They were, arguably, among the best you could buy in those days, but the limited market for commercial 4x4 trucks would not bear the Marmon-Herrington price tag. In 1935, Walter Marmon realized the need to cut costs or die and conceived the idea of using an existing line of trucks and converting them to all-wheel drive.

Marmon-Herringtons were built for work. This 1939 LD-4 1/2-ton pickup is shown in Colombia in the early 1940s, sporting the dents and dings of honest labor. One of the reasons Marmon-Herringtons are rare is that many were sent overseas. *Marmon-Herrington via the Don Chew collection*

This 1950 Ranger has a fascinating family history. According to its owner, David Edwards, it was purchased by his stepfather, Dr. Robert Goulding, who bought it new. Apparently, it was the first Ranger built and was used in his practice in the back country of North Dakota. It was famous for being able to get him where he needed to be despite the extremely adverse weather conditions of North Dakota. *David Edwards*

Ford trucks went to No. 1 on the list of candidates because of their competitive pricing, powerful V-8 engine, solid reputation, and vast production capability. As a test, Assistant Chief Engineer Bob Wallace was given the job of converting a 1935 Ford 1 1/2 ton. After installing a Marmon-Herrington transfer case and modifying the center section of a Ford differential to accept Marmon-Herrington steering knuckles and constant velocity joints, the truck was given a severe test under the watchful eyes of Ford representatives. The tests were an unmitigated success, and a marketing strategy was hashed out whereby the converted trucks were sold via the Ford dealer network. By September 1935, the hybrid trucks were beginning to emerge from the Marmon-Herrington plant.

By 1936, Ford-based 4x4, 6x4, and 6x6 trucks were in production, as well as half-tracks, various pieces of military specialty equipment, and even a line of light tanks. Thus far, the trucks had been 1 1/2 ton or larger, but on a July sales trip to Belgium, Col. Herrington began the light-duty 4x4 era with a telegram to the factory and a special request for a 1/2-ton four-wheel drive utility vehicle.

An ordinary 1936 4x2 Ford pickup was procured from a local dealer and Bob Wallace went back to work. His efforts yielded a powerful, lightweight 4x4 vehicle that was to prove a pivotal development in the all-wheel drive world. The cut-down truck proved more nimble and capable than any previous design. It proved that it could outperform any 4x4 of the day. Its capacity was limited to a handful of men and a light anti-tank gun—but that was enough.

Just a year later, 1937 Ford car and truck models could be ordered in four-wheel drive. Imagine having a 4x4 Ford woody or coupe. They existed, though many of them were sold overseas. The Arab-American Oil Company, ARAMCO, bought converted Ford cars and trucks and used them in the huge drilling and exploration projects in the Saudi desert.

The 1953 Ranger used the new "fat-fendered" body style that has become so popular in recent years. Only about six 1953 Rangers were built, according to a retired Shop of Siebert employee with a very good memory. None are known to have survived. *Marmon-Herrington via the Don Chew collection*

Business was so good that in 1937, Marmon-Herrington moved into the old Duesenburg Factory on Washington Street in Indianapolis.

World War II brought even more prosperity to Marmon-Herrington, but the competition became fierce by much larger companies, like Dodge and Willys, which jumped into the four-wheel drive arena with both feet. Still, with Allied nations clamoring for vehicles, there was more than enough business to go around.

After the war, new light-duty 4x4 sales slumped a bit due to the influx of surplus military trucks. The Marmon-Herrington/Ford

relationship stayed strong through 1958, when Ford decided to build 1959 and later light-duty 4x4s in-house. The Ford/Marmon-Herrington relationship had lasted 23 years on just a handshake, but it was time for both companies to move on.

Though Marmon-Herrington continued converting Ford's large trucks (and other makes), the loss of business caused management to lay off a significant number of workers, and in 1963, the company moved out of the huge old Duesenburg factory and into a smaller facility in Lebanon, Indiana.

A lean and mean Marmon-Herrington built business back up to profitable levels by the late 1960s, and even though a tornado destroyed the Indiana factory in 1974, big trucks remained moneymakers. Today, Marmon-Herrington continues its legacy of all-wheel drive by converting large Ford, Freightliner, GM, Volvo, and Navistar trucks in their Louisville, Kentucky, plant. They also supply all-wheel drive conversion parts for Mack, Advance Mixer, Kenworth, Peterbilt, Western Star, Duplex, HME, and Spartan. Though much of Marmon-Herrington's business was overseas, a goodly number of the Marmon-Herrington vehicles have survived. Of the 1930s conversions, just a handful remain in the United States.

By the last year of the Marmon-Herrington relationship, 1958, only a limited number of light-duty trucks were being converted. This 1/2 ton is a rare bird, especially since it is complete with the Marmon-Herrington badges on the hood, just behind the Ford arrow. These badges are a vital element in the purchase of any conversion because they are so difficult to obtain or reproduce. *Fred Scharff*

Dos Hombres! Butch Gehrig's 1951 Chevy 3600 3/4-ton (right) is currently the earliest known NAPCO conversion in existence. He bought the truck in 1981, used it as a truck for a while and then took a year to restore it to like-new condition. It's been a consistent show-winner ever since. The truck on the left is a very nice, original, 1954 3600 3/4-ton NAPCO that Butch acquired in 1994 from the original owner. In 1954, the NAPCO kit retailed for $1,185, plus installation. The truck cost $1,582 so the four-wheel drive just about doubled the price of the truck. Gehrig's 1951 is powered by its original 216.5-cid, 85-horsepower "Thriftmaster" six. In 1954, the light truck line got a boost to the more powerful 112-horsepower 235.5-cid six and Gehrig's 1954 3/4-ton is so equipped. Through most of this era, the engines were pretty standardized across the 1/2- to 1-ton line. The heavier loads were handled by changes in gearing. Half-tons used 4.11; 3/4-tons used 4.57s; and 1-tons used 5.13s. *Trisha Gehrig*

One of the earliest GMC-based NAPCO trucks to be found is Kris Krieg's 1954 GMC 1-ton, Series 150-24. The running gear is complete with the twin-stick Rockwell transfer case, Warner Gear T-98 transmission and NAPCO front axle. Gearing is 4.57-1. The original 248-cid six was replaced by a later model 292 Chevy about 15 years ago. Kris found the NAPCO in Wyoming, spruced it up and has been using it ever since in his sign painting business.

In this 1957 Chevrolet advertising shot, a model 3100 shortbed pickup climbs a steep ramp built on one of GM's proving grounds. Even with a capacity load, the 7.05-1 first gear multiplied by the 1.94 low range in the transfer case and the 1/2 ton's standard 3.90-1 axle ratio made it possible for the truck to practically idle up the slope. *GM Historical Archives*

A large number of trucks were built for World War II, many of them large-capacity units. The postwar and early 1950s trucks seem to have survived in some quantity but most of them are medium-duty or larger.

In the light-duty realm, the most likely finds are pickups, with the higher capacity 3/4 and 1 ton being most common. Among the choice finds are the Ranger models. Basically a panel truck to which Marmon-Herrington added four-wheel drive, the interiors were converted to carry passengers and windows were added. Voila! A Suburban-like 4x4.

The Ranger concept began in 1942, when a few Ford panel trucks with Marmon-Herrington 4x4 conversions were modified by adding windows and seating for seven. These were done by specialty coach builders, such as Proctor-Keefe, on a custom basis and they were well liked. The Ranger name was not applied then, but Marmon-Herrington took note. At least one of these 1942 trucks has survived.

In 1949, Marmon-Herrington got around to offering a similar setup that they officially named the Ranger (and you thought it was a 1983-on Ford mini-truck!). Unlike the 1942 rigs that were built on a panel delivery chassis (essentially a beefed up station wagon), the 1950 Rangers were built on real 1/2-ton, F-1 truck chassis. These Rangers were built on Ford's postwar F-series trucks that had debuted in 1948. Marmon-Herrington did the 4x4 conversion and Shop of Siebert in Ohio altered the bodies. The Ranger stayed in the lineup through 1956. They found a particular niche with surveyors, on remote construction sites like Thule, Greenland, and with oil exploration teams.

According to sources at Shop of Siebert, fewer than 100 Rangers were built between 1949 and 1956. The number quoted was 86. Amazingly, 15 are known to still exist, and they are all 1950 models, of which there were approximately 35 built. Marmon-Herrington built a vast number of big trucks but the light-duty rigs only averaged at about 200 per year in 1940 and 1941 and from 1946 to 1958. Prior to 1940, fewer than 200 were built in total.

Parts are difficult to find for Marmon-Herringtons, but unlike the Coleman, they did not use an exotic design, so fabrication of unavailable parts is not a major undertaking—relatively speaking. Look for vehicles that are complete, at least in terms of the 4x4 conversion parts. The Ford truck parts are not particularly difficult to find, making that part of the resto fairly easy. As with the other conversions, the 4x4 parts can be transferred from a hopeless truck into a better unit and retain the originality.

Most Marmon-Herringtons were converted in the Indiana factory but some were done by dealers who purchased the kits. The kits were not particularly easy to install and necessitated removing the body and making some chassis modifications. The trucks usually carry badging on either side of the hood, though a lazy workman at a local conversion facility might have left them off. From 1935 to 1938, the badge was an upside-down triangle, but after 1938 it was an oval badge. In addition, some screwed-on instruction plates were added to the dash and a serial number plate was added to either the left or right A-pillar.

Marmon-Herringtons are timeless classics that are still very reasonable. So far, there has been only moderate collector interest, but this is beginning to change. There is a small collector/enthusiast network for Marmon-Herrington that can be of aid in procuring parts and information.

NAPCO

The Northwestern Auto Parts Company, NAPCO, started business around the turn of the century as a major parts warehouse, under another name. In 1918, they reorganized into NAPCO and apparently became known as a place to find "hard-to-get" obsolete parts. During World War II, they got into manufacturing and built a variety of specialty automotive products for the war effort. After World War II, they bought some 1/2-ton axle tooling from Dodge and in late 1950, started offering a four-wheel drive conversion they called the "Powr-Pak."

It appears that until 1954, these were exclusively Chevrolet and GMC trucks and only 3/4-ton or larger units. The 1/2 tons built into 1955 used an enclosed driveshaft assembly, and the conversion was next to impossible without major work. A few 1/2-ton trucks have been found with 3/4-ton rear axles installed.

The Chevy and GMC trucks were particularly easy to retrofit, so unlike Marmon-Herrington, most early NAPCO kits were installed outside the Minneapolis, Minnesota, plant. A shop could sign up to become a NAPCO distributor and install the kits locally. Many of the NAPCO distributors were Chevy and GMC truck dealers. The kit could also be installed at the NAPCO facility in Detroit.

In 1956, GMC offered a four-wheel drive option and the undercarriage was none other than NAPCO. The NAPCO kits were installed on the assembly line, allowing GMC to claim a "factory" 4x4. The installation was sans the customary NAPCO badging, of course, though the axle housings are still marked with a cast-in "NAPCO." The 4x4 option was available in the 1/2-ton long- and short-wheelbase trucks, as well as the Suburban and Panel. The 3/4-ton and 1-tons came in pickup, stake, or panel configuration. GMCs could be ordered with either the six or the V-8.

In 1957, Chevrolet followed suit and offered a 4x4 "factory" option. Unlike the "Jimmies," the Chevrolets came only with the 235-cid six. The V-8 models could be converted locally as before, and some

When you get into the collectable NAPCO Chevys, Suburbans are the hot ticket. This 1958 Suburban is in near original condition. Mike Hyatt, of Grand Junction, Colorado, is only the second owner and has a full restoration planned. It's a model 3156 1/2 ton with rear doors (tailgates were optional). As with all of the factory 4x4s, only a 235-six was available. Mike has installed a slightly warmed period 283 V-8 for the extra power. The six-seater Suburbans of this era shared the 1/2-ton pickup's 114-inch wheelbase and came standard with 6.50x16 tires.

The GMC NAPCOs were significantly different from the Chevrolet variety. In those days, GMC retained a fair bit of autonomy in choosing components for its trucks and the drivetrain choices were significantly different—and more powerful. Kirby's 1959 Model 102-8 is an example of this. Showing only 47,000 miles on the clock, the 123-inch wheelbase 1/2 ton has stayed very original.

Unlike its Chevrolet brethren, the 1956–1959 GMC truck could be ordered with a V-8. For 1959, that V-8 was a Pontiac transplant. The 336-cid engine is a direct ancestor of the now-famous mid-1960s 389-cid V-8 that powered, among other Pontiacs, the GTO. In two-barrel form, the 336 made an honest 200 horsepower and, more importantly to truck owners, a very substantial 307 pound-feet of torque.

were, but the majority of the late 1950s NAPCO/Chevys were factory-assembled, six-cylinder models.

The NAPCO/Chevrolets continued being assembled at GM through the 1959 model year. In 1960, General Motors debuted a new line of trucks and the 4x2s used an independent front torsion bar suspension. This made conversion nearly impossible and a separate chassis was designed for four-wheel drive applications. GM also got wise that they could source the front axle and transfer cases from vendors like Spicer or Rockwell. While NAPCO continued converting trucks, 1960 marked the end of their heyday with GM. NAPCO was absorbed into the Dana-Spicer Corporation in 1976.

In general, the GM trucks are divided into three categories, the 1947–1954 "First Series" trucks were followed by the 1954–mid-1955 "Second Series," which were similar in appearance. In mid-1955, these trucks were superseded by the all-new "Task Force" trucks. The two types (before and after 1955) of trucks used slightly different equipment.

The shortbed Chevy/NAPCO trucks are among the most attractive. This 1959 Chevy/NAPCO, in near original condition, spent its life in Texas. Now it's owned by early Chevy guru Jim Carter. Jim Carter has reproduced NAPCO manuals, brochures, and badging and carries some NAPCO NOS parts, in addition to a large supply of reproduction and used parts for all 1934–1972 Chevy trucks.

The Livingood Model-T conversion was a good unit that offered many features. It had what amounted to a two-speed transfer case when Livingood combines his transfer case with a dual range Warford auxiliary transmission. With the body removed, weight could be dropped to about 1,400 pounds. Oddly enough, the Livingood conversions are still being sold by the inventor's son, Jesse, using the original tooling and equipment. *Jesse Livingood*

The nuts and bolts of a pre-1955 conversion included a Rockwell transfer case with a 1.94-to-1 low range that was mounted separately from the transmission and connected by a short driveshaft. This transfer case is expensive to rebuild but the parts are available. As mentioned earlier, the 1/2 tons were not converted because of their enclosed driveshafts, with the exception of a few 1955 Second Series trucks. These transitional rigs had an open shaft like the Task Force trucks and a few 1955 1/2 tons have surfaced with NAPCO kits.

Another difference was that the First and Second Series trucks (with the exception of the transitional 1955 1/2 tons just mentioned) had the front differential offset to the left. The later setups were similar, though the front differential was offset to the right and the T-case was a Spicer 23 with a 1.87-to-1 low. The kits from both included driveshafts, various mounting brackets, and hardware.

The front axle housing was a NAPCO item that contained a standard GM differential. One of the features of the NAPCO conversions was the Rzeppa (pronounced "Cheppa"), five-ball constant-velocity joints in the steering knuckles. These parts are now unavailable and, as fate would have it, the Rzeppas are usually worn out because the trucks did not mount free-wheeling hubs. Even with no load applied, the Rzeppas were churning all the time. Age, miles, and neglect do the joints in by the time the trucks are restored. With some effort, the axle can be converted to use a modern Spicer U-joint, but an axle rebuild for a NAPCO can be in the $800 range.

The NAPCO-converted Chevrolets are the most popular of the conversions, primarily because the Chevy trucks themselves are very popular. They were built in fairly large numbers so there are still good examples to be found. The main enemy is rust, but a plethora of outfits deal with the reproduction Chevrolet parts, so the only hitch may be some of the NAPCO hardware. The repair and parts manuals have been reproduced. The NAPCO/Suburbans are currently on the hot list but they are the scarcest of the bunch.

The best part is that if a collector had a good Chevy 4x2 truck and a bad but complete NAPCO truck, he or she could install the 4x4 kit into the better truck and be within the limits of originality. If the donor NAPCO was a factory assembled unit, he or she could add the badging to make it an after-market kit.

The enthusiast network is fairly large in the NAPCO arena, making the restoration a little less lonely than with the other conversions.

NAPCO Fords

After Ford separated with Marmon-Herrington at the end of 1958, they offered "factory-built" 4x4s for the 1959 and 1960 model years. Before and after this time, NAPCO offered kits for the Ford light-duty trucks and these were common enough conversions in some parts of the country. Since Ford offered four-wheel drive only in 1/2-ton or 3/4-ton trucks until about 1974, anything larger would have been a conversion, and depending on whether the dealership was a die-hard Marmon-Herrington supporter or a NAPCO supporter, either was available.

Depending upon the era and the weight rating, these conversions would have used either the standard NAPCO front housing with a Chevy drop-out carrier or a Spicer 44 axle. The lighter units used the Spicer axle and the heavier used the NAPCO.

There has been a persistent rumor that the 1959–1960 Ford trucks used assembly line-installed NAPCO kits. This has been proven untrue and it's easy to tell them apart. The big NAPCO drop-out axle is a dead giveaway but the Spicer-equipped NAPCOs had the differentials offset to the left, whereas the factory Ford trucks were offset to the right. Also, NAPCO used a Spicer 23 transfer case with a NAPCO tag, and Ford used a Spicer 24 box.

While there is nothing inherently wrong with the NAPCO Fords, they are regarded as orphans by the collector community. Nobody seems to want them. The Ford folks don't like the idea of Chevy parts appearing under their Ford, and the Chevy camp doesn't want a Ford attached to their Chevy parts. Collector value is likely to stay very low but, nonetheless, they are interesting trucks.

NAPCO Studebakers

Little is documented about the Studebaker 4x4s. Though not generally known for four-wheel drive products, Studebaker was not a complete stranger to all-wheel drive, having built large numbers of 2 1/2-ton 6x6 trucks in World War II. In 1941, Studebaker built two prototype 4x4 trucks, called the T27, one mounting a 75-mm gun and the other built as a cargo/personnel vehicle. In 1943, they also built an innovative 1 1/2-ton low-silhouette 4x4 that resembled a giant version of the M-274 "Mechanical Mule." Studebaker is most famous in the World War II era for building the M-29 and M-29C "Weasel," a small, fully tracked amphibian that became famous in the Arctic and Antarctic.

An imposing sight! Lee Eidem's 1959 Studebaker NAPCO 4x4 is in original condition. Bought from the Paasch family in northern Oregon, the original owners, the truck is a model 4E7D 1/2 ton. It came equipped with 4.89 gears, four-speed manual transmission, two-speed Spicer transfer case and a rare option, the 289-cid V-8. The 259-cid was the more common V-8 choice. The 289 had been used in Studebaker's medium-duty truck line until it was offered in light-duty trucks for 1959. A limited slip differential, called the "Twin Traction" but actually a Spicer Powr-Lok, is installed in the rear. This truck was originally shod with 6.50-16 Firestone All-Traction tires. *Lee Eidem*

This is reputedly the first 4x4 Studebaker built, produced in 1957 as a 1958 model. It was used for testing and photography, and is now owned by an employee of Newman & Altman, a firm specializing in Studebaker parts and information. *Richard Quinn*

Most of Studebaker's records are intact. Newman & Altman, of South Bend, Indiana, is probably *the* Studebaker parts source (see sources in appendix) and can look up your Studebaker truck and furnish you with a copy of the production order. Here is the order for Lee Eidem's 1959. Newman & Altman is housed in part of Studebaker's old factory.

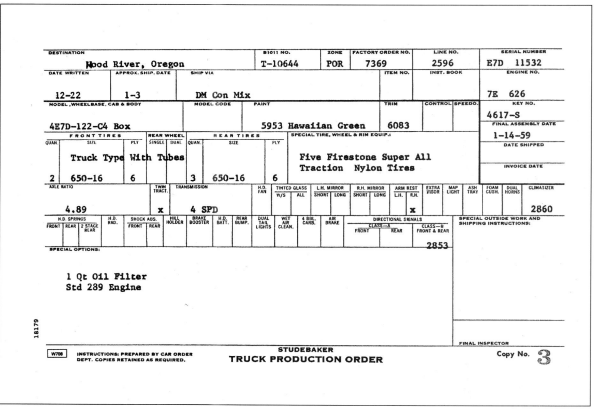

DESTINATION					B1011 NO.	ZONE	FACTORY ORDER NO.		LINE NO.		SERIAL NUMBER
Hood River, Oregon					T-10644	POR	7369		2596		E7D 11532

DATE WRITTEN	APPROX. SHIP. DATE	SHIP VIA				ITEM NO.	INST. BOOK		ENGINE NO.
12-22	1-3	DM Con Mix							7E 626

MODEL ,WHEELBASE, CAB & BODY / MODEL CODE / PAINT / TRIM / CONTROL / SPEEDO. / KEY NO.

4E7D-122-C4 Box — 5953 Hawaiian Green — 6083 — 4617-S

FINAL ASSEMBLY DATE: 1-14-59

FRONT TIRES / REAR WHEEL / REAR TIRES / SPECIAL TIRE, WHEEL & RIM EQUIP.:

Truck Type With Tubes — Five Firestone Super All Traction Nylon Tires

DATE SHIPPED

QUAN.	SIZE	PLY	SINGLE	DUAL	QUAN.	SIZE	PLY
2	650-16	6			3	650-16	6

INVOICE DATE

AXLE RATIO / TWIN TRACT. / TRANSMISSION / H.D. FAN / TINTED GLASS W/S ALL / L.H. MIRROR SHORT LONG / R.H. MIRROR SHORT LONG / ARM REST L.H. R.H. / EXTRA VISOR / MAP LIGHT / ASH TRAY / FOAM CUSH. / DUAL HORNS / CLIMATIZER

4.89 — x — 4 SPD — x — 2860

H.D. SPRINGS FRONT REAR 2 STAGE 2 REAR / H.D. RAD. / SHOCK ABS. FRONT REAR / HILL HOLDER / BRAKE BOOSTER / H.D. BATT. / REAR BUMP. / DUAL TAIL LIGHTS / WET AIR CLEAN. / 4 BBL. CARB. / AIR BRAKE / DIRECTIONAL SIGNALS CLASS—A FRONT REAR / CLASS—B FRONT & REAR / SPECIAL OUTSIDE WORK AND SHIPPING INSTRUCTIONS:

2853

SPECIAL OPTIONS:

1 Qt Oil Filter
Std 289 Engine

18179

FINAL INSPECTOR

| W706 | INSTRUCTIONS: PREPARED BY CAR ORDER DEPT. COPIES RETAINED AS REQUIRED.

STUDEBAKER
TRUCK PRODUCTION ORDER

Copy No. 3

1938
Alma Motor Company
Alma, Michigan

Alma marketed a simple four-wheel drive conversion they called the Alco Four Wheel Drive system, possibly as early as 1936. Designed mostly for low-speed work, it used a power take-off built into the transmission to drive the front axle, instead of a transfer case. The kit was said to be extremely easy to install. It was marketed to fit 1936–1938 Ford trucks and perhaps later models. The transmission was replaced with an eight-speed unit that had an output shaft for the front axle built into the main housing. The lowest first gear had an 84:1 creeper gear. The front differential was a worm gear style. The unit was reputed to take only four hours to install. Few were sold.

1932–1939
Asam Truck Company/ Asam Motor Company
Detroit, Michigan

Designed by F. H. Asam, the conversions used an unusual, low-profile front axle called a "Turret Drive." The axle was designed by Asam for the late 1920s Freeman trucks and featured a low profile, spur-gear differential with gear reduction at the ends. When Freeman went belly up, Asam marketed the design himself as a conversion for Ford trucks. The army tested a Ford Model AA 1 1/2-ton 4x4 in the early 1930s with good results but didn't offer Asam a contract. A converted Ford truck was again tested by the army in 1937 and just a year later, a converted 1937 Chevy was run through the mill. Both trucks were rated as inferior to the Dodge and Marmon-Herrington 1 1/2-ton 4x4 trucks then in service with the army. Between 1932 and 1939, an unknown number of trucks were converted and it isn't clear if any were produced for commercial use. No Asam trucks are known to have survived.

1955–1977
Fabco
Oakland, California

Really a truck builder, the Oakland, California, company primarily manufactured all-wheel drive agricultural equipment. At last report, it is still in business, manufacturing driving front axles and other hardware and the occasional custom-built truck.

The Asam turret drive front axle was a mechanical wonder that offered easy installation, stock ride height, and low gearing. This unit was installed on a Ford AA truck and tested by the U.S. Army. The front brake was a 16-inch hydraulic drum on the front driveline. The rear used the vehicle's existing brakes. *U.S. Army*

Asam's final entrant in the quest for a government contract was this 1937 Chevy 1 1/2-ton. It was converted using the Asam kit and then thoroughly tested by the army, starting in June of 1938 and ending in February of 1939. Though the truck performed well, it was rated as unsuitable as a prime mover for the 105-mm howitzer and inferior to the Marmon-Herrington T-2 Squad Car of the same capacity. It was not recommended for procurement.

After the war, Studebaker experimented with light-duty 4x4s by building two prototypes for the Arab American Oil Company, ARAMCO. The project began in 1949 and two 4x4 vehicles were built, a 1950 Deluxe Commander four-door sedan and a 1/2-ton pickup. This project apparently went nowhere and, considering Studebaker's problems maintaining a share in the American motor vehicle market, it probably was the result of the lack of resources rather than an inferior product. The company also built an undetermined number of 2 1/2-ton 4x4 trucks for a military contract, probably of overseas origin.

In 1958, Studebaker again entered the 4x4 arena with a line of 1/2-, 3/4-, and 1-ton "Transtar" trucks. Offered in two wheelbase lengths, 112 and 122 inches, they could be ordered in six variations from chassis-cabs to stakebeds. These trucks used NAPCO kits that were almost certainly assembled on the Studebaker assembly line. Available with either a 170-cid L-head six, a 245-cid L-head six, or an OHV, 259-cid V-8, these trucks had an impressive list of available options.

In 1959, Studebaker dropped the Transtar name but upped the ante again by offering the more powerful 289-cid V-8 as an option. They also included the 4x4 option in their "Scotsman" line, which were advertised as the lowest priced pickups in the United States. A number of the 4x4 Scotsmans were apparently shipped overseas. The 1/2- and 3/4-ton 4x4 models were last manufactured in 1959.

When the new "Champ" line (called the "T-cab" and resembling the moderately successful Lark car line) debuted for 1960, the all-wheel drive option wasn't on the list, though two prototypes were reputedly built. The 1-ton and larger trucks used the old body style, called the "C-cab," and the Transtar name. Four-wheel drive was an available option into 1964. According to available records, no 4x4s were produced after that year. Total production of the 1958–1964 4x4 Studebakers was 358 units, and at least 95 went overseas; 64 went to the U.S. Navy and 5 were used in the factory fleet. That doesn't leave many for collectors. Newman & Altman, the premier authority and parts source for Studebakers of all types, has preserved the Studebaker production records and supplied much detail information.

The death of Studebaker marked the final victory in the battle for market dominance by the "Big Three" against the smaller manufacturers. By the late 1950s, Studebaker was on its last legs and truck sales were in an even sorrier state. The lack of sales was due less to the quality of the trucks than with the marketing schemes (or lack thereof) of the Studebaker Company itself. The company and its dealer network, such as it was, simply did not promote the truck lines.

There appear to be more 1959 4x4s around nowadays than any other year, but all the Stude 4x4s are commanding incredible prices. The Studebaker name has an admirable support organization for enthusiasts, but experts on the 4x4s are few and far between. Parts for Studebaker trucks are moderately difficult to obtain, but fortunately, the NAPCO four-wheel drive kits used the Spicer 44 style axle and Spicer 23 transfer case, making drivetrain restoration a bit easier. The primary restoration focus becomes the rest of the truck.

Expect to pay a high price for a Studebaker 4x4 but with a very high investment potential and a fabulous look, they are a choice pick.

SPECIFICATIONS
1937 MARMON-HERRINGTON LD1-4

Engine:

Type	V8, L-head
Displacement	221cid
Power	85hp @ 3,800rpm
Torque	150lbs-ft @ 1,800rpm
B&S	3.03x3.75in
CR	6.12:1

Transmission:

Type	4-speed, Ford

Transfer Case:

Type	1-speed, Marmon-Herrington

Axles:

Front type	Full-floating, Marmon-Herrington
Rear type	Semi-floating, Ford Corp.
Ratios	4.44:1

Dimensions & Capacities:

Length	189.6
Wheelbase	113in
Shipping weight	2,719lbs
Fuel capacity	16gal
GVW	3,900lbs

1954 GMC NAPCO

Engine:

Type	6-cyl OHV
Displacement	248cid
Power	125hp @ 3,600rpm
Torque	215lbs-ft @ 1,550rpm
B&S	3.71x3.81in
CR	7.5:1

Transmisssion:

Type	4-speed, Muncie SM-420
Ratios	1=7.06, 2=3.58, 3=1.71, 4=1.0, R=6.78

Transfer Case:

Type	2-speed, Rockwell
Ratios	Low=1.94, High 1.0

Axles:

Front type	Full-floating, NAPCO
Rear type	Full-floating, GM Corp.
Ratios	4.57:1

Dimensions & Capacities:

Length	206in
Wheelbase	125.25in
Curb weight	4,100lbs
Fuel capacity	17.5gal
GVW	5,600lbs

1958 CHEVY/NAPCO SUBURBAN

Engine:

Type	6-cyl, OHV
Displacement	235cid
Power	123hp @ 4,000rpm
Torque	195lbs-ft @ 2,000rpm
B&S	3.56x3.94in
CR	8.0:1

Transmission:

Type	4-speed, Muncie SM-420
Ratios	1=7.06, 2=3.58, 3=1.71, 4=1.0, R=6.78

Transfer Case:

Type	2-speed, Spicer 23
Ratios	Low=1.87, High 1.0

Axles:

Front type	Full-floating, NAPCO
Rear type	Semi-floating, GM Corporate
Ratios	3.90:1

Dimensions & Capacities:

LxWxH	197.87x76.37x79.68in
Wheelbase	114in
c	17.5gal
GVW	5,400lbs

Chapter 3

Dodge—The Power and the Glory

Of the Big Three truck makers, Dodge has had the longest continuous run of factory built 4x4s. With 63 years in the four-wheel drive business, Dodge has a long and rich history of doing it in the dirt. As with many other manufacturers of all-wheel drive trucks, the military proved to be Dodge's major motivation. From 1939 to the early 1960s, Dodge produced a series of 1/2- and 3/4-ton tactical military trucks that were as reliable as gravity and as popular with the troops as taking the next breath. These trucks demonstrated feats of strength that became the subject of "war stories" told by service veterans from World War II to Vietnam.

The roots of the Dodge 4x4 story go back to 1916, and long before Dodge became a division of Chrysler Corporation. Dodge Brothers cars were used in the short but explosive 1916–1917 Punitive Expedition into Mexico. Despite ham-fisted drivers, blistering heat, and hostile terrain—not to mention gunfire—the reliable Dodge Brothers Touring Cars showed that motorized transport was the wave of the future.

Because of this sterling service, the Dodge name got cemented into the minds of military planners. When the U.S. Army scrambled for vehicles at the beginning of World War I, Dodge Brothers became a major supplier of light-duty vehicles. Some estimates say that the government purchased as many as 20,000 Dodge Brothers vehicles between 1916 and 1918. These Dodges quickly became the Doughboy's best friend, and much was learned about motorized transport in wartime. One of the biggest lessons was the need for all-wheel drive on the battlefield.

In July 1928, Walter P. Chrysler purchased the still booming Dodge Brothers Company, and it became a division of the Chrysler Corporation. Chrysler also got the Graham Brothers truck line that Dodge Brothers had absorbed earlier in the year. W. P. Chrysler already had a fledgling truck company in the newly created Fargo Motor Corporation but, because it didn't come with a reputation like Dodge, it took an immediate back seat.

Dodge Brothers and Graham merged into one division called simply, Dodge. Fargo retained a separate identity within Chrysler Corporation for a time. At first, the Fargo trucks were distinctly different but by 1933 they were simply rebadged Dodges and eventually the Fargo name was used exclusively on export, foreign-built, and fleet models, and for models built and sold in Canada. The DeSoto name was used in the same fashion.

The First 4x4s

Dodge was approached by the army in 1933 for militarized 4x2 versions of their Model HC 1 1/2-ton cargo trucks as well as 4x2 1/2 tons. These were designed to replace the aging fleet of World War I era trucks. The next year, a 4x4 version of the 1 1/2-ton truck was built and called the K-39-X-4USA. This 143-inch wheelbase truck utilized the first mass-produced version of the part-time four-wheel drive system that we still use today.

Unlike the full-time systems offered by other 4x4 manufacturers of the day, the Dodge setup allowed the front axle to freewheel when not in use. This improved fuel economy, lessened wear and tear, and made the trucks easier to drive on the highway. A total of 796 of the K-39-X-4USA trucks were built in 1934, including an artillery version with a center-mounted, double-capstan winch.

This first foray into all-wheel drive proved to be an easy and simple one. The conversion utilized a special Timken transfer case and a front axle that incorporated most of the standard Dodge differential. The early trucks were so successful that another batch of similar trucks was purchased in 1938. This time, 1,700 of the RF-40-X-4USA trucks were produced, again resulting in accolades from the military. Many of these 1930s-era trucks stayed in service until after World War II. Few, if any, of these trucks have survived.

Half-Ton 4x4s

By 1939, it was generally acknowledged that war of one form or another was on the horizon. The government finally loosened the purse strings enough to let the woefully unprepared U.S. Army start a buildup. Among many other things, the army badly needed 1/2-ton 4x4s. With a brand-new truck factory in operation, Dodge was ready to jump on the 1/2-ton contracts with both feet. The new Mound Road truck plant had been in operation since 1938 but had been running at only a small portion of its capacity.

Marmon-Herrington had been producing superb 1/2-ton 4x4 conversions on Ford chassis for the Army as far back as 1937, although these were in fairly limited numbers. When the call went out for 1/2 tons, not only did Marmon-Herrington respond, so did GMC, Ford and, of course, Dodge. When the smoke cleared, Dodge emerged as the clear winner and immediately went into production with a 1/2-ton model. Though Marmon-Herrington had built the first 1/2-ton 4x4 with their 1936 conversions of 1/2-ton Fords, Dodge became the first manufacturer to mass produce purpose-built light-duty four-wheel drive trucks.

Dodge had debuted a totally new commercial truck design late in 1938, as 1939 models, and these TC models became the basis for the new military trucks. The 1940 VC series (V=1940, C=1/2 ton) 4x4s carried the engineering designation of T202. Four distinct body styles were produced: a command reconnaissance/radio car; open and closed cab pickups; and a carryall. Though the trucks were rated as 1/2 tons, they were built on a 1-ton chassis that gave the army plenty of leeway

The first production 4x4 Dodge was the K-39-X-4USA 1 1/2-ton. A total of 796 units were built in a variety of configurations, including this artillery special that mounted a center capstan winch. The trucks had a 143-inch wheelbase and were powered by the commercial truck 241-cid, 80-horsepower flathead six used in larger trucks. Timken supplied the front axle and transfer case. It used 7.00x20 tires. *U.S. Army*

The VC was a model code in which the V stood for 1940 and the C for 1/2 ton. In reality, the chassis of the VCs were one-ton units derated for severe service. At least three VC-1s have survived the years. *Chrysler Historical*

In addition to the command and radio cars, the VC series was available as open- and closed-cab pickups and carryall. Shown here is a VC-5 posed at the Dodge Mound Road factory prior to delivery. *Chrysler Historical*

for abuse. A similar 1 1/2-ton model was built concurrently using the same civilian sheet metal. This truck used the T203 engineering moniker, and their model designations were VF-401-406.

Though much of the design and testing of the VC series was done in 1939, all production models appear to have been built in 1940. Thus far, no collector has found a military VC Dodge that can be documented to have been produced in 1939. A total of 4,640 VC 4x4 models were manufactured and only about 14 are currently known to have survived. The rarest of them is the carryall, of which 24 were produced and only one is known to remain. A total of 6,470 of the VF models were manufactured. As far as records show, most of the VC and VF trucks were used Stateside.

When the war surplus bonanza started in 1945, many VC and VF Dodges were bought and used up in commercial and farm roles. No doubt, there are a few of these rare and valuable gems still hiding in the weeds somewhere. Because they look very much like the prewar and immediate postwar WC civilian trucks, they could be easy to miss.

If you are lucky enough to locate a VC Series, you will find that some parts can still be found in NOS condition, although the selection is spotty. While many parts interchange among the 1938–1940 R, T, and V series civilian trucks or the later WC military 1/2 tons, there are some very oddball pieces that may be difficult, if not impossible, to find. Still, a VC is a worthy restoration project and due to their scarcity, they are highly prized collectables.

"Dodge—An Original Jeep"

The name "Jeep" has been the source of controversy since the beginning of World War II. In army parlance, the term dates back to World War I, where a jeep was either a new, unproven motor vehicle or a new recruit in basic training. When applied to the recruits, it was somewhat less than complimentary. The term stayed in army vocabulary until the buildup for World

The Dodge WC series represented a leap ahead from the VC trucks. They used a military pattern body and uprated mechanicals. The entire Dodge 1/2-ton line is very collectable these days, especially the closed-cab models like Floyd Suit's 1941 WC-12. This truck has a fascinating history, most likely having been assigned to the atomic test site at Alamagordo, New Mexico. No, it does not glow in the dark.

War II. Along the way, a cartoon character was created called Eugene-the-Jeep. He appeared in the Popeye-the-Sailor comic strip by E. C. Segar late in 1936 and became an instant hit. Eugene could do just about anything, so the name became synonymous with great feats.

When the VC Dodges entered service, they acquired the nickname "jeeps." Up to that point, there had already been several other motorized "jeeps" and at least two flying "jeeps." It would be logical to presume that the name was stuck on the Dodge to follow old army motorpool slang as much as it was a comparison with Eugene. The Dodges were definitely at the cutting edge of 4x4 performance of the day. With "jeep" in common

usage as a colloquial description for amazing deeds, it's easy to see why the Dodge got the name. The term seems to have been mostly applied to the command reconnaissance version that captured the fancy of press photographers.

When the WC series 1/2 tons appeared, the nickname followed. At the same time, the 1/4-ton 4x4 that we now call the Jeep went into production. "Peep" appears to have been its most common nickname, but it's well documented that Jeep was also popular. A media blitz over the Willys, Bantam, and Ford 4x4s got the Jeep name glued firmly to the 1/4-ton and with millions of new GIs entering service, the old-timers usage of the word was overwhelmed. By the time the 3/4-ton Dodges emerged as standard equipment, they were known more or less officially as "Beeps," short for Big-Jeeps.

1941–1942 WC Series 1/2-Ton Military

While the VC Series Dodges were generally regarded as very successful, their civilian sheet metal was considered a liability on a tactical vehicle. Late in 1940, a military style body was adopted. The new series of Dodge 4x4s,

The WC-21 open cab pickup is fairly common but a great collectable nonetheless. Ben Rehder's 1941 has been in the family since 1946. It was purchased surplus by Ben's Uncle Henry that year and used as a hunting vehicle in Colorado until 1987. At that time, it was rough but very complete, almost unaltered and still wearing its original paint. Ben undertook a complete restoration and by 1989 was winning "Best of Show" at military vehicle meets. The restoration was so detailed that even the accessories bear a 1941 date. The truck was delivered on November 23, 1941, and shows 25,221 original miles since new.

A Dodge VC-1—
Back From the Brink

Steve Greenberg, a long-time collector of military vehicles, owns a very rare VC-1 command reconnaissance vehicle that he restored in 1990. When he bought the truck, its original body had been removed and a VC-3 pickup body installed. The change had been made many years previously, when this sort of butchery was a fairly common fate for command cars of all series. Surplus buyers were usually interested in carrying cargo, not passengers, so the command car bodies were often hacked into pickups or had their bodies removed altogether. Certain parts, such as tailgates, rear seats, and top bows, are always in short supply. WhenSteve bought the VC, he was told that the original body had been dumped into a ravine decades before and presumably was still there. This proved to be true. After a 100-mile drive to a remote location, Steve and some friends managed to recover the body, complete with original unit markings and in relatively good condition.

The WC 1/2 tons were still pretty civilian under the hood. With the exception of a military standard generator and carburetor, the 217-cid was pretty much the same unit as you would get in a truck on civvy street. Later in the war, closed crankcase systems and suppressed or waterproofed ignition systems complicated them a bit.

designated the WC (W=1941, C=1/2 ton) series, began production in 1941. The new body used the cab from the previous models but the hood, fenders, and grille were all GI in appearance and operation. Few mechanical changes were made to the first of nearly 80,000 WC series 1/2 tons. The first batch of the "Military Pattern" Dodges got the engineering code of T207.

The number of body styles was expanded on the T207 Dodges. In addition to the command reconnaissance, carryall, and open and closed cab pickups, a new all-metal ambulance body was produced, as well as a panel delivery. The new trucks sat on the same 116-inch wheelbase of the previous VC series, but the ambulance and the panel came on a 123-inch wheelbase. All the trucks used a 6-volt electrical system, except the radio cars which were 12-volt.

The drivetrains were very similar between the types, though the lockout device on the VC shifter that prevented shifting into first or reverse without also being in 4WD was eliminated on the later rigs. The axle housings were improved on the WCs and the wheel bolt pattern enlarged, though the differential unit remained the same. A larger 217-cid flathead six-cylinder was installed in the T207 that gave about the same power as the 202-cid but more torque. Altogether, 33,346 WC models were built in the T207 range.

A new batch of 1/2 tons was produced later in 1941 and designated T211, but there was little to mark them from the T207s. Built in the same body styles as the previous units, they received new WC numbers and very little else. A long wheelbase, closed-cab truck, less the rear body, became the basis for a number of specialty conversions. The larger 230-cid six replaced the 217-cid late in the run (at engine No. 42,001). A total of 17,560 T211s were built.

Ambulances were the only 1/2 tons to see frontline service throughout the war. Just over 6,000 were built, but they are fairly common and not particularly valuable compared to other models in the 1/2-ton line. This complete WC-18 awaits a new owner and some TLC at Vintage Power Wagons, Fairfield, Iowa.

The 3/4-ton WC-52 weapons carrier was Dodge's World War II *pièce de résistance*. Beloved of GIs nearly as much as the Jeep, it served in every theater of combat. This rig belongs to John Smith, who purchased it from Norway. The Norwegian military kept it virtually stock, with the exception of a screen in front of the radiator. It had very few miles on it and had been in storage for at least two decades.

Among the rarest and most sought after 3/4-ton military Dodges are the carryalls. These were often used as mobile command posts and had 12-volt electrical systems to accommodate radio sets. An extremely rare variant of this was called the WC-53, or field limousine, and was essentially a carryall to which a set of rear doors, a divider between the front and rear compartments and leather seats had been added, as well as a rear heater and extra dome lights. Before you get all excited and start looking, only two were made.

Dodge capitalized on the popularity of the World War II Dodges by producing a civilianized version of their 4x4 in 1946. This very early model, probably a prototype, is equipped with military combat wheels, an item not offered on standard production rigs. *Chrysler Historical*

The first postwar military success for Dodge came with the 1950 intro of the M-37. Generally regarded as the best of the military Dodges, they make a good 4x4 as well as a collectable. They are extremely capable in many forms of terrain, as proven by Duane and Nicole Bartley in their 1953 vintage M-37 they nicknamed "Eeore." This stock rig tackled some of the worst terrain in Moab, Utah, with an ease that surprised many.

When the T215 models debuted late in 1941, they had some significant changes. The standard military round gauges replaced the old civvy rectangular units. A utility body was added to the model range and was used as a telephone installation truck. These rigs continued production into 1942, even as the new 3/4-ton truck debuted. A good number of T215 models were never even assigned government registration numbers and were sent directly overseas to England or the Soviet Union under the Lend-Lease program. Just over 29,000 T-215s were built, and at least a quarter of these went to war through Lend-Lease.

The 1/2-ton Dodge W-Series saw combat in Africa with both the Americans and the British. They were used in the tense moments at the beginning of the Pacific Campaign against the Japanese. The 3/4-tons began replacing 1/2 tons with combat units in the spring of 1942. By mid-1943, there were few to be found serving with front-line units except the ambulance versions. Many 1/2 tons served Stateside, and as a result, a goodly number have survived to become collectors' items.

Among the rarest are the command cars and the closed-cab pickups. Panels are popular as well as ambulances. Command cars and ambulances seem to have suffered the most from "hackers" who converted them to unimaginable home-made pickups. Mechanical parts are plentiful but, as you'll hear over and over, body parts are the most difficult to find. Some reproduction pieces are available. The trucks are popular and, for the most part, modestly priced.

1942–1945 WC Series 3/4-Ton Military

The final evolution of the WC series Dodges came in the form of the 3/4-ton models. By this time, Dodge had frozen the WC term despite the change of years and weight rating. Much had been learned in two years of production, and these were the best Dodges to that time. The 1/2 tons had essentially been peacetime developments, but when a declared war ensued on two fronts, the government was ready to freeze the 1/2-ton design as it was to avoid complications. Dodge reckoned that more improvements could be made without disrupting the efforts to standardize truck production into a few specific types.

The army had divided its tactical vehicle fleet into standard capacities. Starting with the 1/4 ton, it jumped to 1/2 ton, 1 1/2 ton, 2 1/2, and so on. When the 3/4-ton truck idea was announced, it seemed to strike at the roots of the government's efforts at standardization.

The T214 series 3/4-ton trucks expanded the line, but without major upset to army supply rooms and motorpools. More than 80 percent of the 1/2-ton components were used in the newer truck. Dodge focused on narrowing the number of models and making each truck more useful in its assigned role.

Fred Coldwell's 1947 WDX is a classic example of a Power Wagon. His is equipped with 11.00-16 Michelin tires in place of the standard 9.00-16. With a Braden winch, a sun visor, and a host of other goodies you can't see, Fred enjoys some truly classic four-wheeling.

One of the earliest tactical uses of the 1/2-ton Dodges had been to carry a heavy weapons squad. In 1940, this consisted of eight men and a .30 or .50 caliber machine gun or a mortar. The open-topped truck offered the squad mobility to move quickly to areas where their extra firepower was needed. The lower profile open truck was also more easily concealed. This type of truck became known as a "weapons carrier," though this term didn't become official until the advent of the WC-51 and 52 3/4-ton Dodges.

The new truck was distinctly different in appearance to the previous models. It was lower and smaller. The WC-51 and 52 weapons carriers sat on a short 98-inch wheelbase, which improved cross-country performance and maneuverability. The rear body was wider and more capacious. The T214s were shod with beefy 9.00-16, 10-ply nondirectional tires that also enhanced off-road performance. The new "combat" wheels allowed emergency run flat capability, as well as easier mount and dismount. The mechanicals were largely the same as had appeared on the last of the 1/2 tons.

The vast majority of 3/4-tons were built in the weapons carrier style. The 1942 WC-55 variant mounted a 37-mm anti-tank gun, though by 1943 it was realized that this popgun was of little use against the heavily armored German tanks, and most of them were converted back to weapons carrier configuration. A command car was built in moderate numbers on the 98-inch wheelbase and ambulances and various specialty service bodies were installed on the 121-inch wheelbase. In 1945, 3,500 long-wheelbase WC64 "knockdown" (KD) ambulances were produced and are now very rare. A shortage of 1 1/2-ton trucks encouraged Dodge to adopt a 6x6 configuration and the WC63 was born. It used many of the standard 3/4-ton components but had the extra driving axle and a two-speed transfer case. More than 40,000 were built.

Of the more than 250,000 3/4-ton Dodges built from 1942 to 1945, many thousands have survived for collectors. The most sought after are carryalls and command cars. The ambulances and weapons carriers are very easy to find, purchase, and restore. Parts are plentiful, with many NOS and reproduction parts available.

The Power Wagon chassis was fitted out in a variety of special ways. About 800 buses were built from about 1948 to 1956 by three companies, Carpenter, Gillig Brothers, and Hicks. The bodies were all slightly different but the basic Dodge 4x4 chassis was the same 126-inch wheelbase unit you could buy from your friendly, neighborhood dealer. Extensions were welded onto the rear chassis to support the extra overhang. The buses came equipped with the optional 8,700 GVW package that included beefier springs, 9.00-16 eight-ply tires and 5.83-1 gears. Many of the buses were equipped with 7,500-pound PTO winches. The Power Wagon buses were used primarily in rural school districts around the country and were built to carry 14–16 students in any weather or road condition. This bus is a Carpenter-bodied unit that spent its life in the Selma School District near Fairfield, Iowa. The chassis is a 1949, but the Carpenter data plate shows it was completed in 1950. Recently, the bus was purchased by Peter Wilkin as a restoration project. His intentions are to restore the exterior to factory fresh appearance but to turn the interior into a camper. A classic all-wheel drive motorhome? Hmm!

1950–1968 M37 3/4-Ton Military

After World War II, Dodge attempted to one-up themselves by building an even better military truck. After numerous high-tech prototypes, what the government bought was an updated version of the World War II WC-Series trucks, designated by the army as M37 and by Dodge as the T245. The first series of the truck was produced from 1950 to 1954 and was on-line in some numbers for the Korean War. There was a fair bit of parts carryover from the older trucks. The second series, the M-37B1, was produced from 1958 to 1968 with a few minor improvements.

The M-37s took the good qualities of the W-Series and enhanced them. They were bigger, stronger, and much better performers. Time has judged them the best of the Dodge tactical military trucks. Mechanical changes from the World War II trucks included a stronger chassis, improved suspension, a two-speed transfer case, and a bit more power from the same 230-cid flathead six. The electricals were military standard 24-volt in waterproof harnesses.

Two basic body styles were manufactured, the M-37 cargo truck and the M-43 ambulance. There were a few minor adaptations, of which the most common were the M-42 command truck, simply a regular cargo truck set up with a special shelter on the bed, and the M-201 maintenance truck, which mounted a utility body. Two wheelbases were used, 112 inches for the cargo trucks and 126 inches for the ambulance and maintenance truck. More than 90,000 of all types were built.

These trucks began to be replaced in service during the late 1960s by the generally inferior M-715 Kaiser but were still seen into the late 1970s. A great number are in the marketplace, and prices are rea-

The Power Wagon continued virtually unchanged until the end of its run in the United States. This 1968 WM-300 belongs to Roger Adlisson and represents the last year of Power Wagon sales in the United States. It's showing a mere 44,000 miles on the clock, after spending its life as a Fort Collins, Colorado, Public Utilities workhorse. Roger bought the truck in 1987 and began a restoration that took five years to complete. The truck was an immediate showstopper but also proved the "Power" part of its name by taking first place in the six-cylinder class at a tractor pull.

sonable. Many experts in the field have plotted the M-37's growing desirability among collectors and predict it will soon eclipse the World War II-era trucks in popularity. Parts are plentiful and easily found.

1946–1968 Power Wagon

With the success of the military trucks behind them, Dodge sought to capitalize on the reputation by building a postwar commercial 4x4. At that time, the four-wheel drive market was a limited one, with several companies competing and thousands of ex-GI trucks on the market at bargain basement prices.

Despite all the obstacles, the new Dodge was a modest success. The name chosen for this rig was Power Wagon. This was not an entirely new name, having been used previously by Grabowsky in the early 1900s, but 50 years later, "Power Wagon" still inspires confidence born of many years of legendary service.

More than 95,000 were produced from 1946 until domestic sales ended in 1968. Production for overseas markets continued as late as 1978, with a batch of Slant Six powered variants going to Israel. The M-601 variant, built from about 1962 to about 1970, was a militarized, soft-top Power Wagon produced especially for the Military Defense Assistance Program (MDAP), under which "needy" friendly governments were supplied military equipment. More than 13,000 M-601s were built, but they are extremely rare in the United States.

The Power Wagon combined the chassis of the World War II-era 4x4 with the prewar cab of the VC truck. Front sheet metal was part WC-Series military and part "Burma Road" 3-ton Dodge truck, of which 15,000 were built for the Chinese government in 1945 and 1946. A new heavy-duty 8-foot bed was designed to accommodate the Power Wagon's 1-ton optional payload.

Mechanically, there were a few changes from the GI trucks. Most notable among them was the two-speed transfer case that had originally been designed for the WC-63 6x6 and modified by lowering the low-range ratio. The engine was the same tried and true 230-cid six, but uprated in civilian service to 102 horsepower. Electricals started with a six-volt system but was uprated to 12 volts in 1956.

As with most trucks of the era, these were Spartan rigs. The deluxe cab, available as an option from 1946–1960, offered the supreme comfort and convenience of vent windows, a dome light, dual sun visors, and dual electric wipers. The package later added some extra seat padding. In those early days, even the heater was optional! By 1961, the deluxe cab package was standard. The last U.S. Power Wagons of 1968 featured a few items mandated by federal law—a padded dash, seat belts, and hazard flashers.

Mechanically, the Power Wagon offered a buyer only a few choices through most of the 22-year run. Through 1956, two GVW packages were offered, 7,600 pounds and 8,700 pounds. In 1957 the higher capacity rig was

The venerable flathead Dodge soldiered on long after most other L-head engines were but a memory. It was produced for the U.S. market all the way to the WM series Power Wagon's demise in 1968. The 251-cid made an honest low-revving 125 horsepower and 216 pound-feet of torque.

Some owners have transformed the Spartan interiors into luxury with felt and mohair. Roger Adlisson's 1968 Power Wagon is so adorned, and the effect is pleasing, both to observers and riders.

This 1957 W-100 is a true family heirloom. This truck belonged to Kelley Wich's father. Equipped with a 315 V-8, four-speed and 4.89 gears, it spent several years as a work truck. One day in the early 1960s, it was caught in a flood and nearly washed away permanently. Kelley's dad resurrected the machine and continued to use it. When the elder Wich passed away, Kelley inherited the truck and has been renovating it just short of a full restoration.

The 1957 4x4 truck on the left presents an interesting question. A cursory examination would show it to be a factory 3/4-ton W-200 dually with a flatbed installed. In almost every respect, it appears genuine. If you look at the front fenders and compare them to the fenders on the truck above, you'll see they are missing the eyebrows. The eyebrows were a 4x4 feature. After reviewing the VIN, it turned out to be a 4x2 number. The most likely scenario is that the original owner had the four-wheel drive installed at a later date using factory parts or pieced two trucks together. This was done many years ago, so it appears genuine. This is a great truck and well worth owning but if you were looking for a factory original 1957 4x4, or, more importantly, paying more for it, you'd be upset. It pays to do your homework.

The 1-ton W-300 debuted in 1958. This factory photo shows a preproduction truck with "Dodge 8" in the spot where "Power Wagon" should be. *Chrysler Historical*

Slight restyling gave the 1958–1960 trucks more of a "Bulldog" look. Ben Rehder's 1958 W-100 has been restored to better than new condition. It was a "cherry" when purchased and had only 35,000 miles on it. It was optioned out almost to the maximum level possible with a 315 V-8, four-speed transmission, heavy-duty axles (essentially 3/4-ton pieces), dual headlights, chrome bumpers, turn signals, and a bunch of interior goodies.

upped to 9,500 pounds. Until 1958, the lighter package came with 7.50-16 eight-ply tires and 4.89 axle ratios. The heavier capacity unit was equipped with 9.00-16 10-ply meats and 5.83 gears. In 1958, the 9.00-16 tire and 5.83 gears became the standard combo, with the difference in GVW accounted for by eight-ply versus 10-ply tires. The rear springs of the lighter rated unit were rated at 2,500 pounds and the higher rating got 3,000-pound springs. Power steering and brakes became options in 1957.

A variety of go-to-work options gave the Power Wagon great versatility on the farm, ranch, or job site. First among these were the Braden power take-off winches. Powered by the engine via a power take-off attachment on the transmission, these winches came in 7,500 and later 10,000-pound capacities. Other goodies included a rear PTO for running equipment, a drawbar, and a pintle hitch. With the right equipment, the old Power Wagon could pull a 14-inch, three-bottom plow. A few Power Wagon owners have been seen recently at tractor plowing days, showing off the Dodge's capacity to work like a medium tractor.

The old-style Power Wagon is probably at the top of the Dodge collector's hot list. They are fairly readily available, but scarce enough to make them special. Since the trucks were usually worked very hard, they are often found in rough shape. They are, however, a straightforward restoration that will evolve into a truck that is still useful for work or play. Despite their heavy suspension, they are capable off-roaders, though they can be very tough on passengers if driven fast in the dirt.

The earlier WDX models, seem to be the most sought after Power Wagons because of their four-pocket bed and the fact that they were often heavily accessorized. The last-of-the-breed 1967 and 1968 rigs are a close second-place finisher. There is little logic to the order of these preferences, since the later trucks are marginally better units. Parts are readily available for all Power Wagons and suppliers are beginning to reproduce certain hard-to-find cosmetic and interior items. Body parts are the hardest bits to find so look for a rust-free example if possible. Accessories, such as the Braden winch, are very desirable options.

1957–1960 "Civilian" Power Wagon

By the late 1950s, four-wheel drive was on the sales upswing, even though, generally, truck sales were down industrywide. With Dodge in a definite No. 3 position, management looked for every edge to nibble away at Chevrolet and Ford sales leads. One of the means to this end was to offer a 4x4 version of their conventional truck line.

In 1957, Chrysler Corporation debuted a new truck that was touted as the "Forward Look" in styling. The 4x4 variant came with an options package no other factory builder could match. A 315-cid V-8 and a cast iron three-speed Loadflite automatic (available only with the V-8) were optional, as well as power steering and power brakes. Half the Dodge trucks sold in 1957 were V-8s. These were items not available in GM or Ford 4x4s until much later. The trend towards "Plain Jane" 4x4 work trucks was still very much evident with the two sales leaders.

In addition, a healthy list of useful work options was available for the Dodges that included a 6,000-pound PTO winch, a brush guard, tow hooks, a drawbar, and a pintle hitch. You could even order the 3/4-ton with dual rear wheels or a factory-installed flatbed.

The trucks came in 1/2- (W100) and 3/4-ton (W200) capacities with the old-style Power Wagon (designated W300) as the 1-ton option. Body styles included the long and short-wheelbase pickups, as well as a stake bed. The Suburban-like Town Wagon debuted this year in a 1/2-ton version and offered all-wheel drive seating for nine.

The 1957 Dodge 4x4s came standard with a 230-cid, 120-horsepower flathead six and a three-on-the-tree. A New Process No. 420 four-speed was optional, as was the automatic. A version of the venerable Dana 44F axle was used up front and a corporate axle was used in the back. The 4.89 axle ratios were standard, though some sources show 5.83 ratios being available. On the 1/2 tons,

Debuting in 1957, the Town Wagon was Dodge's answer to the Chevy Suburban. This early model 1958 mounts single front headlights. Dual lights were optional at the beginning of the year but later became standard.

Most people don't realize that Power Wagon panels were available in the 1958–1966 era. Shown here is a 1960s Town Panel that was found in the old files of *Four Wheeler* magazine. Because it has a 1958 grille, it's difficult to pin an exact year on this truck.

17.5-inch tires and wheels were standard, while the 19.5-inch was the standard size on the 3/4-ton.

For 1958, a civilian 1-ton became the W300 and the old military job became the W300M (later WM300). Mechanically, the 1958s were similar to the 1957, except that the W300 used the nearly indestructible Dana 70 axles front and rear in 4.89 or 5.83 ratios. Cosmetically, the 1958s were quite different with their extra body lines and optional dual headlights, but the general body outline remained similar though the 1960 model year.

Unfortunately for Dodge, sales remained slow through the 1960 model year. This is good for us now because these attractive Dodges are rare enough to be collectable, though parts, especially body parts, can be somewhat difficult to obtain.

The Town Wagon—Dodge's Answer to the Suburban

Among the most collectable Dodge 4x4s are the Town Wagons. Introduced late in 1955 as a 4x2 truck, the 4x4 Town Wagon entered the fray along with the other Power Giant trucks in 1957. They offered all-terrain seating for eight in a 1/2-ton capacity. This old-style body remained in pro-

The 1961 Power Wagons hit the trail with an all new look that was more than skin deep. The 225-cid OHV Slant Six replaced the old flathead (except in the 1961 W-300) and a 318 V-8 replaced the previous 315.

duction nearly unchanged from 1958 until 1966, even after new bodied Sweptline trucks debuted in 1961.

They shared the mechanicals with the 1/2-ton pickups of their particular era. The wheelbase stretched from 108 inches to 114 inches when the new "Sweptline" trucks debuted in 1961. The Slant Six replaced the flathead 251 as the standard Town Wagon powerplant in 1961. The 318 became the optional V-8.

Town Wagons are a useful collectable because of their large passenger capacity. They have an unfortunate vulnerability to rust, however, in their rear fender area. This has severely culled the number of remaining trucks.

1961–1972 Sweptline Power Wagons

After the disastrous sales drop of the late 1950s, Dodge bounced back with a new line of trucks. These were wider, longer and had more cargo capacity than the previous trucks. The trend toward more comfortable trucks took one step closer to blurring the car-truck lines.

Among the mechanical improvements that debuted in 1961 was the now-famous Slant Six. It had debuted in Chrysler Corporation cars the year before and was available in 170-cid and 225-cid sizes. You shouldn't find a 170-cid in the 4x4s, as this smaller powerplant was reserved for the very lightest duty trucks. The venerable 251-cid flathead soldiered on in the old-style WM300 Power Wagons as well as in the big W300 1-ton for 1961 and 1962. It featured a forged steel crank, stellite valves, and a roller timing chain. The 225 Slant Six finally found its way into the 1-ton Dodge in 1963.

The W-series Power Wagons evolved through the 1960s into comfortable, hard-working trucks. An increasing number of creature comforts came to the options list, such as air conditioning in 1969, plush seating, carpeting and snazzy paint. Chrysler did a vast amount of market research that uncovered a need for recreationally useful trucks and this translated into offering Camper Special models to maximize playtime for customers. The 4x2 trucks got more of the comfort and play packages, such as the Custom Sports Special and the Adventurer. There were still the go-to-work options like winches, power take-offs, and brush guards.

The 318 remained the biggest powerplant available until 1967, when the 383 took over as top dog. This gave the 1/2-ton and 3/4-ton 4x4s some serious muscles to flex. Transmission options ranged from the venerable A745 three-on-the-tree, through four-speed manuals and Loadflite automatics. About the time the Camper Specials debuted, Dodge realized that the average Joe with a camper found the stump-pulling 6.68-1 first gear of the four-speed manual more of a liability than an asset, due to the wide spacing between first and second. The close ratio NP445 box offered in 1971 had a more manageable 4.5-1 first.

The 1961–1971 Dodge 4x4s were great trucks but have been overlooked by most collectors. Their current collector market is very marginal,

If you want a vintage pickup with seating for six, consider a 1963–1972 Crew Cab W-200. With the turning radius of a Mack, they probably aren't for everyone but they are fairly rare. Many were built for the military, as was this 1966 that belongs to Don Evans. It has a slant six, four speed, and 4.56 gears.

As the 1960s rolled by, pickup design focused more and more on recreational aspects. This 1966 factory photo shows off the W-200 Power Wagons camper carrying abilities.

49

Evolution of the Power Wagon

Model Designations

Year	Model
1946–1947	WDX
1948–1949	B-1-PW
1950	B-2-PW
1951–1952	B-3-PW
1953	B-4-PW
1954	C-1-PW
1955	C-3-PW
1956	C-4-PW
1957	W300
1958–1959	W300M
1960–1968	WM300

Changes

1949- Transmission uprated to unit used on 1 1/2-ton trucks.

1950- Four-blade radiator fan replaced the six-blade unit.

1951- Uprated axles, uprated springs, pickup box redesigned, brake improvements, dash revised to match "civilian" style B-Series trucks, improved fuel pump and starter.

1952- Revised carburetor.

1953- Tinted windows and power-assisted brakes optional, compression ratio boosted from 6.7-to-1 to 7.0-to-1 for a 1-horsepower increase to 103.

1954- Compression increased again from 7.0 to 7.25. Intake manifold redesigned for better flow and camshaft duration increased. New power rating, 110 horsepower.

1955- Syncromesh transmission.

1956- Electricals uprated from 6 to 12 volts.

1957- Power steering optional. Key start standard. Turn signals standard. 230-cid compression boosted again to 7.9-to-1 for 113 horsepower.

1961- 251-cid with 125 horsepower flathead replaces 230-cid. 12-volt alternator installed as standard.

1962- Optional locking front hubs were available.

1963- Spring rates increased front and rear.

The burly W-300 continued into the 1960s with its beefy drivetrain. This 1969 is equipped with a 10,000-pound PTO winch and is used as a shop truck at Vintage Power Wagons in Iowa.

with the low production W300s probably having the most interest. Trucks of this era are prone to rust and can be very scarce in environments where this is a potential problem. They are easy trucks to live with and mechanical parts are not difficult to find. Due to their proclivity to corrode, body parts can be very hard to find. Original accessories such as winches and brush guards add to the collectability. The government bought a great number of these trucks, so don't be surprised to find a little olive drab paint under the current paint job. Most of the GI issue trucks were six-cylinder.

The slant-six was one of Chrysler Corporation's triumphs. A 1961 variety is shown here, complete with oil bath air filter.

The "Poly Head" 318 was used in trucks from 1960 to 1966. One of the distinguishing features of this engine was its polyspherical combustion chambers and mechanical tappets. The valve covers are wide and have a serrated looking edge along the bottom.

The old Poly-heads were replaced with a wedge type head in 1967. The lower end was very similar, though the solid lifters had been replaced by hydraulics. This engine is a heavy-duty variant in a 1969 W-300.

CLASSIC DODGE CHARTS

Years	Models	Engine	Gearbox	Axles	LxWxH	Tires
1940	VC-1-6	201.3cid-L6 79hp 154lbs-ft	4-speed main 1-speed transfer	full-floating 4.89-1	116in WB 188x74x88	7.50-16 directional
1941	WC-2-20 (T207, T211)	217.7cid 78hp 164lbs-ft	4-speed main 1-speed transfer	full-floating 4.89-1	116in or 123in WB 181x76x88	7.50-16 non- directional
1941–1942	WC-21-43 (T215)	230.2cid 92hp 180lbs-ft	4-speed main 1-speed transfer	full-floating 4.89-1	116in or 123in WB 181x76x88	7.50-16 non-directional
1942–1945	WC-51-64	230.2cid 92hp 180lbs-ft	4-speed main 1-speed transfer	full- floating 5.83-1	98,114 or 121in WB 167x78.5x81.5	9.00-16 non- directional

MODEL DESIGNATION AND PRODUCTION OF VC SERIES 1/2 TONS

VC-1 (T202)	Command Reconnaissance	2,155 units
VC-2 (T202)	Radio (similar to C&R but fitted w/radio)	34 units
VC-3 (T202)	Pickup, Closed Cab w/Troop Seats	816 units
VC-4 (T202)	Pickup, Closed Cab W/O Troop Seats	4 units
VC-5 (T202)	Pickup, Open Cab	1,607 units
VC-6 (T202)	Carryall	24 units

MODEL DESIGNATION AND PRODUCTION OF T207 WC SERIES 1/2 TONS, 1941

WC-1	Closed Cab Pickup w/longitudinal troop seats	2,573 units
WC-3	Open Cab Pickup w/transverse troop seats	7,808 units
WC-4	Open Cab Pickup w/transverse troop seats w/winch	5,570 units
WC-5	Closed Cab Pickup w/o troop seats	60 units
WC-6	Command Reconnaissance	9,365 units
WC-7	Command Reconnaissance w/winch	1,438 units
WC-8	Radio Body (similar to C&R)	548 units
WC-9	Ambulance	2,288 units
WC-10	Carryall	1,643 units
WC-11	Panel Delivery	353 units

MODEL DESIGNATIONS AND PRODUCTION OF T211 WC SERIES 1/2 TONS, 1941

WC-12	Closed Cab Pickup	6,047 units
WC-13	Open Cab Pickup	4,019 units
WC-14	Closed Cab Pickup	268 units
WC-15	Command Reconnaissance	3,980 units
WC-16	Radio (similar to C&R)	1,284 units
WC-17	Carryall	274 units
WC-18	Ambulance	1,555 units
WC-19	Panel	103 units
WC-20	Closed Cab no rear body	30 units

MODEL DESIGNATIONS AND PRODUCTION OF T215 WC SERIES 1/2 TONS, 1941–1942

WC-21	Open Cab Pickup	11,823units 2,464 Lend Lease
WC-22	Open Cab Pickup	1,900 units
WC-23	Command Reconnaissance	1,500 units 1,137 Lend Lease
WC-24	Command Reconnaissance w/winch	500 units 912 Lend Lease
WC-25	Radio (similar to C&R)	1,400 units 230 Lend Lease
WC-26	Carryall	2,600 units 300 Lend Lease
WC-27	Ambulance	2,181 units 400 Lend Lease
WC-40	Closed Cab Pickup	275 units
WC-41	Closed Cab no rear body	383 units
WC-42	Panel Radio	650 Lend Lease
WC-43	Telephone Installation	370 units

MODEL DESIGNATIONS AND PRODUCTION OF T214 WC-SERIES 3/4 TONS, 1942–1945

Model	Description	Production
WC-51	Weapons Carrier	48,300
WC-52	Weapons Carrier with winch	41,396
WC-53	Carryall	8,400
WC-54	Ambulance	22,007
WC-55	Gun Motor Carriage 37mm	5,380
WC-56	Command Car	15,687
WC-57	Command Car with winch	6,010
WC-58	Radio	2,344
WC-59	Telephone Maint.	549
WC-60	Chassis Cab for Maint. Conv.	296
WC-62	6x6 Personnel & Cargo	31,344
WC-63	6x6 Personnel & Cargo with winch	13,656
WC-64	Ambulance, KD	-

SPECIFICATIONS T245 M-SERIES 3/4 TONS, 1950–1968

Years	Models	Engine	Gearboxes	Axles	LxWxH	Tires
1950–1954, 1958–1968	M-37-42-53 and B1 models	230.2cid 94hp 188lbs-ft	4-speed 2-speed transfer	full- floating 5.83-1	112in WB 185x73.5x89.5in	9.00-16 non- directional
1950–1954, 1958–1968	M-43-52-56-201 and B1 models	230.2cid 94hp 188lbs-ft	4-speed 2-speed transfer	full- floating 5.83-1	126in WB 198.7x73.5x 92in	9.00-16 non- directional

PRODUCTION FIGURES
1950–1964 M37 AND M37B1 SERIES
(DOES NOT INCLUDE CHASSIS-CAB OR EXPERIMENTAL)

M37	47,404 total (1950–1954)
M37B1	43,975 total (1958–1968)
M42	8,079 total (1950–1954)
M43	6,305 (1950–1954)
M43B1	1,902(1958–1968)
M56(R2)	308 (early 1960s)
V41	599 (1950–1954)
M201B1	519 (1958–1968)

MODEL DESIGNATION AND PRODUCTION OF M-SERIES 3/4 TONS, 1950–1964

Model	Description	Production
M-37	Personnel & Cargo	47,404 (1950–1954)
M37B1	Personnel & Cargo	43,975 (1958–1964)
M-42	Command Post	8,079 (1950–1954)
M-43	Ambulance	- (1950–1954)
M-43B1	Ambulance	- (1958–1964)
M-53	Cab & Chassis 112in WB	-
M-53-B1	Cab & Chassis 112in WB	-
M-56	Cab & Chassis 126in WB	-
M-56B1	Cab & Chassis 126in WB	-
M56C	Maintenance, Heavy Duty, with winch "#3 Shop Set"	-
M52(R2)	Airport Fire Truck	308
M-56	Chassis Cab	-
M-201	Maintenance	-
M-201B1	Maintenance with winch	-

SPECIFICATIONS POWER WAGON, 1946–1968

Years	Models	Engine	Gearboxes	Axles	LxWxH	Tires std./opt
1946–1952	WDX B-1-PW B-1-PW B-3-PW	230cid 102hp 185lbs-ft	4-speed 2-speed transfer	full- floating 4.89/5.83	126in WB 209x79x76	7.50-16 9.00-16
1953	B-4-PW	230cid 103hp 190lbs-ft	4-speed 2-speed transfer	full- floating 4.89/5.83	126in WB 209x70x76	7.50-16 9.00-16
1954–1957	C-1-PW C-3-PW W300	230cid 103hp 190lbs-ft	4-speed 2-speed transfer	full- floating 4.89/5.83	126in WB 209x70x76	7.50-16 9.00-16
1954–1956	C-1-PW C-3-PW	230cid 103hp 190lbs-ft	4-speed 2-speed transfer	full- floating 4.89/5.83	126in WB 209x70x76	7.50-16 9.00-16
1957	W300	230cid 110hp 198lbs-ft	4-speed 2-speed transfer	full- floating 4.89/5.83	126in WB 209x70x76	7.50-16 9.00-16
1958–1960	W300M WM300	230cid 110hp 198lbs-ft	4-speed 2-speed transfer	full- floating 4.89/5.83	126in WB 209x70x76	9.00-16
1961–1968	WM300	251cid 125hp 216lbs-ft	4-speed 2-speed transfer	full- floating 4.89/5.83	126in WB 209x70x76	9.00-16

MODEL DESIGNATIONS AND PRODUCTION POWER WAGON, 194–1968

Years	Model	Production Domestic/Export/ MDAP
1946–1947	WDX	4,608/842
1948–1949	B-1-PW	5,280/2,918
1950	B-2-PW	2,577/2,316
1951–1952	B-3-PW	4,844/5,809
1953	B-4-PW	1,215/2,781
1954	C-1-PW	2,275/3,326
1955	C-3-PW	1,892/3,166
1956	C-4-PW	868/1,862
1957	W300	6,812/1,892
1958	W300M	2,387 total
1959	W300M	1,592/1,106
1960	WM300	405/1,112
1961	WM300	281/1,087
1962	WM300 M-601 (MDAP)	397/1,794/1,544
1963	WM300 M-601	490/2,896/1,302
1964	WM300 M-601	742/4,686/486
1965	WM300 M-601	884/1,513/2,496
1966	WM300 M-601	873/372/3,371
1967	WM300 M-601	832/500/2,303
1968	WM300 M-601	1,087/1,374/1,958

SPECIFICATIONS W-SERIES "POWER GIANT," 1957–1960

Years	Models	Engine std./opt.	Gearboxes std./opt.	Axles std./opt.	LxW	Tires std./opt.
1957	W100-200 Town Wagon	230/315ci 120/204hp 202/290lbs-ft	3-speed/ 4-speed/ Auto.	semi/ full- floating 4.89	108 or 116in WB	7x17.5 8x19.5 185.2 or 197x79.7
1958–1960	W100-200-300 Town Wagon	230/251/ 315ci 120/125 204hp 202/216/ 290lbs-ft	3-speed/ . 4-speed/ Auto	semi/ full- floating 4.89/4.88/5.87	108/116/ 129in WB	7x17.5 8x19.5 185.2 or 197 or 204x79.7

MODEL DESIGNATION AND PRODUCTION W-SERIES "POWER GIANT," 1957–1960

Years	Model	Production 6/V8
1957	W100 SWB	166/205
1957	W100 LWB	131/427
1957	W200	105/202
1958	W100 SWB	406/290
1958	W100 LWB	196/564
1958	W200	396/331
1958	W300	143/194
1959	W100 SWB	298/211
1959	W100 LWB	199/327
1959	W200	213/253
1959	W300	96/99
1960	W100 SWB	333/153
1960	W100 LWB	182/251
1960	W200	262/150
1960	W300	119/119

SPECIFICATIONS W-SERIES "SWEPTLINE" 1961–1971

Years	Models	Engines std./opt.	Gearboxes std./opt	Axles std./opt.	LxWxH	Tires std./opt.
1961	W100-200	225ci-6/ 318ci-V8 140/200hp 215/286l-f	3-speed 4-speed 2-speed transfer	semi/full- floating 4.10/4.88	114 or 122in WB 186 or 206x82x75	7.00-16/ 7.00-17.5/ 8.00-19.5
1961	W300	251cid-6 125hp 216lbs-ft	3-speed 4-speed 2-speed transfer	full- floating 4.88/5.87	129in WB 8.00-19.5 204.5x79x75	8.00-19.5/ 8.00-17.5
1962–1965	W100-200-300	225ci-6/ 318ci-V8 140/200hp 215/286l-f	3-speed 4-speed 2-speed transfer	semi/full- floating 4.10/4.88/5.87	114 or 122in WB 186 or 206x82x75	7.00-16/ 7.00-17.5/ 8.00-19.5/ 9.00-16
1966–1971	W100-200-300	225ci-6/ 318ci-V8/ 383ci-V8 140/210/ 258hp 215/310/ 375lbs-ft	3-speed 4-speed Auto. 2-speed transfer	semi/full- floating 4.10/4.88/5.87	114 or 122in WB 186 or 206x82x75	7.00-16/ 7.00-17.5/ 8.00-19.5

MODEL DESIGNATIONS AND PRODUCTION SWEPTLINE POWER WAGON, 1961–1971

Years	Model	Production 6/V8
1961	W100 W200 W300	426/239 273/258 215/173
1962	W100 W200 W300	411/273 805/375 198/258
1963	W100 W200 W300	877/412 2,385/764 269/287
1964	W100 W200 W300	842/454 2,058/989 245/272
1965	W100 W200 W200 Crew Cab W300	692/563 596/550 - 201/272
1966	W100 W200 W200 Crew Cab W300	1,389/659 1,010/2,107 - 200/536
1967	W100 W200 W200 Crew Cab W300	570/530 2,099/1,997 - 214/528
1968	W100 W200 W200 Crew Cab W300	721/752 2,569/3,178 - 175/693
1969	W100 SWB & LWB W200 W200 Crew Cab W300	766/1,007 1,091/3,427 698/438 749/901
1970	W100 SWB &LWB W200 W200 Crew Cab W300	1,500 total 5,719 total 914 total 1,053 total
1971	W100 SWB W100 LWB W200 W200 Crew Cab W300	1,626 total 2,026 total 4,814 total 334 total 783 total

Chapter 4

Jeep—The American Icon

Whether you speak German or gibberish, Jeep is a word that gets instant understanding all over the world. In many ways, the Jeep has become a symbol of America, and one that reflects well on us as a nation. As a collectable 4x4, it has fanatics all over the globe dedicated to its preservation and enjoyment. If it isn't the most popular 4x4 collectable, it's got to be near the top of the list.

The name Jeep is now a highly coveted trademark of Chrysler Corporation. Using the term generically (meaning a lower case *jeep* instead of *Jeep*), 1/4-ton jeeps were built by Bantam, Ford, Willys-Overland, Kaiser, AMC and now Chrysler. The development of the vehicle we now know as the Jeep was full of political chest pounding, dirty deals, and controversy. Willys finally emerged from the fray carrying the brass ring. Along the way, they established a dynasty of 4x4 performance that has few equals in history.

It's All in the Name: Jeep Etymology

The source of the Jeep name has been debated, both privately and in court, for nearly six decades. Those four letters have become a valuable commodity, so the debates will probably never stop. The following discussion will not end the furor, but bear in mind that it is well researched.

The most likely answers to this controversy over origins comes from two sources. As early as World War I, the term "jeep" was in use with army motorpool personnel as a slang term for a new, unproven vehicle received for tests. It was also used as a less-than-complimentary term for a new, unproved human recruit! This term still was in use by career soldiers to the beginning of World War II.

The second source comes from the introduction of the Eugene-the-Jeep character in the March 16, 1936, *Popeye the Sailor* comic strip. Eugene was a mythical creature, about the size of a small dog, though he walked upright, who ate orchids and could do just about anything except tell a lie. He became immensely popular and soon the term "Jeep" became a slang word for something extraordinary.

Using the Eugene reference as a source, there were a variety of other vehicles that acquired the "Jeep" nickname before our revered 1/4-ton, including two aircraft, a 4x4 artillery prime mover, a 4x4 geological survey truck, a 1/2-ton 4x4 truck, and an electric tunnel repair vehicle, among a few others. All these rigs were reputed to be able to "do anything," just like Eugene. Enter the 1/4-tons.

It's not hard to put two and two together and figure out why a bunch of grizzled GIs would call a new untried 4x4 with extraordinary capabilities a

"Jeep." There were a variety of other nicknames for the 1/4-ton, the most common being "Peep." The army already had a semiofficial "Jeep" in the form of the popular 1/2-ton Dodge 4x4.

It all came to a head in February of 1941, when a prototype Willys was being demonstrated climbing up the steps of the Capitol. When a bystander asked Willys test driver "Red" Housman what the odd little vehicle was called, he replied, "It's a Jeep." Reporter Kathryn Hillyer reported the incident in her syndicated column and the civilian public came to know the 1/4-ton as the Jeep. As hundreds of thousands of men were drafted, they overwhelmed the old-timers who knew it by other names and there you have it. Willys also contributed to the usage with a big ad campaign in the early 1940s, but the name came by popular demand as much as anything else.

A common and easily refuted reference claims that "Jeep" came from a slurring of the term GP for General Purpose. Geep? There is not a shred of evidence to support this, since the term "general purpose" was never applied to the 1/4-ton. The Ford GP or GPW is often cited as the source but GP was a Ford engineering moniker, with "G" standing for "government contract" and P for "80-inch wheelbase Reconnaissance Car." The "W" in GPW stood for "Willys," the vehicle being a Ford manufactured version of the Willys design.

Bantam and Minneapolis-Moline, manufacturers of other vehicles nicknamed "Jeep," took Willys to task with the Federal Trade Commission during and after the war. Despite being chastised for being over-exuberant with the use of the Jeep name, Willys managed to end up with the name anyway and gained full legal rights in 1950. The public had spoken. The Willys 1/4-ton was a Jeep and would forever remain so.

The First 1/4-ton: Bantam No. 1

Bantam started all the jeep hoopla in September 1940 by completing the first prototype of the 1/4-ton 4x4 that so enamored the military and eventually much of the world. The roots of the Bantam involvement go back to 1930, when the American Austin Car Company began building a version of the British Austin 7 mini car under license. After an initial sales spurt, the 50-mile per gallon small cars were cold-shouldered by the American public.

In a major slump, Bantam looked at every possible avenue that sold cars. In 1933, they submitted a 4x2 version of their mini-pickup for testing by the U.S. Army. The fragile vehicle was generally unsatisfactory but the army spent some time trying to improve cross-country performance by adding aircraft tires. They liked the small size and nimble performance but the two-wheel drive Bantam was far too fragile for front-line work.

In 1936, American Austin reorganized with new owners into the American Bantam Car Company, and they put the whole line through a serious facelifting operation. The new owners placed high hopes on the redesigned small cars, but once again, the idea was ignored by the American public. Bantam hung on through the 1930s, again submitting a few prototype 4x2

Bantam Pilot No. 1, the vehicle that started it all. It's shown here undergoing tests at Camp Holabird sometime after 23 September 1940. After tests, this pivotal vehicle was damaged in a collision with a utility truck in early 1941 and was never repaired. *U.S. Army*

The Bantam Mark II models were very similar to the Pilot Model but the front fenders were more military in appearance. Sixty-nine were built to this basic design. One Mark II, serial number 007, survives and is displayed at the U.S. Army Transportation Museum, Ft. Eustis, Virginia. *U.S. Army*

"Scout Cars" to the army but by 1940, their facility in Butler, Pennsylvania, was down to a staff of 15 people—including executives.

Some serious prebankruptcy lobbying got the Army interested in a pickup version of their latest cars. The idea progressed to the point where a contract seemed a real possibility, when, again, the liabilities of two-wheel drive on the battlefield were discussed. This time, members of the Army Ordnance subcommittee worked with Bantam to flesh out the design for a lightweight 4x4 vehicle. After a great deal of turmoil involving Willys, who also wanted the business, Bantam finally won a contract for 70 vehicles, the first of which had to be delivered in a mere 49 days.

A Bantam BRC-40 gets a GI bath in 1941. The BRC-40 was the last Bantam Jeep. Some 2,600 were built before production ended in December of 1941. *U.S. Army*

The Ford GP took the Pygmy design to a production-level vehicle. Though still powered by the troublesome 119-cid NNA tractor engine, it proved to be a serviceable machine. Altogether, 4,458 were built, and many have survived. The GP is the most common of the prototype jeeps. *FWD*

The Willys Quad was regarded as having the worst overall body layout but it had an engine with 15 more horsepower than the nearest competitor and a good drivetrain to boot. Two were built to this general design. These rigs were also seriously overweight, so Barney Roos tore one of the Quads down and lightened every piece he could. They even went to the point of installing shorter bolts where threads protruded and even saved a few pounds on paint. The Willys squeaked by just a few ounces under the limit. *Chrysler Historical*.

At first, Bantam had hoped to use a large number of their own existing components. In the end, beyond a few body parts and miscellaneous small parts, little was usable. Still, Bantam succeeded in delivering the prototype, often referred to as "Number One" or "Old Number One," just 30 minutes before the deadline. The vehicle was mercilessly tested by the staff at Camp Holabird, Maryland, and it endured. The performance of this new breed of military vehicle captured the imagination of every branch of the military. In 1940, Bantam Number One had no equal.

The Bantam pilot model was built upon an inverted U-section chassis. The rear body was fabricated but the front end and cowl came from the Bantam car parts bin. The bicycle-style front fenders, also modified Bantam car pieces, gave it a toy car look. The engine was a 45-horsepower Continental that was backed up by a Warner Gear T-84 three-speed and a Spicer Model 18 transfer case. The front and rear axles were Spicer 25 models that Spicer modified for the purpose. With the exception of the engine, this is the same drivetrain combination that was used for the Ford GP and the Willys prototypes and even the production Willys MB and Ford GPW. Bantam gets the credit for using this particular combination first.

The Bantam pilot has passed into history. After being wrecked in an early 1941 traffic accident, it was disassembled and many of its parts were likely recycled into the Mark II models then in production. According to legend, the unusable parts of the vehicle were buried with a load of scrap on the Bantam grounds. This has never been verified but it's a comforting thought.

Field Tests: Bantam Mark II

The initial tests of the Bantam prototype had yielded some weak links and improvements were incorporated into the Mark II models. Among the visual differences were the more military looking, squared-off front fenders. A variety of minor improvements were made, but essentially, the 69 Mark IIs were a copy of the original. A few were built as four-wheel steer models.

The majority of the Bantams were issued to operational army units for field tests and for the GIs, it was love at first sight. The little "Blitz Buggies" were mounted with machine guns and 37-mm antitank guns. Period photos show them getting frequent flyer miles with exuberant GIs at the wheel. While all this was going on, Willys and Ford were in a fierce fight with Bantam for the potentially lucrative 1/4-ton contract.

The Mark IIs were thoroughly tested and remained in service until replaced by the Willys MB or Ford GPW models. At present, only one Mark II is known to have survived. Owned by the Smithsonian Institution, it's currently on display at the Army Transportation Museum, Fort Eustis, Virginia. Some of the 69 vehicles were known to have been sold surplus at Berg's in

The MA was the second-generation 1/4-ton from Willys that embodied many of the lessons learned from the first tests. This vehicle is probably the design that won Willys the 16,000-vehicle contract. Only 1,550 MAs were built and with most of these going overseas, there aren't many left for collectors. This restored example, along with the 37-mm antitank gun, belongs to the Alabama Center for Military History. *Alabama Center for Military History*

The slat grille was the earliest version of the MB and was built to the tune of about 25,000 units. The earliest used the column-shift arrangement favored by Willys but not the Army. The slat grilles are a mixed bag of unusual features but they gradually standardize to MB spec by the time the stamped grille MB emerged in early 1942. Few slat grille Willys remain. *Reg Hodgeson*

The final version of the Willys MB emerged in 1942 and from there, Willys stamped 'em out faster than they could be shot up in battle. Tony Standefer's beautifully restored 1944 MB is unusual because it's painted in USMC markings. *Tony Standefer*

The best part about owning a World War II Jeep is that you can play with markings. If you can discover the original markings and want to maintain them, okay. You can also play around and give it markings from a particular unit, individual, or era. Maurizio Berretta, of Milan, Italy, painted his 1943 to match a Jeep in which the British General Montgomery and Canadian General Crerar were seated in a 1944 photo at the Normandy beachhead. Berretta's Jeep was used by the U.S. Army in the Italian Campaign and then given to the Italian Army in 1945. It was used by them until 1955. *Maurizio Berretta*

Chicago, a military surplus dealer, during the war, along with other prototype jeeps. It seems likely that there may be others hiding in the weeds somewhere. Good luck!

The Last Bantam: BRC-40

To end some of the squabbling, and further the development of the 1/4-ton, the government ordered 1,500 improved models each from Bantam, Willys, and Ford. Bantam responded with the BRC-40. The BRC stood for Bantam Reconnaissance Car. The development of a standardized 1/4-ton model put the Lend-Lease production behind schedule. In order to satisfy these pressing and ever-growing obligations, more orders were made from Ford and Bantam. Bantam ended up building 2,605 BRC-40s. At least 207 of these went to the British Army, others went to the Russians and elsewhere.

The BRC-40 was the highest evolution of the Bantam design. It still carried the same, albeit slightly improved, engine and drivetrain but the body had been simplified, the chassis beefed up and the unit was built to a more military standard.

It was known for being a nimble performer and was considerably lighter than the later MB models that became standard.

The Bantam contracts ended when the last BRC-40 was shipped in December of 1941, and Bantam never built another 1/4-ton. The company spent the rest of the war building the ubiquitous 1/4-ton jeep trailer, torpedo

motors, and aircraft landing gear. This situation is regarded by many historians as one of the great "raw deals" of the war. Considering the success that history has brought to the producers of the jeep, the originator deserved a better fate.

Bantam BRC-40s are fairly common, with somewhere between 50 and 100, depending on which expert you ask, still in existence around the world. There are others occasionally being found and restored. As with any of the early jeeps, they get pricy to restore because parts are not readily available. Some parts have been reproduced for the early units, but with very low production, they don't come cheap.

The Winner: Willys Quad

Willys' entrant into the jeep race was called the Quad. Two were built initially to compete in the army tests and were delivered on November 11, 1940, more than a month after the Bantam Pilot. By that time, the Mark II Bantams were rolling off the line and it is likely these improved Bantams went toe-to-toe with the Quad in tests along with the pilot model.

The Quad had a secret weapon that took the others by storm. The 60-horsepower "Go-Devil" four-cylinder was head and shoulders above the Ford or Bantam powerplants. The biggest problem with the Quad, as the Army saw it, was weight. It was several hundred pounds over the 2,160-pound weight limit. Willys put the Quad on a diet and squeaked by with only ounces to spare.

As mentioned earlier, the Quad used the same Spicer axles and Model 18 transfer case and Warner T-84 transmission as the Bantam and Fords (the earliest Ford used a Model A transmission but later units had the Warner). Willys was fond of the column shift and the Quad was so equipped. This later proved to be a major bugaboo to the army, who disliked the complexity and the fact that in rough terrain, the lever could be bumped by a flailing knee.

The two Quads were extensively tested, and every Jeep historian knows that Willys got the contract. What happened to the Quads is a question that has titillated historians for decades. One is known to have survived into the early 1950s, when it was photographed alongside a 1950 Willys M-38 and a 1953 M-38A1. After that, it's anyone's guess. It's possible that the Quad rests in a barn or field somewhere but most likely, it went to the smelter.

The Transition Willys: Willys MA

Willys was pretty slow on the draw getting an improved model out. With the army's needs and specifications changing by the week, this is not surprising. When the 1,500-unit order came, Willys stared pumping out an updated rig, which they called the MA. About 1,550 were built before they were superseded by the Willys MB. While the MA bore some of the improvements mandated by the army, it was still as much Quad as anything else.

The basic mechanical hard parts were very nearly the same pieces that would be used in the later MB. In the looks department, any observant person will note the similarities between the MA and the Bantam designs. It needs to be remembered that the Bantam plans had been freely passed around when the MA was on the drawing boards, along with the Army's notes on its shortcomings. Both Willys and Ford had ample opportunity to use the other company's experience to their own benefit.

The MA was a transitional vehicle and one that Willys was not 100 percent behind. Barney Roos, the chief engineer at Willys, had serious reservations about the weight limits imposed on the design. The MA, with its com-

The production amphibian was built by Ford and called the GPA. Nicknamed the "Seep," it was notorious for going to the bottom in any chop. The sea bottom off the Normandy beachhead is still littered with the remains of the GPAs that attempted a landing there and didn't make it.

The M-38, or Willys MC model, was a short-term replacement for the World War II era MBs. Introduced in 1950, it was heavy, underpowered and was soon replaced by the M-38A1. With only about 62,000 built (more than half going for export) it's the rarest production military Jeep. Reg Hodgson's M-38 is decked out in Korean War vintage Canadian colors. *Reg Hodgson*

A nicely restored M-38A1 like this is a collectable piece. With parts relatively plentiful, they are an easy restoration. George Baxter, of Army Jeep Parts, can be justifiably proud of the work done on this vintage soldier. *George Baxter*

The development of the civilian jeep started in 1944. The first 12 or so were called Agrijeeps, and this is the only restored one. This is CJ-2-09 and it was built in the summer of 1944. The Agrijeeps were a unique experiment that combined the military Jeep with the features Willys thought would be desired after the war, including a tailgate, drawbar, and PTO. The mounting of the spare tire and the brass "Jeep" emblems are the Agrijeep giveaways, as well as the VIN plate which is so marked. The records are unavailable and do not confirm this, but it appears that 12 Agrijeeps were built in 1944. Owned by noted early civilian Jeep expert and author Fred Coldwell, the CJ-2 was restored by Charles Ellis and is one of three remaining Agrijeeps. Note the column shift. *Fred Coldwell*

bination of light weight (under 2,200 pounds) and powerful engine, was a real hot rod but the lightening up process brought problems. For example, the spare tire mounting on the rear body would tear away, because the thinner metal wasn't quite strong enough to carry the weight. The army also announced a dislike for the MA's column shift and under-dash parking brake, though these items were not to change until later.

Most of the Willys MA rigs went overseas, a great many to Russia. They are now the rarest of the first series Jeeps, with perhaps as few as 20–25 in existence. Many of those are still overseas. An MA is most Jeep collectors' dream vehicle. Expect to pay a high price for an MA—if one ever comes up for sale. An MA would be an advanced restoration because so little is documented and parts are nearly impossible to find, beyond those it shares with the later Jeeps. There exists only one parts source to the prototype jeep restorer; Ken Hake's Jeep Parts (see source list). This outfit has restored many prototype jeeps (all three makes) and has made patterns of body parts as well as locating NOS parts and sourcing many hard-to-find items.

Almost Standard: Slat Grille MB

As the military studied the MA, and the other jeeps, they began to realize that Barney Roos at Willys had been right. The tradeoffs for light weight were not worth the cost. They realized that a multitude of other details had been ignored. In July of 1941, while production of the MAs was ongoing, Willys was awarded a contract for 16,000 vehicles but was also given a whole batch of improvements to make. The controversial weight limit was subsequently waived in favor of an improved design. In the end, the new MB model tipped the scales at nearly 2,500 pounds.

In August of 1941, the MA production line was shut down to retool for the MB. Production of the new model began in December. Among the improvements was a payload increase from the MA's 650 pounds to an often-to-be-exceeded 800 pounds. A new towing arrangement was fitted as well as larger tires, a more powerful 40-amp charging system, and a 116 amp/hour battery. The body design represented a homogenization of Willys, Ford, and

Bantam ideas, as well as some all-new ones. Despite the army's objections, the first slat grilles came with column shifts.

The contract was soon amended to increase the numbers of MBs being built. This was in direct response to the December 7 bombing of Pearl Harbor and the declaration of war that followed. The first 25,000 MBs were called "slat grilles" because they used a welded steel grille similar to the Ford GP. In a way, they were also transitional vehicles, because they rapidly evolved according to experience gained in operational use and combat.

There were numerous differences between the slat grille and the stamped grille MB, but a later slat grille will differ from an early one because there were so many running changes. Besides the grille, some of the differences included the air cleaner design, the absence of a glove box in the dash, brass dash plaques on the earliest units, and "Willys" stamped into the rear body. The wheels were solid 16-inch jobs instead of the later bolted-together combat rims, there was no fender mounted blackout light, and the earliest MB slat grilles had an MA style windshield that was lower than the later pieces. Lastly, the serial numbers on many slat grilles were stamped on an oval shaped tag on the inside of the left front chassis rail, but unlike the later MBs, its serial number was not preceded by an "MB."

Several experts were queried as to the remaining number of slat grilles, and the answers average to about 200. Either way, the slat grille MB is a very collectable variation of the standard MB for those who like to be a little different. You will find some slat grille parts very difficult to obtain, the air filter being one such item, and the running changes made in them makes it difficult to research a 100 percent correct restoration.

Genuine Hero: Willys MB

Once the final design was determined, Willys went to work stamping out Jeeps as fast as they could. Eventually, some 335,531 were manufactured. While there were minor variations and adaptation, most of the stamped grille MBs are the same. Among the sought-after variations are the very earliest models that, like the slat grille, bear a stamped "Willys" on the left rear. Beyond this, the goal becomes outfitting the classic Willys with some of the variety of add-ons that were available to adapt the vehicle to a multitude of tasks.

As America geared up, our allies got to be the first to subject the jeep to the rigors of war. In the 1941 and 1942 North African Desert Campaign, the elite British Long Range Desert Group arm of the SAS (Special Air Service) outfitted Jeeps for raids behind the German lines to disrupt supply lines, sever command and control links and, in general, give the Germans a hard time. Equipped with up to four heavy machine guns and loaded beyond capacity with ammo and fuel, the jeeps were famous for their ability to keep going. The German commanders were impressed

This is Art Carey's masterful 1946 CJ-2A resto that was designed to reproduce a family heirloom. A summer spent with his Grandfather and an early CJ-2A Jeep put an indelible mark on Art. Many years later, after trying unsuccessfully to find the original CJ-2A, Art built his own. *Art Carey*

Here's a peach of a CJ-3A. Still resplendent in its original Luzon Red paint, this 1950 model is distinguishable as a 3A by its one-piece windshield and air vent just below it, in the center. A Jeep in this almost 100 percent original and non-rusty condition is a rare find.

The CJ-3B introduced the more powerful F-head engine into the production CJ lineup for 1953. In order to clear the carburetor and air cleaner, the hood and cowl was raised. The stamped reinforcement along the side of the hood of Bob Mohan's pristine 1962 is the approximate location of the top of the earlier low-hood design. Late CJ-3Bs are very scarce. The hardtop is an aftermarket unit, probably from Sears.

On the left is the original Willys Go-Devil L-head engine and to the right is the Hurricane that replaced it in 1953 CJ models (1952 for the military). The old flathead (L-head) had both intake and exhaust valves in the block, as was common practice for engines designed in the 1930s and 1940s. These engines were low-power units and were fairly inefficient breathers due to the tortuous path the incoming air had to take into the cylinder. The high compression version of this engine made about 63 horsepower. The F-head (right) kept the exhaust valves in the block but the intake valves were contained in a new cylinder head assembly. Not only was this conducive to breathing, it allowed an even bigger intake valve to be used. Power jumped to 75 horsepower for the high compression engines. The F-head was still not an ideal engine. The overhead valve engines of today are much more efficient. The Hurricane design, however, allowed Willys to use about 80 percent of the old L-head and saved a lot of development and retooling costs. The old L-head could be retrofitted with an F-head kit, though this was possible only on vehicles that had the hood space, such as the Willys trucks.

enough to issue a general order that captured jeeps should be used wherever possible to replace their own inadequate machines.

Early jeeps were used in the defense of the Philippines to pull rail cars of ammunition to the front after the locomotives were destroyed. Equipped with flanged wheels, the jeeps pulled 20-ton rail cars around the clock to keep the troops supplied with ammo. The Japanese captured many jeeps in their early successes and sent some of them home to be copied. These rigs became the inspiration for the postwar entrance of the Japanese into the world 4x4 market.

One battered jeep was officially issued a Purple Heart medal after being damaged in two successive Pacific beach landings and was sent home. Another was credited with destroying four Japanese tanks. There are enough stories of this kind to fill a book.

Adaptation was another key advantage to the jeep. The jeep was half-tracked, armor plated, stretched, shortened, lightened, mounted with heavy machine guns and light artillery, and used as a stationary powerhouse. In 1943 Sicily, bereft of electric power, army units supplied a local olive oil producer a jeep to power his olive processing machine. A belt was used from the jeep's rear wheel to drive the machinery. This act of good will resulted in 44 tons of virgin olive oil for the starving Italian people.

Derek Redmond's 1961 CJ-3B is a masterpiece of restoration but is still used on a near daily basis—weather permitting. Derek is probably the first authority on CJ-3Bs and his Website at http://www.film.queens.ca/CJ3B/index .html is chock full of CJ-3B info. *Derek Redmond*

The jeep also offered the GI an outlet for his youthful exuberance in the form of a pseudo sports car. Sports car? The jeep had a better power-to-weight ratio than many contemporary automobiles. Light and low slung, it actually cornered well for the day. Unfortunately, without a roll cage or roof, it was usually fatal in a rollover, as many GIs found out. Bill Mauldin, the famous World War II cartoonist, was quoted as saying, "Jeeps killed about as many people as any weapon in World War II. You have to drive it with respect."

Production of MBs stopped in 1945 and even before that, Willys was hard at work designing the civilian version. The World War II-era jeeps were used into the Korean War, when they were replaced by the M38 models. Many foreign armies bought surplus jeeps and some of them were used almost to the current day. Many were bought surplus by starry-eyed ex-GIs.

The Willys MB Jeeps are still very common today. Many have been turned into trail machines but the trend now is to restore them to factory original appearance. A vast array of new parts and new old stock is available for the restorer. It's almost possible to build a new jeep out of pieces. This is about as close as you can come to the "jeep-in-a-crate" myth that has hung around almost as long as the jeep itself.

The World War II jeep scene is incredibly active. Not only are there a vast array of clubs dedicated to the marque all over the world, but vast amounts of research has been done to aid the restorer in getting every detail meticulously correct. Ray Cowdery's books on jeeps, *All American Wonder, Volumes I and II*, are masterpieces of detail on the World War II jeep. The Willys Jeep is an ideal first restoration for anyone.

Ford's 4x4 Flivver: Pygmy

Ford was a little slow to build up speed on the 1/4-ton project but once started, it nearly rolled over and crushed all the others competing for a contract. Their first prototypes, delivered to Camp Holabird on November 23, 1940, most closely resembled the final jeep design—at least on the outside. The Fords were powered by the NNA four-cylinder that displaced 119 cubic inches and made 45 horsepower. The axles and transfer case were all Spicer

The CJ-5, introduced late in 1954 for the 1955 model year, can be distinguished from the later units by the battery box on the cowl and the cut-out on the passenger side hood. The battery box disappeared after the 1965 model year, when the battery was located under the hood, and the cut-out, a leftover from the military M-38A1 (used for the fording snorkel), was gone after 1965 as well. This 1955 model is shown fitted with a PTO-driven air compressor. *Jeep Public Relations*

pieces but the first transmission was a variant of their Model A car gearbox, and it proved to be troublesome.

Of the two vehicles Ford submitted, only one was accepted for testing. One version had a body that was built by Budd, and this unit was not accepted. Though similar, it had been independently designed and did not share all the Ford's desirable features. So, the Ford-built machine went into the not-so-tender hands of Captain Mosling and the rest of the torture specialists at Camp Holabird for serious evaluation. They quickly uncovered a number of defects, not the least of which was a tendency for the engine to come unglued. The Ford NNA powerplant had been designed for a constant speed application in tractors and suffered from bearing failures, vapor locking, and ignition system problems. It was also not very powerful, especially compared to the Willys. It had even less oomph than the Bantam's modest Continental powerplant, despite the fact that they had virtually the same rated output.

In spite of the problems, the Ford unit was praised for many fine features, not the least of which was the basic layout of the body and controls. These features were emulated in many ways in all the future jeep designs. Still, after Ford proved far inferior to the Willys in performance and reliability, it was a big shock for the other competitors to learn Ford was offered a contract. No doubt, the government was banking on Ford's being able to solve the problems. There was no doubt of Ford's ability to produce the goods in quantity. With Willys howling "foul," the contract was quickly rescinded and given to Willys. More squabbling ensued and three 1,500 vehicle contracts were issued to all three competitors to further evaluate each type.

The CJ-6 was introduced in late 1955, a year after the CJ-5. It was essentially the same rig as a CJ-5 but stretched 20 inches. They were not built in large numbers and many of those produced went for export or into commercial hands. Few remain. This is a 1975 model hard at work.

The first Ford prototype has survived. After testing, it was used for publicity during the war and donated to the Henry Ford Museum in 1948. In 1982, it was offered up for sale in one of the museum's periodic auctions and purchased by Randy Withrow. The vehicle has been on display periodically at various military vehicle shows around the country, but will soon be enshrined in the Alabama Center for Miliary History, as soon as that organization has a permanent home.

Improved Ford: The GP

Ford's second design was somewhat improved over the Pygmy. It still bore the NNA engine, only slightly improved and still troublesome, but the Model A gearbox had been replaced by the same Warner Gear T-84 that was being used in the Bantam and Willys rigs. All in all, it was a satisfactory machine in this guise and Ford proceeded to stamp them out as only Ford can.

Ford finished up with the last of their 1,500 in March 1941 and was promptly issued a contract for another for 1,150 more. In June, another bid was requested, given, and accepted for another 1,000 units. Both these and the preceding contracted vehicles were completed in November. A special batch of 50 four-wheel steer version was ordered and completed in October. The official tally of Ford GPs is listed as 4,458 units.

Many of these were shipped overseas, with 33 going to Brazil, 403 to the Netherlands East Indies, 144 to Great Britain, 6 to the Polish Army in Canada, and 1,000 to China. The remainder served in the U.S. Army Stateside. Some were sold surplus during the war and became the first jeeps in civilian hands. Others served with nontactical units or government agencies until finally replaced by MBs.

The Ford GP is the most numerous of the prototype jeeps, with almost 200 in private hands around the world. As with the other prototypes, parts and expertise are in short supply, but the Ford GP makes a fine, historic, and unique collectable.

Under License: Ford GPW

With the issuance of the 16,000-vehicle contract to Willys, Ford was approached as to whether it would be willing to produce jeeps to the Willys pattern. Despite the obvious retooling costs and difficulties, the answer was yes. A contract was issued in October 1941 for 15,000 vehicles. With the war fever rapidly gaining momentum, the government knew that more than one supplier was needed. This proved to be valuable foresight when war was declared in December.

After some initial teething difficulties replicating the chassis design, the Ford GPW emerged as fully interchangeable with the Willys in every major sense but with quite a number of small detail changes. Just like Willys, Ford embossed its name on the rear of the vehicle. The government frowned on what they considered blatant commercialism and ordered the practice stopped. Still, the first batch of GPWs were so marked and the last of these were delivered in April 1942. The Ford "Script" models are highly sought after and quite rare. After they were denied the Ford name on the rear, many Ford small parts and vital nuts and bolts were marked with an embossed "F. " Reputedly, this was done on Henry Ford's orders so his company would not accidentally have to honor warranties on a Willys-made part.

Though this statement may be debatable in the circles where such things are argued, Ford-built jeeps are the equal of the Willys-built units and share the same performance characteristics. It is commonly thought that Ford-made engine blocks are prone to cracking and not the Willys castings. Apparently, Ford blocks are now difficult to come by, and many GPWs are found with Willys-made engines.

Ford built 277,896 GPWs. The final contract was terminated in August of 1945, and Ford went on to other pursuits. GPWs are somewhat more common than Willys Jeeps but their value on the market is essentially the same. While there was some friendly rivalry between the MB and GPW camps, they are on a level playing field pricewise. For GPW restorers, having the correctly marked Ford script parts is important to the restoration. Often, Ford scripted nuts and small parts can be sold or traded.

Fully Floating: GPA Amphibian

As early as 1940, there was discussion of building an amphibious version of the 1/4-ton. It progressed to the specifications stage by 1941 and by late that year, two companies, Marmon-Herrington and Ford, were actively pursuing designs.

In Marmon-Herrington's case, outside aid was enlisted in the form of the prestigious yacht designers at Sparkman & Stevens of New York. Mar-

The 1970 Renegade 1 models came with a roll bar, a swing-away spare tire carrier, extra gauges, and 8-inch rim fitted with G70-15 Polyglas tires, which were definitely not an off-highway tread. This Renegade was also fitted with the V6. *Jeep Public Relations*

In 1972, the Renegade took on new life with the introduction of the V-8. Alloy wheels, off-highway tires, the roll cage, a limited-slip rear axle, and the 304-cid gave this new Jeep some serious punch. These limited production units were built in a similar package through 1979. This is a 1973 model. *Jeep Public Relations*

mon-Herrington built up a prototype utilizing a standard 1/4-ton chassis and a floating body that was built out of welded sheet steel and called the QMC-4. It was successfully tested by both Marmon-Herrington and the army in early 1942.

Ford's first design was launched sometime after Marmon-Herrington's and it was based on the Ford GP chassis. It was successfully "launched" in April of 1942. This unit was tested and approval was given for a revised pilot model based upon the GPW. This design was eventually accepted and production began on the model dubbed the GPA, the A for amphibian.

With its extra weight and bulk, the GPA was an ungainly beast. It was like driving a mini motorhome. On land it struggled to reach 55 miles per hour. In the water, it was designed for about 7 miles per hour but you had to make it scream to run at 5.5 miles per hour, its rated speed. The hull was an assemblage of stamped pieces welded together. The flat surfaces were ribbed to provide structural rigidity.

The water drive was achieved by means of a power take-off that operated both the prop and a bilge pump. Second gear was used in the water. The engine was cooled via a hatch on the front deck which could be closed for rough weather. There was also a splash shield on the bow. The GPA was notorious for overheating while running in the water. The GPA mounted a 3,500-pound, engine-driven capstan winch on the bow to help it waddle ashore.

This design was rushed into service, mainly for the invasion of Italy—which it missed anyway due to teething problems. Some 12,778 were ordered in 1942 and 1943, though fewer than this number were actually built due to problems in design. They were sent out into the field before they were adequately tested. Between the design problems and an inadequate training program for operators, the army regarded them as a "technical and tactical failure," to quote a U.S. Army Material Command pamphlet. They were used in the Normandy beach landings in June 1944, and most of them sank on the way to the beach. The nickname of "Seep" was aptly put.

Jumping forward about 50 years, the GPA is a popular collectable, though definitely for a niche market. Properly handled in a fair weather situation, they can be fun water toys as well as historic military rigs. They are uncommon and usually expensive. The hulls are usually rusted out and require a great deal of fabrication skill to put into floatable shape.

Oddballs: The Military Jeep Variants

There are a number of variants built upon the basic MB or GPW chassis that may still be occasionally found. Most of them were built in very small numbers. First would be the four-wheel steer variety. Most of these were in the prototype models but a few were built in the MB and GPW lines. The idea was to improve maneuverability but the system created other problems and added complexity. While a couple of Ford and Bantam four-wheel steer jeeps have survived, this writer could not find any MBs or GPWs extant that were so equipped.

When the need for a snow tractor arose, the jeep was looked at as a possible basis for modification. Search and Rescue units needed a vehicle capable of getting them across expanses of snow, especially in places like Canada, Alaska, and Greenland, over which large numbers of military aircraft flew and some crashed. The T-28 and T-29 snow tractors were nothing more than Willys MBs with half-tracks added to the rear. The T-28 used the standard wheels and front end while the T-29 replaced them with skis. Not particularly successful, they were not built in any numbers. The eventual production vehicle was the M7 Snow Tractor, which was built by Allis Chalmers, using the jeep's engine and much of its drivetrain.

Willys experimented with a 6x6 version of the Jeep, for which they had high hopes of building in large numbers. Nicknamed the "Super Jeep" it was optimistically rated as a 3/4-ton and tested in 1943. Cargo/personnel, ambulance, and an anti-aircraft gun carrying version were built, but the design never went into production.

At least six jeep "tanks" were manufactured by Marmon-Herrington in Canada for use as light, air portable armored vehicles. The Willys engine, gearbox, and axle were used as a powertrain. The idea never progressed beyond the six. One of the vehicles survives in a collection in England.

The Marine Corps converted jeeps for use as ambulances by modifying the body and adding litter racks and a special top. The passenger seat in front was replaced by a large storage box accessible from the outside. The litter rack was a tubular cage that rose above the height of the windshield, which was pushed forward to vertical. Apparently these USMC rigs were modified in some quantity for use in the Pacific.

In an attempt to save materials, jeep bodies were built of wood on an experimental basis. Several prototypes were built by a couple of companies, but the wood was heavier than steel and tended to swell when wet. The idea was abandoned in 1943. It's doubtful that any "firewood" jeeps have survived.

Developing the Peacetime Jeep

By 1944, it was no secret that Willys-Overland had postwar plans for the Jeep. Peacetime planning was well under way early in the year, and a few prototypes were built using MBs as the basis for the changes. Adapting the unit to agricultural use became one of the first priorities. Many of the meticulous records kept in this era have disappeared and until recently, it wasn't clear how these first prototypes were designated.

It had always seemed likely that the first units, or at least the planning stage vehicles would have been called CJ-1. This has now been proven to be the case. Lately, some Willys blueprints were unearthed, dated June 1944, where the Jeep was designated CJ-1. Previously found records verified that a CJ-2 designation existed for as many as 45 vehicles. CJ-2 #9, #11, #12, #32, and #37 exist and have been verified. There is a good chance that some others have survived, in whole or part, for the dedicated searcher/collector to uncover.

The earliest CJ-2s, Numbers 1–12 according to the available records, were dubbed the "Agrijeeps" and bear this name on their data plates. They are distinctly different than the CJ-2s. The Agrijeeps were built in 1944 and tested at agricultural centers around the country. The spare tire is mounted in front of the rear wheel arch on the passenger side. The later CJ-2, like all the

Under the hood, the 304-cid powered CJs were clean and neat. The 304 is interchangeable with the 360 or 401 V-8s of the same era, as well as the earlier AMC 290, 343, and 390. Using parts available from Jeep, an AMC V-8 can be bolted, that's right, bolted, in place of a 232 or 258 six.

In 1976, the Renegade package no longer included the V-8, though it was available as a separate option. From 1975 on, the option also included the Levi interior. This is a 1977 CJ-5 that used the new Renegade graphics. Note the "Levi's" decal above the Jeep name on the cowl. Note also the absence of the V-8 emblem.

following CJs, had the tire mounted aft of the wheel arch. They came equipped with a semicircular front brush guard, though this appeared on some of the later CJ-2s also. The Agrijeeps also mounted brass "Jeep" plates on the sides of the hood, on the rear body, and on the windshield frame. They were equipped with power take-offs and the tailgates had three vertical ribs. Mechanically, they were nearly identical to the MB, with the exception of the stronger T-90 gearbox.

Later CJ-2s had "Jeep" stamped on the hood sides or tailgate. CJ-32 and 37 exist and are under restoration. If you find a derelict early Jeep with an "x" prefix serial number, odds are you have found a prototype and you've hit the collector's jackpot. Prototypes can be either incredibly valuable or worth nothing. There is no established market value. More often than not, they are valuable to a dedicated collector. Beware that prototypes can be very difficult to properly restore accurately due to lack of records and corn-cobbing by the test engineers.

Jeeps in Civvies: The CJ-2A

The CJ-2A was the first production version of the civilian adaptation of the Willys 1/4-ton. Production began in late 1945, just days after the war in Europe ended, and the public got its first look in July of that year. Just under 2,000 units were produced for the 1945 model year, but more than 70,000 were built in 1946. In the face of a bevy of war surplus MBs and GPWs, the 2As sold well. They were produced into the 1949 model year (only about 100 2As were made in 1949) until the upgraded CJ-3A replaced them. Just over 210,000 CJ-2As rolled down the line in the three and a half-year run. The letter "A" at the end of the model designation is taken from military nomenclature and denotes a significant upgrade on an existing model.

There were a variety of differences between the early and later 2As. One of the most interesting was the column-shift models. From the beginning units into the early part of 1946, to serial number 38,221, Willys used a "three-on-the-tree" column shift on the CJ-2As. Willys had long been enamored of this complicated apparatus and had even tried selling it to the army for the wartime Jeeps. Well, the army didn't buy and apparently neither did the public. The column-shift models are very rare and a "eureka" find for a Jeep collector.

Also, the first 29,000 or so 2As had the tool indents in the body like the wartime MB. These were phased out to the common flat-sided look, but many an early 2A has been mistaken for an MB. The dead CJ-2A giveaways, of course, are the tailgate, the protruding headlights, seven grille slots instead of nine and "Willys" embossed on the hood sides, windshield frame and tailgate. The early 2As also had a limited range of color options available, gray, blue, tan and brown. Soon a more vibrant range of hues came available.

There were also a number of running changes in the line. The first CJ-2As came with the wartime Spicer 23-2 full-floating rear axle. This was soon changed to the Spicer 41-2 semifloating unit. A number of engine changes also took place, including a new one-piece forged crankshaft, a revision of the cylinder head, timing gears replacing the chain, and carburetor changes. The transmission was upgraded to the beefier Warner Gear T-90 and the Model 18 transfer case saw some improvements as well. All in all, the CJ-2As were an improvement over the wartime Jeeps in most respects. Very few of the early 2As have survived and finding one in original condition is tough. The later 2As are more easily found but the years have taken a toll.

Here is the 1949 station wagon lineup, with the 4x4 in the center. This was the intro year for the 4x4 station wagon line and before long, they were outselling the two-wheelers by a big margin. *Jeep House Museum*

Last of the Low Hoods: CJ-3A

Following the successful run of the CJ-2A, the 1949–1953 CJ-3As came to the market. Actually introduced late in 1948, the CJ-2A and 3A models were sold concurrently for a time. The changes were few. One major upgrade was the Spicer 44-2 axle that replaced the 41-2. Visually, the CJ-3A can be identified by its one-piece windshield and the air vent, known to some as the "1-60" air conditioning unit (open one vent and go 60!), just below it. There were some very minor physical dimension differences and a few more available options.

Late in 1951, the CJ-3A could be ordered with the Farm Jeep package. This package came standard with a drawbar and a power take-off and was available until the end of 1953 and items like lights, passenger seat, horn, etc. were deleted. The vehicle was intended never to be used on the road. Just over 150,000 CJ-3As were built in the four-year run. The last year of production, they were built alongside the "high-hood" CJ-3B. The 3A represents a good value and clean examples can be found at reasonable prices. They lack the collector potential of the 2A but have every bit as much charm. This is a good, entry level early Jeep.

The CJ is Drafted: The M-38

When the military came looking for a replacement for its aging World War II era MBs, naturally Willys wanted to produce it. It actually was a fairly easy proposition. The Willys model MC, known by the military as the M-38, was an adaptation of the CJ-3A. The MC used a stronger chassis and suspension than its CJ cousins. The bodywork partially reverted back to the MB style with the addition of tool notches on the side. It used the same CJ-3A vented, one-piece windshield and frame. The headlights were protected by a one-piece guard.

Mechanically, the major changes included a 24-volt electrical system, and a semi-floating Dana 44 rear axle. A new waterproof, shielded ignition system was installed and the instrumentation was the military standard type. The stronger T-90 gearbox and upgraded Model 18 transfer case followed from the CJ line and a bigger 9.5 inch clutch was used.

The M-38 was produced from 1950–1952 and many saw combat in the Korean War. Just over 62,000 were built for domestic use, making them one of the least common Jeeps and *the* least common military Jeep type. Some additional units were built from 1953–1955 for export.

Though highly collectable, the M-38s have not gained the following of World War II-era Jeeps. This is beginning to change. M-38s still represent a good investment but the prices are going up for this fairly rare Jeep. Parts peculiar to this limited production GI Jeep are getting increasingly hard to find.

The Missing Link: CJ-4

Not generally known is that Willys worked on a CJ-4 project. You and many other Jeep fans have wondered about that missing number! Before you get all excited, it appears that only one was constructed. Built upon an 81-inch chassis, the CJ-4 was developed concurrently, with the MD, or M-38A1 model that also became the CJ-5. The pilot models of the M-38A1 project, called the M-38E1, wore the same unique front sheet metal as did the CJ-4. The oddball CJ-4 and its military cousins may have the distinction of being the first CJ to carry the Willys F-head "Hurricane" engine, but the few avail-

Some of the Tiny Detail Differences Between Ford and Willys Jeeps

1) The most readily visible difference is the front crossmember. The GPW has a C-channel piece while the MB uses a tubular member.
2) The GPW serial number is stamped on the top of the chassis, between the front crossmember and the motor mount bracket on the driver's side. Occasionally, it is found on the top rail between the bumper gusset and the radiator support bracket. The Willys number is on a tag riveted to a plate that is welded to the inside of the frame horn just behind the bumper area on the driver's side.
3) The transfer case shifter makes a rapid change in diameter at the top for the knob on the GPW. MB has a gradual taper. The GPW part is also marked with script.
4) The GPW rear crossmember has a small hole to the right of the bumperette. The MB does not.
5) The GPW engine hand crank is marked with Ford script instead of with a W.O. (for Willys Overland). Same goes for the jack handle.
6) The GPW toe board gussets have two smaller round holes and one large oval hole, while the Willys has five round holes of varying sizes. The body number can be found on the underside of the toe board also.
7) The GPW uses bolt clips on the springs, whereas the MB uses clamps.
8) The ground strap from the generator to the regulator is separate on a GPW, but wrapped up in a harness with the armature and field wires on an MB.
9) The reinforcing flange on the hinge end of the hood has no drain hole and the MB does. The general construction of the piece is distinctly different for each, although the hoods interchange.
10) The rear shock brackets on a GPW are a two-piece stamping welded together. The MB uses an open channel.
11) The rear seat supports on a GPW are roughly triangular in shape. The MB supports are roughly U-shaped.
12) The front frame horns on the GPW have a larger hole at the leading edge than the MB.
13) The radiators on a GPW have fewer depressions on the top tank than the MB, and the MBs run continuously around the outer surface.
14) The GPW front fender is attached to the step at the lower edge with two bolts. The MB is attached by one.
15) The GPW firewall has an embossed reinforcing bar on the driver's side above the steering column.
16) The toolbox lid in the rear body of a GPW has ridges stamped into the cover. The MB is a solid piece. Also, the GPW has a rectangular depression on the latch and the MB has a round one.
17) The battery space in the right inner fender is stamped on the GPW and spot welded on the MB.
18) The footrests on a GPW have a triangular shaped end bracket and the MBs have a U-shaped end bracket.
19) The insulation webbing on the gas tank hold-down straps on a GPW is riveted on. The MB's is stapled.
20) The inner fenders on the rear of a GPW just behind the shock mounts have vertical bars stamped in. The MB does not.
21) The GPW uses cast clutch and brake pedals. The MB used stamped pieces that are seldom seen these days.

able records don't indicate the exact year of production. Preliminary data shows about 1951 for the CJ-4. The back half is pretty standard CJ-3A. The front is a mix of MD, and some custom fenderwork that gives it an odd appearance. Mechanically, it has pretty standard Jeep goodies. The CJ-4 survives in a private collection by sheer luck alone but the records of its development seem to be missing. This rig is worth a mention because few records exist of this era, and there may be more than one CJ-4, so keep your eyes open.

High Hoods: CJ-3B

The advent of the F-head engine left the CJ compromised. It was too tall for the current CJ body. The solution was simple—a "hoodectomy." The hood and cowl were simply raised the required amount to fit the F-head. Obviously, it was a transitional model to carry the line through to the intro of the CJ-5. More than 71,000 were produced between its 1953 intro and the debut of the CJ-5 for the 1955 model year.

Besides the engine, hood, and cowl, there is little to mark them from the CJ-3A and, mechanically, even the early CJ-5. While the 3B used the shorter 80-inch wheelbase, it used many of the same mechanical parts as its older and newer brethren. It was the last true flat-fendered Jeep and is cherished by many for that reason. Others find it an odd looking duck.

Odd or not, the 3B stayed in production, though at drastically lower levels, until 1968, when it was finally discontinued. Most of the more than 84,000 produced after the CJ-5 intro were exported or put into commercial livery. Mahindra, in India, continued to produce them under license until the 1990s. Under the MAP (Military Assistance Program), thousands of militarized CJ-3Bs, designated M-606, were given to "friendly" nations for military use and accounted for many of the 3Bs sold in later years.

While the CJ-3B is every bit the equal of any other Jeep, it has a smaller following than the other flat fenders. Low availability has something to do with this and looks another. You either like 'em or you don't. Parts are no more difficult to obtain than any other vintage Jeep and complete bodies, as well as other

The introduction of the Jeep 4x4 pickup in 1947 gave Willys a big piece of a small but growing market. Initially, they were available only with the old Go-Devil four-banger and were grossly underpowered. This is a very early unit, perhaps a prototype. The front end was very CJ-like before early 1950. In mid-1949, "4-Wheel Drive" was added to the sides of the hood. *Jeep House Museum*

1976 saw the introduction of the CJ-7 and this rig proved to be one of the most popular Jeeps ever produced. It was just big enough—but not too big. Plus it also came with hard doors, roll up windows, removable hardtop, and air-conditioning (1977-on). Through 1979, the CJ-7 was also available with the V-8, automatic and Quadra-Trac combination. Shown here is a 1977 Renegade. *Jeep Public Relations*

In 1954, the grille changed from the 1950 second series nine vertical bars and five horizontal to one with nine vertical slots and three horizontal bars. The captions tag of this factory photo identifies it as a 1950 but it's obviously a 1954 or later by the grille design. *Jeep Public Relations*

body parts, are available from overseas sources, though their quality is often suspect.

Round Fenders: M-38A1 & M-170

The army was unsatisfied with the performance of the M-38 models. The M-38, or MC, model had gained about 350 pounds and was designed for a larger 1,200-pound payload. The old 60-horsepower Go-Devil flathead had run out of go. When the army gearheads had a chance to drive the newly introduced F-head engines as mounted in the Jeep pickups of 1950, they very impressed with the 15-horsepower boost. A development program began almost immediately after the introduction of the MC for a model MD, which was called the M-38E1.

The very first version had the same rear body and flat front fenders of the MC but a higher rounded hood and cowl. This soon translated into a more stylish set of fenders, with a rounded edge and a neater transition into the cowl. The CJ-4 prototype was a nearly identical but civilianized version of this.

Initially, two MD prototypes were built, a standard 81-inch wheelbase rig and a longer 101-inch wheelbase unit. This program may have started as early as 1950, with some of the prototypes photographed in May 1951. These designs gradually metamorphosed into the now-familiar shape of the M-38A1 and M-170 rigs and went into service in 1952, replacing the M-38 as rapidly as possible. This development program had direct offshoots into the civilian market with the CJ-5 and CJ-6.

The M-38A1 was all GI, using a 24-volt electrical system, military style tops and bows, tow hooks, standardized military gauges, pintle and tow hooks, plus a full-floating rear axle. One variant, called the M-38A1C, had a split windshield and was fitted with a 105-mm recoilless rifle. This gave the Jeep the firepower of a small tank, though canvas and sheet metal offered little protection from return fire.

The MD was produced until 1958 for domestic military use and until 1968 for export. Total build was just over 100,000 units, with about half going to the U.S. Armed Forces. The M-38A1 was replaced by the M-151 about 1960 but the old MD stayed in service well into the 1970s with National Guard units and government agencies. They were generally better liked than the M-151.

Unlike the World War II Jeeps, the M-38A1's following is more prone to drop in a V-8 than restore it to military splendor. This is probably because of its ties with the CJ-5. As far as the early round fenders go, it's a better basis for such modifications than the actual early CJ-5. It has a better chassis than the civilian Jeeps and the reversed front spring shackles make for a better front suspension.

The MD is readily available, as are NOS parts and a few reproduction pieces. Prices run about the same, or slightly higher, than a CJ-5 of a similar era.

Round Fenders in Civvies: CJ-5

The CJ-5 was introduced on October 11, 1954, and the curvy new body revitalized the utility line. This was just short of two years after Kaiser purchased Willys-Overland (by coincidence, on its 50th birthday) and no doubt, that company wanted to justify its investment by increased sales. The

CJ-5 was very much like the MD (M-38A1) model that preceded it but the mechanicals were a step or two lower in beef to keep the price down. It used a lighter chassis, a semifloating rear axle and had the spring shackles leading the front axle.

The CJ-5's 81-inch wheelbase and wider body afforded a bit more room than had the earlier CJs, but it was only a few pounds heavier. The little F-head didn't have to huff and puff much harder with the new Jeep. A new "All-Weather" optional top afforded marginally more weather protection than the earlier CJs but the new style seats were a big jump ahead, with coil springs and extra padding. The CJ-5 soon became the flagship of the utility line.

In the early days, go-to-work options were the order of the day. You had to order a passenger seat and top, as well as a heater and a rear seat. The Warner T-98A four-speed was introduced as an option in 1957, with the "granny" 6.4:1 first gear giving the little F-head 134-cid a gearing advantage. Spicer Trac-Lok limited-slips went on the options list at about the same time. Jeep dealers offered a great number of aftermarket goodies as well, from hardtops, to winches and a variety of farm and construction implements.

There isn't much CJ-5 stuff to talk about, other than the special models that are covered in a later section, until 1966, when the 225-cid V-6 engine was introduced. Finally, some power for the Jeep! This 160-horsepower, 235-pound-feet engine more than doubled the power and torque of the F-head four-cylinder. The cast-iron engine had powered some Buick and Pontiac compacts in the early 1960s and was a derivative of the GM 215-cid aluminum block V-8 that dated back to 1961. Kaiser-Jeep bought the tooling from GM and used the lightweight engine to good effect all the way to 1971, when AMC installed their own line of engines into the Jeep. The V-6 designs were later sold back to GM during the later part of the gas crunch years.

In 1969, Jeep offered a camper option that used a half cab and had an overhead camper attached in the bed of the CJ-5. A subframe with a set of weight-carrying bogie wheels trailed out the back and carried most of the overhanging weight. The camper was as large as the 8-foot overhead pickup units of the day. Jeep recommended it be used with the V-6 engine and 4.88 gears. No doubt it was an ungainly behemoth to drive but in theory, the camper could be detached at a campsite and the jeep could then be used independently. This rig was available only in 1969 and 1970 and did not sell well.

In 1972, AMC replaced the F-head four and the V-6 with engines from their own stable. The AMC 232-cid six became the baseline CJ powerplant with the 258-cid being the medium option. These were both superior powerplants. Both had seven main bearings and were as modern as any inline six of the day. Power outputs for both were on par with the V-6 and the 258 had the V-6 beat on torque. In order to fit the new powerplants, the wheelbase was lengthened to 84 inches.

The biggest news was the availability of the 304-cid AMC V-8. This was the first V-8 offered in a CJ—and also the last. It was available through the 1979 model year. The 304 made an honest 150 net horsepower (about 210 horsepower gross—remember that the horsepower and torque ratings for domestic vehicles went from SAE gross to SAE net in

In 1957, Willys marketed a new vehicle called the Forward Control. It came in two sizes, the 81-inch FC-150, and the 103.5-inch FC-170. This is Craig Brockhaus' low-mileage, original-down-to-the-tires 1957 FC-150. It is equipped with a front winch and a set of aftermarket dual rear wheels. *Craig Brockhaus*

- **BIGGER PAYLOADS—UP TO 4,159 LBS.**
- **TOUGHER, FULL-FLOATING REAR AXLE**
- **DUAL REAR WHEELS, HEAVY-DUTY SPRINGS & SHOCKS**
- **PLATFORM STAKE & CAB-CHASSIS OPTIONS**
- **OPTIONAL 8,000—9,000 LB.—G.V.W.'S**

FORWARD CONTROL
Jeep FC-170
DUAL WHEEL PLATFORM STAKE

HIGH TORQUE "SUPER HURRICANE" ENGINE

Here is high-powered performance at lowest operating cost. High Torque "Super Hurricane" engine features tough alloy block, chromium rings, Stellite valves with positive exhaust rotation, aluminum alloy pistons, heavy-duty bearings, floating oil intake. Easily accessible between seats in cab. Heavy glass fiber insulation cuts all heat and noise.

165 H.P. @ 3600 R.P.M., 190 lbs. ft. torque at 1400 R.P.M., 226.2 cu. in. displacement, 6-cyl. L-Head design.

WE HAVE A 'JEEP' VEHICLE FOR YOUR TOUGHEST JOB!

WILLYS MOTORS, INC.
Willys-Overland Export Corp.
TOLEDO, OHIO

One of the rarer finds in the FC-170 realm are the 1-ton dual rear wheel models. Introduced in 1959, few were built, perhaps as few as just a couple of thousand. With a 226-cid six, a T-98 four-speed and a Dana 70 rear axle, this is a formidable truck by any standard!

1972). The 304 was backed up by a Warner gear T-15A three speed. The Warner T18 was optional for six-cylinder models, though it was a close ratio model with a "tall" 4.02-1 first gear.

The transfer case changed in 1972 from the venerable model 18 to the stronger model 20. The front axle changed from the Model 27 to the beefier Spicer Model 30 and the rear axle went from the Dana 44 to an AMC Corporate 20 with tapered axle shafts. This has often been lamented as a big step back . The shafts are a source of trouble on the trail but several fixes have been marketed for the AMC-20 axle to make it equal to the Dana 44.

Through the 1970s, the CJ-5 struggled to bring itself into the modern era of comfortable 4x4s and never totally succeeded. For the purposes of the book, we are ending major discussion of the CJs with the end of the V-8s but it should be mentioned that the CJ-5 lasted only a few years past that and died after 1983. A campaign by TV's *60 Minutes* and a consumer-oriented magazine inspired some lawsuits that made AMC gun-shy about rollovers. It was the final nail in the coffin of the venerable CJ-5.

With the exception of the special models, CJ-5s don't have much collector/restorer interest but as hard-working, hard-core 4x4s, they still have a huge following. With over 600,000 built in nearly 30 years of production, there are good examples from every era to suit every taste. Look for the very earliest rigs and the original V-8 models to go up in collector value first. The CJ-5 is a true classic and whether or not they achieve collector status, they are still a capable, durable 4x4 with an impeccable pedigree, and you won't regret owning one.

Longer Jeeps: CJ-6

In order to address requests for more room, Willys introduced the CJ-6 in late 1955 for the 1956 model year. A direct offshoot of the military M-170 ambulance, the CJ-6 design took the standard Jeep and stretched the wheelbase 20 inches from 81 to 101. This added considerably to the room without hampering the off-pavement qualities much. While it could carry more volume, it was not rated for any more weight capacity. Its GVW increased only to cover the 200 pounds of extra weight generated by the stretch job. No doubt the low power four-banger dictated capacity.

Other than its wheelbase, the CJ-6 shared almost every characteristic and option with the CJ-5, which doesn't leave too much nitty-gritty stuff to talk about. When the CJ-5 stretched to 84 inches for the 1972 model year, the CJ-6 was lengthened a corresponding amount to 104 inches. It was not a huge seller, with a sales low of 244 in 1961 and a high of 3,521 in 1966. The CJ-6 lasted from 1956 to 1975 in the domestic arena and to 1981 as an export model. A total of 50,172 were built, many of these going overseas.

As a collectable, the CJ-6 has drawn little interest, except as a modified trail machine. Hard-core four-wheelers have found it an ideal basis for a buildups because its longer wheelbase offers more room to fit various engine and drivetrain combos.

The Last CJ: CJ-7

Introduced for the 1976 model year, the CJ-7 replaced the CJ-6 as the longer wheelbase variant. With a 93.5 inch wheelbase, it was a bit shorter than the CJ-6 but proved a very popular Jeep. The door openings were enlarged, making ingress and egress easier and also allowing for solid doors and—hang on to your hats—roll-up windows! This was a first for the CJ line. The CJ-7s were often ordered with a polycarbonate hardtop that was the most weathertight ever fitted to a Jeep. When air conditioning was offered just the next year, along with many other luxury items (this is a relative term), the CJ-7 became the first CJ that wasn't totally painful to drive.

Other goodies found their way into the CJ-7, including the TH-400 automatic and the Quadra-Trac full-time four-wheel drive transfer case. Both the V-8 and the Renegade package were available on the CJ-7. In 1977, front disc brakes went on the option list

The CJ-7 continued to 1986, when it was replaced by the new Wrangler. Thus it had the honor to be the last CJ. CJ-7s have not acquired much, if any, value as a classic but are immensely popular nonetheless. Built in large numbers, they are Jeeps that are easy to own and drive on a day-to-day basis. A vast array of parts are available and they are popular as the basis for trail buildups. The early V-8 models in original condition are quite rare, even though many six-cylinder CJ-7 owners have installed the AMC 304, 360, and 401 V-8s into them. This is an easy swap that is virtually a bolt-in.

It may be a long time before the CJ-7 goes into classic Jeep status but they hold their value and continue to be popular. Good examples are easy to find.

High Zoot Jeep CJs: Specials

Special models did not become an issue until the signs were clear that people were buying Jeeps for more than just hard work. The first attempt at sprucing up a CJ came in 1961, with the Tuxedo Park package. This consisted of chrome bumpers, "turbine" style wheels, chrome hood hinges, and mirror arms, as well as whitewall tires. The package was denoted by a special Tuxedo Park emblem.

The first year was designated, on paper at least, as the Tuxedo Park Mark I, with the 1962s being Mark II, and the 1963s being Mark III. In 1964, the Tuxedo Park Mark IV was introduced, and the differences in trim were taken a bit more seriously than with its predecessors. The package retained the Mark IV title until it was dropped in 1968. The "Mark IV" was added to the Tuxedo Park hood emblem.

The Tuxedo Park Mark IV package was available in the CJ-5 and CJ-6 lines. There were enough basic changes for them to be dubbed CJ-5A and CJ-6A. Willys called it, "a new idea in sports cars." The new rigs came with a cushy 60-40 front seat and a column shift for the three-speed models (the optional four-speed shifter stayed on the floor). It used softer springs for a better ride and had some minute differences in the electrical system to accommodate a slightly different lighting arrangement. It also got a chrome treatment that included the bumpers, mirrors, light bezels, hood hinges, and gas cap. A special parts list was published by Kaiser-Jeep to denote the differences:

Among the most interesting and most sought after FC trucks are the M-Series military rigs. Two of the most collectable are shown here, the M-679 Ambulance and the M-677 crew cab pickup. The crew cab is a clean, original unit that belongs to Fred Williams. The production numbers of the military contract have not been uncovered yet, but most of them were built in 1963 or 1964. Many of them went to the Navy and the Air Force. There were four basic models produced, and estimates are that fewer than 600 of each were manufactured. All were equipped with Cerlist diesel engines. *Jeep House Museum/Fred Williams*

Parts List W-1175. It listed parts peculiar to the Tuxedo Park Mark IV, CJ-5A, and CJ-6A. The 1964 CJ-5A cost less than $100 more than a standard model but was a limited production deal. The CJ-5A and CJ-6A were offered from 1964–1968 and could be had with other options, including the V-6 engine from 1966.

Few people remember that a Perkins diesel was on the options list from 1961 through 1969. The 192-cid, four-cylinder diesel cranked out 62 horsepower and 143 pound-feet of torque at 1,350 rpm. It was seldom ordered by customers other than commercial ones. It was slower than the gasoline four-cylinder but got fantastic fuel mileage, in the neighborhood of 30 miles per gallon. An estimated 3,000 CJs so equipped were sold in the eight years of production, some going overseas.

An options package was offered in 1969 that heralded a whole new concept—high-performance off-roaders. The "462" package came with a roll bar, swing-away tire carrier, Polyglass tires, skid plates, and extra gauges. Ordered with the V-6 and limited-slip differentials, it made a formidable trail package. Unfortunately, the four-speed option was not available in combination with the V-6.

The 462 package transitioned into the Renegade I in 1970. It was similar in its goodies package but came with a white hood stripe that ran along the side of the hood onto the cowl that said "Renegade 1." Again, ordered with the V-6 and other goodies, it made a very sportable package.

The year 1971 saw the Renegade II package that was similar to the 1970 offering. It came in one color, called "Big-Bad Orange," had charcoal striping and a tach was included.

After the 1970 purchase of Kaiser-Jeep, the AMC influence was beginning to be felt in some of the marketing schemes. In 1972, AMC injected some serious fresh blood into Jeep CJ by offering their version of a Renegade model that featured the AMC 304-cid V-8. It was similar to the previous specials in that it had a stripe along the hood announcing "Renegade" but it also had American Racing alloy wheels, H78-15 whitewall tires and fender flares. Along with the rear seat, passenger grab handle, dual sun visors, and the roll bar, the package included a limited-slip rear differential. The Warner T-15A three-speed was standard but a close-ratio, T-18 four-speed was optional but only for six-cylinder models. A fuel tank skid plate was included and the model came sans tailgate and fitted with the swing-away carrier. Not much chrome on this job.

The Renegade package continued past the end of the V-8 in 1979, though that is beyond our realm of discussion. Initially, it was available in only three colors, yellow (sort of a Gatorade hue), orange, and plum. Later, the full range of colors was possible. In 1975, the Levi option was packaged into the Renegade. The Renegade offered a great deal of performance and was one of the few really effective four-wheeling packages offered by any manufacturer.

The 1975-on Levi option consisted of heavy-grade vinyl with Levi-style stitching. It was available in blue or tan and came with a Levi's decal above the Jeep emblem on the cowl. It was a popular option though the 1970s.

In 1972, a "Super Jeep" package was offered that consisted mainly of a lurid paint scheme with red, white, and blue stripes curving back off the hood that also had a field of stars. The 1977-on Golden Eagle package featured a gold paint job over which a giant eagle was applied on the hood. It also came with styled wheels and big tires. The interior of the Golden Eagle was all the Levi pieces in tan, with a roll bar. The convenience group and decor group options were included for good measure.

All the special edition jeeps have potential collector value. None are particularly easy to find and finding an original with all striping and bric-a-brac intact can be even more of a problem. Striping can be reproduced, though it isn't particularly cheap. The special badging and hardware is another matter. The Renegade II with the V-6 and the 1972-1974 V-8 Renegade have the most potential. A Super Jeep is an almost unheard of commodity. Tuxedo Park IVs are scarce but available. No one this writer has spoken with has seen a 1961–1963 Tuxedo Park in recent years.

Pug-Nosed Jeep: Forward Control Jeeps

If you want something a little off the conventional Jeep mark, have a look at the Forward Control models. Offered from the 1957 through the 1965 model years, these cab-over rigs came in two wheelbase lengths. The FC-150s, introduced in November of 1956, were built upon a standard CJ-5 chassis and used the CJ's 81-inch wheelbase. The longer FC-170, which debuted in May of 1957, used a 103.5-inch wheelbase. All the FCs were four-wheel drive.

The FCs were intended as an innovative answer to the light commercial needs of the day. Despite a promising initial sales spurt, they were not a commercial success. Only about 30,000 units were produced (many for military contracts) in the eight-year run. Brooks Stevens, the forward thinking designer of the FCs, was probably a little ahead of the mark.

Despite their odd, pug-nosed look, the FCs made practical use of limited space. The FC-150s 74-by-36-inch bed and the FC-170's 110-by-48-inch bed approximated the capacity of much larger pickups. The little FCs, however, could easily outmaneuver the bigger rigs in tight quarters. This made them a handy addition to many contractors' fleets.

Mechanically, the FCs were right out of the everyday Jeep parts catalog. The FC-150 came with Jeep's F-head four-banger, while the longer rig was powered by the "Super Hurricane" flathead six. Warner Gear three-speed T-90 gearboxes came standard, with a Warner four-speed T-98 as an option. Axles were from Spicer, and Powr-Lok limited-slip differentials were available as an option. In 1959, an HD option was offered for FC-170s that featured a beefy Dana 70 axle, dual rear wheels, and a GVW up to 9,000 pounds.

Driving an FC could be called "different!" Driver and passenger are perched right over the front axle. Visibility is superb, with over 2,747 square

This 1968 J-3000 must be a very late year model because it's powered by the 350-cid Dauntless engine that was officially offered for the 1969–1970 model years. Other than this inconsistency, it's a pretty normal 120-inch wheelbase Townside with a four-speed.

inches of glass in the Deluxe cab. Though the cab has a surprising amount of room, most of it is taken up by the engine box. The engine rests between the two seats and is accessed via a hinged lid.

The early FC-150s had some handling quirks of which a prospective buyer needs to be wary. Because they were based on a CJ-5 platform, the FC-150 used a narrow 48.4 inch track. For a low slung, lightweight 4-by like the CJ, this was fine. For a taller, heavier rig with the FC's unusual distribution of weight, this made for a very tippy vehicle. In 1959, from chassis number 65548-18206, the axles were changed to give a 57-inch track and more stability. This fact makes the later "wide track" FC-150s the most desirable and sought after. The extremely short FC-150s of any year were also notorious for being nose heavy and you needed to take care going steeply downhill in an unloaded condition. The long FC-170s were a lot more forgiving in this regard and with their 63-inch track, much less tippy as well.

The FCs had a staggering amount of body options, from specialty utility bodies, stake beds, a "Dump-o-Matic" hydraulic box, and fire truck bodies, to the M-series line of military trucks. The military trucks were equipped with a three-cylinder Cerlist diesel and came in four body styles, pickup, crew-cab pickup, carryall, and ambulance. These military rigs have turned up all over the country, having been used mainly by the U.S. Army and Air Force.

The FC Jeeps are fairly scarce and are just now attracting the attention of collectors. Because of their commercial use, good examples are getting hard to find. While mechanical parts (with the exception of Cerlist engine parts) are easily found, replacement body parts are almost nonexistent. It often takes two rough bodies to make one good one. As with the other older Jeeps, the FCs are very prone to rust.

FC-150s are noted by experts as being the most common, with the M-series crew cabs the least common and most sought after. The dual rear wheel FC-170s are also very scarce. At this writing, prices are still reasonable, making the FC Jeeps an affordable and unusual 4x4 collectable with moderate appreciation possible in the next few years.

Willys Pickups and Station Wagons: 1947–1965

As far as the perennial Jeep went, Willys had the postwar SWB utility market locked up with the CJ-2A. That left trucks. Willys Overland was flush with war profits and so began designing a line of trucks and a station wagon that took design cues from the Jeep. The 4x2 station wagon debuted first in 1946. In June of 1947, the new pickup hit the streets as a 4x2, followed just a month later by the 4x4 version.

With only the Dodge Power Wagon as direct competition, Willys figured an inexpensive 4x4 pickup was just what the public ordered. Initially called the 4T, it featured a big "W-O" on the tailgate with a painted-on "Four Wheel Drive" on the right. These trucks were optimistically rated as 1-ton models.

The station wagon 4x4 came in 1949, as well as a panel. Both vehicles were based upon the same basic structure. At first, all the new trucks were powered by a slightly uprated, 63-horsepower version of the "Go-Devil" engine. With heavier vehicles and even heavier payloads, this engine was seriously overmatched. The tried and true T-90 3-speed Warner transmission and Model 18 t-case combo were used as well as a slightly wider version of the CJ's Model 25 front axle. The rear axle was either a Timkin or a Spicer 53 semi-floater in the trucks and a Spicer 25 in the lower GVW wagons.

By the end of the 1940s, it was apparent that something had to be done in the power department. Barney Roos developed an F-head (intake valves in a new head and exhaust valves still in the block) adaptation of the flathead powerplant. With its better breathing characteristics, the 134-cid mill initially made 68 horsepower in low-compression form and 72 in a high-compression guise. The best part was that it used most of the old engine and saved a whole lot of tooling costs.

A kit was developed to retrofit the new cylinder head onto older L-head engines (SW & PU only) for the benefit in power. The new engine appeared in vehicles built after March of 1950. The 1949 designs had carried over into 1950 as transition models and were called "first series" 1950 models. The new F-head models with a revised grille were called the "second series."

Designations were to change with the second series rigs, the pickups becoming 4x473 models and the station wagons 4x463, the "4x" prefix signifying a four-wheel drive model. Other than a few minor styling changes, all remained static until 1954.

After Kaiser-Frazier took over in 1953, they began upgrading the Willys lines. One of the upgrades included the introduction of the 226-cid "Super Hurricane" L-head six as an optional powerplant for the pickups and station wagons. This continued until 1963, when the overhead cam 230cid, 140-horsepower six debuted as an option and the 226 became the standard plant in the pickups. The utility wagons still had the old four-banger available all the way to the end of production.

Over the years, there was little to note in appearance between the years. The earliest pickups had a stamped grille similar to the CJ, with ten vertical slots. In 1950 second series trucks, the V-shaped nose similar to the 4x2 Jeepsters was adopted with eight vertical slots and three horizontal bars. Sometimes the horizontal bars were chromed, depending on model. In 1955, a downmarket version of the station wagon was offered and called the utility wagon. In 1958, the split windshield was replaced by a single piece.

The classic Jeep pickup and station wagon lasted to 1965. For two years, they were produced in ever dwindling numbers alongside the bigger and high-zoot Gladiator pickups and Wagoneers that had debuted in 1963. In 19 years of production, a large number of the old style rigs were produced. They have been popular on a small scale as collectables but are just now beginning to attract more serious attention. Mechanical parts are readily available, since many are shared with the CJ but body parts are a bit more scarce due to their vulnerability to rust. Still, with so many built, finding a good example is not hard and the prices remain reasonable. The six cylinder models are preferred.

Gladiator and Wagoneer: 1963–1970

In November of 1962, Willys introduced a new line of pickups and station wagons called, respectively, the Gladiator and the Wagoneer. They were

Here's a rare one to watch out for. The Super Wagoneer took the basic four-door Wagoneer and added a powerful four-barrel V-8 and every conceivable comfort convenience feature. It was a first in the 4x4 business. Though only about 1,200 were built between 1966 and early 1969, they are still very reasonable if you can find one. *Jeep Public Relations*

pretty up-to-date machines, big and brawny but still with styling cues that reminded the viewer he was looking at a Jeep. The Gladiator and Wagoneer were the first all-new Jeep designs in a very long while. The general hubbub of this introduction almost overshadowed the March 1963 corporate name change. Willys Motors officially changed its name to Kaiser-Jeep.

The Wagoneer, in particular, had the room and comfort of the traditional, big-as-a-boat American station wagon but had four-wheel drive capacity added in as an option. This made it perfect for a variety of purposes, including as a crew hauler for construction gangs or surveyors, police or park ranger use and, of course, as an all-weather family hauler or recreational vehicle. The unit was available in two- or four-wheel drive. The Wagoneer came on a 110-inch wheelbase and could be ordered as a two-door, four-door or as a panel delivery. Both the two- and four-door models were offered in a custom trim that consisted of chrome and stainless steel trim, full carpeting, high-grade headliner, fabric inserted seats with foam padding, high-grade vinyl door trim, and a host of other little, bright goodies.

The pickups came in a Thriftside (call it a stepside) or a Styleside box.

The trucks were offered in three weight ratings, 1/2, 3/4, and 1 ton. Two wheelbases were offered, 120 and 126 inches. The 1/2- and 3/4-tons were available in the 120-inch wheelbase with a seven-foot box and the 126-inch version of the 3/4-ton and the 1-ton had an eight-foot box.

Under the hood of both rigs rested the new 230-cid overhead cam "Tornado" six. While the engine pumped out 140 horsepower, it did not move the 3,500-pound-plus Wagoneer or Gladiator with much authority. It also had a bad reputation for reliability. During the 1965 model year, it was phased out and replaced with the 145-horsepower AMC 232-cid six, which took over as the standard engine for the rest of the Kaiser-Jeep era.

In April of 1965, the first Jeep V-8 was announced and the big Jeeps were fitted with the 327-cid V-8. This was not a Chevy clone, but rather a derivation of a 250-cid engine that had first appeared in the 1956 Nash Ambassador. The "Vigilante" made 250 horsepower (gross) and 340 pound-feet of torque. What it lacked in ultra-modern features, the 600-pound engine made up for in strength and reliability.

The 327 came in two guises, a two-barrel version and the four-barrel unit. The four-barrel was available only in the 1966 to mid-1969 Super Wagoneer and made 270 horsepower and 360 pound-feet using a 9.7:1 compression ratio. The 327 was available through the 1968 model year. In 1969, it was replaced by the 350-cid "Dauntless" V-8, a Buick transplant that churned out 230 horsepower and 350 pound-feet. The Buick was used until AMC replaced it with their V-8 in 1971.

From day one, the standard transmission on both the Wagoneers and the Gladiator was the good old T-90 "three-on-the-tree" or a stronger T-89. The pickup had the option of a Warner T-98A four-speed, and both the pickup and the station wagon could be fitted with a Borg-Warner AS-8F three-speed automatic through 1968. Models from 1969 through 1979 used a GM-built TH-400. A Dana 20 part-time transfer case was used exclusively with manual trans rigs and a Spicer 21 single-speed box was used with autotrans models until the advent of the TH-400. After that the single speed case was dropped for the Model 20.

One of the forward-thinking developments in the big jeep line was the independent front suspension offered as an option from 1963–1966. It used a torsion bar suspension with an A-arm mounted above the axle and a ball joint attached to the upper part of the steering knuckle. The lower end was located by a trailing link and ball joint. It was a bit cranky in service but the ride was reputed to be the most carlike of any 4x4 yet produced. It was available in both the Gladiator and the Wagoneer. The standard suspension for both big Jeeps was the typical live axle, leaf spring setup.

The IFS Wagoneer front axle was a Spicer Model 27AFI (the "I" for independent) with the long side of the housing shortened and replaced with a pivoting CV joint near the differential. It pivoted like a swing arm. The J-series pickups used a similar setup but the drive axle was a stronger Spicer 44FI unit.

In 1966, Kaiser-Jeep introduced the Super Wagoneer. It was produced in very limited numbers until mid-year 1969. Some sources say that only 1,200 were made but this is unconfirmed by hard data. The Super Wagoneer was another pivotal introduction by Jeep and became the first American luxury 4x4. The Super Wagoneer started with the basic four-door Wagoneer and outfitted it with a four-barrel (Holley) version of the 327 and automatic transmission. Power steering was standard, as well as power brakes and air conditioning.

The outside was unique and used a padded black vinyl roof, with a chrome roof rack. On the side, an antique gold strip ran front to rear, widening toward the rear. A smaller, black stripe was just below and both stripes were trimmed in chrome. Available colors were empire blue, glacier white, Indian ceramic, or prairie gold. A new full-width chrome grille was fitted, replacing the narrow centered unit of the standard models. Later this grille design became the norm for all big Jeep models well into the 1970s. Chrome hubcaps, with an alloy wheel look and simulated knockoffs, were mounted on 15x5.5" wheels. Tires were wide 8.45-15 Power Cushions with white sidewalls.

The interior was all 1960s luxo with a seven-way tilt steering column, cushy front bucket and rear bench seats—both in leather. The center console had a padded armrest and floor-mounted shifter. Soft vinyl door panels gave the impression of leather. Auto retracting seatbelts were standard. A transistorized radio used an automatic volume control and extra speakers were fitted. An eight-track tape player was optional.

The Gladiators and Wagoneers of the Kaiser-Jeep era have not reached collectors status. This may change but for now, the full-sized Jeep collector crowd is a small one. The trucks and station wagons are still running around in daily use. They are cheap and plentiful. If any have the potential of appreciating, it will certainly be the Super Wagoneer, which is already selling at premium prices, and possibly the rare IFS models. Parts will be a problem for both of these. As for the others, they can still be a useful addition to the fleet regardless of future status.

The J-Series drafted! This is the XM-715, the predecessor to the M-715 that went into production in 1967. This truck replaced the highly respected Dodge M-series in service but was generally regarded as inferior. More than 20,000 were built for the army and even more for export. Overall, they are a super truck; however, engine problems are their main weakness. The 230-cid OHC six was discontinued in the civvy trucks by 1966 due to these troubles.

The "new" Jeepster Convertible began in 1967, and it very much emulated the flair of the 1948–1950 version but it offered four-wheel drive. Powered by the 225 V6, it offered sport features and more than a little luxury. It even used a top that lowered at the touch of a button. *Jeep House Museum*

Almost Forgotten: 1967–1973 Jeepster Commando

Most experts agree that the 1948–1950 Jeepster was a great idea but a bit ahead of its time. In the mid-1960s recreational 4x4 boom, Kaiser-Jeep revived the idea and the name in the form of a sporty new vehicle. Similar in style to the original, Kaiser-Jeep added what the original lacked—four-wheel drive.

These rigs were offered in two basic varieties, the Jeepster—a rag-topped, two-tone 4-by with a Continental kit and a big resemblance to the original Jeepster. The other version was the Commando—a more modern looking variation that could be outfitted as a convertible, a station wagon, or a pickup. The new rigs were built upon the same 101-inch wheelbase as the CJ-6 and, truth be told, the chassis were very similar. The snazzy Jeepster's convertible top was power-operated.

All the Jeepsters and Commandos to 1972 were powered by the standard F-head four, with the 225-cid V-6 as the popular option. A floor-mounted shifter operated either a Warner T-86 three-speed manual (four-cylinder) or a stronger T-14A three-speed with V-6 engines. The GM TH-400 automatic was optional for V-6 powered units. The Dana 20 transfer case split the power for all transmission and engine combos to 1973. The front axle was the Spicer 27AF and the rear either a Dana 30 or the familiar Spicer 44. The Jeepster/Commando actually had a fair bit of beef built into its driveline for its size and power output.

In 1972, two special editions of the Commando line emerged, the SC-1 and the Hurst Jeepster. The SC-1 came as a mid-year edition and was built upon the fully enclosed station wagon body. It was painted a butterscotch gold with a white top, black rally stripes, and SC-1 badging. It was equipped with all the other goodies available, including the V-6, auto trans, and power steering (introduced in 1970 for the Commando models).

The Hurst Jeepster was a collaboration between American Motors and the Hurst Corporation. In an effort to revitalize the Jeep image, AMC looked at any avenue to generate excitement. Initially planned as a 500-unit run, the all-white units were painted up with blue and red racing stripes and fitted with a hood scoop that mounted an 8,000-rpm tachometer. Raised white letter Goodyear Polyglass F70-15 tires were fitted.

Inside, a padded steering wheel with brushed aluminum spoke was mounted, as well as a Hurst Shifter. The interior was available in charcoal, blue, or buckskin, and bucket seats were standard. The initial plan was for 300 to be automatics and 200 to be sticks. In the end, only about 100 were built, all of them automatics according to available information. Who knows why the deal fell through but a Hurst Jeepster is a very rare bird these days.

By 1972, AMC's influence had spread to the Commando line. The Jeepster model, expensive and a low-volume seller, was finally dropped for 1972. With AMC's engines being fitted to the entire Jeep line, some renovations were in order for the Commando. Just like the CJ-6, the Commando got its wheelbase stretched to 104 inches to accommodate the two AMC sixes and, yowza, the V-8. For 1972 and 1973 (the last year of the Commando), the V-8 was the available top dog powerplant. With V-8 power on tap, the 3,000-pound Commando was a very sprightly performer.

With the stretch job, the Commando got a new front end. The Commando lost its Jeeplike styling cues up front and reverted to a more generic, flat, mesh style grille that was attractive (in this writer's humble opinion) but not popular. An SC-2 version of the new Commando was offered in the butterscotch color that was similar to the 1971 SC-1. It had a woodgrain stripe down the side. Like the previous special, it was dolled up with all the options, V-8, air conditioning, and automatic power brakes and steering.

The Commando line was dropped after the 1973 model year to, as one AMC official put it, "consolidate" the Jeep image. Jeepster/Commandos have been long ignored by most but are beginning to see some collector interest among the rank and file. The Hurst Special and SC-1 and 2 models are low-volume possibilities, as are the high-zoot Jeepster models. According to AMC records, 77,573 Jeepster/Commandos were built. They are available, stylish, and fun. They are also unique enough to have some future collectability.

In 1972, nearly two years after AMC had taken over Jeep, a revised version of the Commando appeared. The "Jeepster" was dropped from the name and the chassis was lengthened three inches to carry the line of AMC engines. Standard was the 232-cid six, with the 258 and the 304 V-8 being options. This is a rare SC-2 version from 1972 that featured a few very appealing features. During the revamping process, the front end got completely restyled and the Commando lost most of its Jeep styling cues up front. This rig is equipped with the 304 V-8.

In the mid-1960s, it came time to update the government's fleet of of M-37 and M-37B1 Dodges. Nearly everyone built a prototype and for the first time in many a year, Dodge missed the contract. Out of the competition drove two prototypes, the Chevrolet XM-705 and the Kaiser Jeep XM-715. The Chevy offering was most definitely the superior of the two, with its V-8 power and high tech design. The Jeep, however, was more than a thousand dollars a copy cheaper, so in 1967 the truck, 1 1/4-ton, 4X4, M-715 Kaiser Jeep went into the service.

One of the advantages of the Jeep truck was that it was based, at least loosely, on the Gladiator pickups of the era. Rated to carry a 1 1/4-ton load, it was soon nicknamed by GIs as the "five-quarter," or "buck-and-a-quarter." It proved to be a good cross-country performer but underpowered. The M-715 had several variants. An ambulance version was designated the M-725 and a utility-bodied variant was the M-726. The initial 1967 order was for just over 20,000 units of all types.

The drivetrain was straight out of the super-HD catalog. The transmission was the venerable and nearly bomb-proof Warner T-98A. The transfer case was an NP-200. The front axle was a Dana 60 unit. The rear axle was a Dana-70. Both axles carried 5.87 gear sets but used an unusual axle and hub arrangement.

The M-715 was powered by the notorious 230-cid, overhead cam six—and if the M-715's reputation has any tarnish, most reports say it was due to this engine. The unit had been dropped from the civvy lineup after the 1964 model year. No doubt, Kaiser-Jeep had large numbers of these engines left to use up.

The M-715 didn't last long in service compared to the Dodge M-37. By 1976, the military had begun replacing large numbers of M-715s in nontactical roles with the M-880 Dodge. The M-880 was a slightly militarized civilian Dodge truck uprated to 1 1/4 tons. The reasoning was that in conditions other than combat, money could be saved by buying and operating standard commercial rigs instead of the oddball and expensive tactical rigs. By then, the vehicle we now know as the HUMVEE was already being tested and soon replaced the M-715 in tactical roles.

Though the M-715 left the U.S. Army livery, a modified version built by the newly formed AM General Corporation (a subsidiary of American Motors) was sold to overseas military markets starting around 1978. Still bearing the Gladiator truck body, it was slightly less militarized and was powered by the 258-cid overhead valve six. Called the AM-715, the weight had been pared down from the M-715's gluttonous 5,200 pounds to a lean 4,700 pounds.

The M-715 has a small following in the military vehicle collecting realm and some have begun to appear as the basis for trail buildups. Small wonder. They have an awe-inspiring look that is pure bulldog toughness! It's very doubtful, however, that they will ever attain collector status in a big way. Most parts are readily available through surplus dealers, thanks to the typical government policy of stockpiling huge amounts of spare parts.

JEEP PRODUCTION
WORLD WAR II MILITARY JEEP PRODUCTION, 1940–1945:

Bantam Mark I and II:	70
Bantam BRC-40:	2, 605
Willys Quad & MA:	1,557
Willys MB Slat Grille:	25,808
Willys MB:	335,531
Ford Pygmy & GP:	4,460
Ford GPW:	277,896
Ford GPA:	3–7,000 (est.)

MILITARY JEEP PRODUCTION, 1950–1971:

	M-38	M-38A1	M-170
1950	1,563	-	-
1951	13,317	-	-
1952	22,972	29,769	-
1953	23,571	29,769	2
1954	-	9,560	1,722
1955	-	8,826	2,271
1956	-	3,166	-
1957	-	1,050	-
1958	-	780	-
1959	-	1,273	-
1960	-	2,673	-
1961	-	434	-
1962	-	2,957	1,155
1963	-	4,369	464
1964	-	2,622	-
1965	-	578	43
1966	-	320	77
1967	-	840	147
1968	-	1,906	-
1971	-	596	-

JEEP CJ PRODUCTION:

From an American Motors list that is in dispute by some experts. This list is relatively close to other production figures and since it listed almost all Jeep vehicles, it is used for consistency.

	CJ-2	CJ-2A	CJ-3A	CJ-3B	CJ-5	CJ-6	CJ-7
1944	15*	-	-	-	-	-	-
1945	29*	1,824	-	-	-	-	-
1946	-	71,455	-	-	-	-	-
1947	-	77,958	-	-	-	-	-
1948	-	62,861	309	-	-	-	-
1949	-	104	31,491	-	-	-	-
1950	-	-	24,060	-	-	-	-
1951	-	-	40,121	-	-	-	-
1952	-	-	34,654	-	-	-	-
1953	-	-	1,208	33,047	-	-	-
1954	-	-	-	35,972	3,883	-	-
1955	-	-	-	12,567	23,595	581	-
1956	-	-	-	10,145	18,441	2,523	-
1957	-	-	-	5,756	20,819	1,248	-
1958	-	-	-	6,178	12,401	1,387	-
1959	-	-	-	5,420	17,488	1,947	-
1960	-	-	-	6,139	19,753	2,201	-
1961	-	-	-	1,147	2,064	244	-
1962	-	-	-	9,416	14,072	2,502	-
1963	-	-	-	9,801	12,499	1,534	-
1964	-	-	-	5,271	16,029	1,702	-
1965	-	-	-	2,847	21,014	2,062	-
1966	-	-	-	5,459	17,974	3,521	-
1967	-	-	-	2,523	18,186	2,295	-
1968	-	-	-	1,446	19,683	2,395	-
1969	-	-	-	-	20,262	2,433	-
1970	-	-	-	-	13,518	2,234	-
1971	-	-	-	-	12,559	1,806	-
1972	-	-	-	-	22,601	1,175	-
1973	-	-	-	-	30,449	1,720	-
1974	-	-	-	-	43,087	2,826	-
1975	-	-	-	-	32,486	2,935	-
1976	-	-	-	-	31,116	2,431	21,016
1977	-	-	-	-	32,996	2,754	25,414
1978	-	-	-	-	37,611	743	38,274
1979	-	-	-	-	41,501	992	55,264

JEEP PICKUP AND STATION WAGON, 1947–1965:

Station wagon numbers include sedan delivery and various special versions. Pickup numbers include stakebed, chassis cab, chassis cowl.

	4cylSW	4cylPU	6cyl SW	6cyl PU	230SW	230PU
1947	-	2,346	-	-	-	-
1948	-	20,957	-	-	-	-
1949	4,472	19,757	-	-	-	-
1950	5,536	12,984	-	-	-	-
1951	11,854	18,343	-	-	-	-
1952	5,683	16,155	-	-	-	-
1953	10,631	16,498	-	-	-	-
1954	3,916	16,498	2,864	-	-	-
1955	1,455	1,513	18,996	12,343	-	-
1956	1,915	1,694	8,011	14,956	-	-
1957	1,627	1,467	8,173	8,127	-	-
1958	760	815	7,051	7,610	-	-
1959	1,492	1,115	8,763	10,627	-	-
1960	1,395	1,125	10,383	12,194	-	-

	4cylSW	4cylPU	6cyl SW	6cyl PU	230SW	230PU
1961	1,451	753	8,790	2,793	-	-
1962	NA	NA	NA	NA	NA	NA
1963	1,054	937	7,273	1,335	108	1,118
1964	NA	NA	NA	NA	NA	NA
1965	NA	NA	NA	NA	NA	NA

FORWARD CONTROL, FC-150, FC-170, M-SERIES, 1957–1965

	FC-150	FC-170	FC-170DRW	M-series
1957	6,637	3,101	-	-
1958	2,070	1,522	-	-
1959	NA	NA	-	-
1960	1,925	2,602	402	-
1961	1,298	2,054	320	-
1962	NA	NA	NA	NA
1963	1,091	2,031	174	NA
1964	NA	NA	NA	NA
1965	NA	NA	NA	NA

JEEPSTER/COMMANDO, 1967–1973:

Total build of all types.

1966	2,345
1967	12,621
1968	13,924
1969	11,289
1970	9,268
1971	7,903
1972	10,685
1973	9,538

*Estimates
Italics are for non -S models

TECHNICAL SPECS BY MODEL AND YEAR:
PROTOTYPE MILITARY JEEPS

	Bantam BRC-40	Ford GP	Willys MA
Engine			
Type	4-cyl L-head	4-cyl L-head	4-cyl L-head
Displacement	134.2cid	112cid	119cid
Power	45hp @ 3,500rpm	45hp @ 3,600rpm	60hp @ 4,000rpm
Torque	86lbs-ft @ 1800rpm	NA	105lbs-ft @ 2,000rpm
Comp. ratio	6.81:1	6.9:1	6.48:1
Drivetrain			
Trans. type	3-speed, Warner T84D		
T-Case type	2-speed Spicer 18		
Front axle	Spicer 25		
Rear axle	Spicer 25, full-floating		
Axle ratios	4.88:1		
Dimensions & Capacities			
Wheelbase	79.5in	80in	80in
LxWxH	126x54x72in	129x62x71in	132 x62x72in
Shipping wt.	2,050lbs	2,100lbs	2,150lbs
GVW	2,600lbs	2,800lbs	3,650lbs
Fuel capacity	10gal	10gal	10gal
Tires	6.00-16	6.00-16	6.00-16

PRODUCTION MILITARY JEEPS

	MB/GPW	MC	MD
Engine			
Type	4-cyl L-head	4-cyl L-head	4-cyl F-head
Displacement	134cid	134cid	134cid
Power	60hp @ 4,000rpm	60hp @ 4,000rpm	72hp @ 4,000rpm
Torque	105lbs-ft @ 2,000rpm	105lbs-ft @ 2,000rpm	118lbs-ft @ 2,000
Comp. ratio	6.48:1	6.48:1	7.4:1
Drivetrain			
Trans type	3-speed, Warner T-84	3-speed, Warner T-90	3-speed, Warner T-90
T-Case type	2-speed, Model 18	2-speed, Model 18	2-speed, Model 18
Front axle	Spicer 25	Spicer 25	Spicer 25
Rear axle	Spicer 23-2, full-floating	Spicer 44, full-floating	Spicer 44, full-floating

	MB/GPW	MC	MD
Axle ratios:	4.88:1	5.38:1	5.38:1
Dimensions & Capacities			
Wheelbase	80in	80in	81in
LxWxH	132x62x72in	133x62x74in	139x61x74in
Shipping wt.	2,315lbs	2,750lbs	2,665lbs
GVW	3,250lbs	3,950lbs	3,870
Fuel capacity	15gal	13gal	17gal
Tires	6.00-16	7.00-16	7.00-16

CJ-2A

Engine
Type	4-cyl L-head
Displacement	134.2cid
Power	60hp @ 4,000rpm
Torque	105lbs-ft @ 2,000rpm
Comp. ratio	6.48-1
Carb. type	1-bbl Carter WO-596-S

Drivetrain
Trans. type	3-speed, Warner T90C
T-Case type	2-speed Spicer 18
Front axle	Spicer 25
Rear axle	Spicer 23-2, full-floating (early)
	Spicer 41-1, semi-floating (late)
Axle ratios	5.38-1

Dimensions & Capacities
Wheelbase	80in
LxWxH	130.8x59x69in
Shipping wt.	2,120lbs
GVW	3,500lbs
Fuel capacity	10.5gal

CJ-3A

Technical Specs
Engine
Type	4-cyl L-head
Displacement	134.2cid
Power	60hp @ 4,000rpm
Torque	105lbs-ft @ 2,000rpm
Comp. ratio	6.48-1
Carb. type	1-bbl Carter 636-SA

Drivetrain
Trans. type	3-speed, Warner T90
T-Case type	2-speed, Spicer 18
Front axle	Spicer 25C
Rear axle	Spicer 44-2 semi-floating
Axle ratios	5.38-1

Dimensions & Capacities
Wheelbase	80in
LxWxH	129.75x68.78x66.75in
Shipping wt.	2,110lbs
GVW	3,500lbs
Fuel capacity	10.5gal

CJ-3B

Engine
Type	4-cyl F-head
Displacement	134.2cid
Power	72hp @ 4,000rpm (75 @ 4,000, opt. hi-comp)
Torque	114lbs-ft @ 2,000rpm
Comp. ratio	6.9-1 (7.4-1 opt)
Carb. type	1-bbl Carter, YF-938-SD

Drivetrain
Trans. type	3-speed, Warner T90
T-Case type	2-speed, Spicer 18
Front axle	Spicer 25
Axle	Spicer 44-2 semi-floating
Axle ratios	5.38-1

Dimensions & Capacities
Wheelbase	80in
LxWxH	130x68.88x66.25in
Shipping wt.	2,132lbs
GVW	3,500lbs
Fuel capacity	10.5gal

CJ-5, CJ-6 - 1955-1965

Engine
Type	4-cyl F-head
Displacement	134.2cid
Power	75 @ 4,000
Torque	115lbs-ft @ 2,000rpm
Comp. ratio	7.4-1 (opt), Std 6.8:1
Carb. type:	1bbl., Carter YF-938-SD

Drivetrain
Trans. type	3-speed, Warner T90
	4-speed, Warner T98A (opt. 1957–1965)
T-Case type	2-speed, Spicer 18
Front axle	Spicer 25
Axle	Spicer 44-2 semi-floating
Axle tatios	5.38:1(to 1960)
	4.27:1 (std), 5.38:1 (opt) (from 1960)

Dimensions & Capacities
Wheelbase	81in/101in
LxWxH	135.5x71.75x67in
	155.5x71.75x67in
Shipping wt.	2,163lbs/2,225
GVW	3,750lbs/3,900lbs
Fuel capacity	10.5gal

	CJ-5 & CJ-6	CJ-7
Engine		
Type	4-cyl, F-head (std '66–71) V6, OHV (opt '66–71) 6-cyl, OHV (std '72–77) 6-cyl, OHV (opt '72–77, std '78–79) V8, OHV (opt '72–79)	6-cyl, OHV (std '76–77) 6-cyl, OHV (opt '76–77, std '78–79) V8, OHV (opt '76–79)
Displacement	134cid 225cid 232cid 258cid 304cid	232cid 258cid 304cid
Power	75hp @ 4,000rpm 160hp @ 4,200rpm 100hp @ 3,600rpm 110hp @ 3,500rpm 150hp @ 4,300rpm	100hp @ 3,600rpm 110hp @ 3,500rpm 150hp @ 4300rpm
Torque	118lbs-ft @ 2,000rpm 235lbs-ft @ 2,400rpm 185lbs-ft @ 1,800rpm 195lbs-ft @ 1,600rpm 245lbs-ft @ 2,500rpm	185lbs-ft @ 1,800rpm 195lbs-ft @ 1,600rpm 245lbs-ft @ 2,500rpm
Comp ratio	7.4:1 9.0:1 8.0:1 8.0:1 8.4:1	8.0:1 8.0:1 8.4:1
Drivetrain		
Trans. type	3-speed, Warner T-90 (std '66–71 4-cyl) 3-speed, Warner T-14A ('70-71 V6), T-15A ('72-79 V-8) 4-speed, Warner T-98A (opt '66–71) 4-speed, Warner T-18 (opt '72–79 6-cyl)	3-speed, Warner T-15A (std) 4-speed, Warner T-18 (opt 6-cyl) 3-speed auto, GM TH-400 (opt)
T-Case type	2-speed, Spicer Model 18 ('66–71) 2-speed, Spicer Model 20 ('72–79)	2-speed, Spicer Model 20
Front axle	Spicer, Model 25 ('66–69) Spicer, Model 27AF ('70–71) Spicer, Model 30 ('72–79)	Spicer, Model 30
Rear axle	Spicer, Model 44-2, semi-floating ('66–71) AMC Model 20, semi-floating ('72–79)	AMC Model 20, semi-floating
Axle ratios	4.27 (4.88, 5.38) (4-cyl '66–71) 3.73 (4.88) (V6 '66–71) 3.73 (4.27) ('72–75) 3.54 (4.10) ('76–79)	3.54(4.10)
Dimensions & Capacities		
Wheelbase	81in/101in ('66–71) 84in/104in ('71–79)	93.5in
LxWxH	135.6x71.75x69.5in (CJ-5 '66–71) 155.6x71.75x68.3in (CJ-6 '66–71) 138.75x71.75x67in (CJ-5 '72–79) 158.75x71.75x67in (CJ-7 '72–75)	147.75x69.1x67.6in
Shipping wt.	2,212lbs/2,274lbs ('66–71) 2,437/2,510 ('72–79)	2,683lbs
GVW	3,730lbs/3,900lbs	3,750 (4,150)
Fuel capacity	10.5gal ('66–69) 15.5gal ('70–79)	15.5gal

	4-cyl	6-226	6-230
Engine			
Type	4-cyl L-head 4-cyl F-head	6-cyl L-head	6-cyl OHV, OHC
Displacement	134cid	226cid	230cid
Power	63hp @ 4,000rpm 72hp @ 4,000rpm	105hp @ 3,600rpm	140hp @ 4,000rpm
Torque	108lbs-ft @ 2,000rpm 118lbs-ft @ 2,000rpm	190lbs-ft @ 1,400rpm	210lbs-ft @ 1,750rpm
Comp. ratio	7.0:1 (opt), 6.5:1 (std)	7.3:1 (opt), 6.8:1 (std)	8.5:1
Drivetrain			
Trans type	3-speed, Warner T-90 (SW) 3-speed, Warner ASI T909E (PU)		
T-Case type	2-speed, Spicer 18		
Front axle	Spicer 25		
Rear axle	Spicer 25, semi-floating (SW) Timken 51540 (PU) Spicer 53 (PU)		
Axle ratios	4.88:1 (std), 5.38:1 (opt)		
Dimensions & Capacities			
Wheelbase	104.5in (SW) 118in (PU)		
LxWxH	176.25x71.75x73.56in (SW) 183.75x66.25x74.38in (PU)		
Shipping Wt.	3,206lb (SW, 6-226) 3,176lbs (PU)		
GVW	4,500lbs (SW) 6,000lbs (PU)		
Fuel capacity	15gal		

	FC-150	FC-170	M-Series
Engine			
Type	4-cyl F-head	6-cyl L-head	3-cyl OHV diesel
Displacement	134.2cid	226.2cid	170cid
Power	72hp @ 4,000rpm	105hp @ 3,600rpm	85hp @ 3,000rpm
Torque	115lbs-ft @ 2,000rpm	190lbs-ft @ 1,400rpm	170 @ 1,900rpm
Comp. ratio	6.9-1 (7.4-1 opt)	6.86-1 (7.3-1 opt)	22-1
Carb. type	1-bbl Carter WA-1	1-bbl Carter WDG	diesel injection
Drivetrain			
Trans. type Warner T90(T-98)	3-speed (4-sp. opt) Warner T90(T98)	3-speed (4-sp. opt) Warner T98	4-speed
T-Case type	2-speed Spicer 18	2-speed Spicer 18	2-speed Spicer 18
Front axle	Spicer 25 (to '59) Spicer 44F ('59-on)	Spicer 44F	Spicer 44F
Rear axle	Spicer 44 Spicer 70 (DRW)	Spicer 53	Spicer 53
Axle ratios	5.38-1	4.88-1	4.88-1
Dimensions & Capacities			
Wheelbase	81in	103.5in	103.5in
LxWxH	147.4 x 71.4 x 77.4in	180.5 x 76.5 x 79.4in	184.3 x 78 x 91in
Shipping wt.	3,020lbs (pickup)	3,331lbs (pickup)	4,585lbs (crew cab)
GVW	5,000lbs 8,000lbs (DRW)	7,000lbs	7,000lbs
Fuel capacity	15gal	22gal	22gal

Engine

Type	6-cyl, OHV, OHC ('63–64)
	6-cyl, OHV (std '65–70)
	V8, OHV (opt '65–70)
Displacement	230cid ('63–64)
	232cid (std '65–70)
	327cid (opt '65–68)
	350cid (opt '69–70)
Power	140hp @ 4,000rpm (230)
	145hp @ 4,300rpm (232)
	250hp @ 4,700rpm (2bbl 327)
	270hp @ 4,700rpm (4bbl 327)
	230hp @ 4,400rpm (350)
Torque	210lbs-ft @ 1,750rpm (230)
	215lbs-ft @ 1,600rpm (232)
	340lbs-ft @ 2,600rpm (2bbl 327)
	360lbs-ft @ 2,600rpm (4bbl 327)
Comp. ratio	8.5:1 (230)
	8.5:1 (232)
	8.7:1 (2bbl 327)
	9.7:1 (4bbl 327)
	9.0:1 (350)

Drivetrain

Trans type	3-speed, Warner T-90 (std SW)
	3-speed, Warner T-89 (std PU)
	4-speed, Warner T-98 (opt PU)
	3-speed, Borg Warner, AS-8F auto. (opt SW, PU, '63–68)
	3-speed, GM, TH-400 auto (opt SW, PU, '69–70)
T-Case type	2-speed, Spicer Model 20 (man. trans)
	1-speed, Spicer Model 21 (auto. trans)
Front axle	Spicer 44F (PU, leaf springs)
	Spicer 44FI (PU, torsion bars)
	Spicer 27AF (SW leaf springs)
	Spicer 27AFI (SW torsion bars)
Rear axle	Spicer 44, semi-floating (SW, PU, 1/2 ton)
	Spicer 70, full-floating (PU, 3/4, 1 ton)

Axle ratios

	3-speed	4-speed	Auto
V8 SW	3.73 (4.09)	-	3.31 (3.73)
Six Sw	4.09 (4.27–4.88)	-	3.73 (4.09)
V8 PU (5,000 GVW)	3.92 (4.27)	3.92 (4.27)	3.54 (3.92)
V8 PU (6,000 GVW)	4.09 (4.27)	4.09 (4.27)	4.09
(7,000 GVW)	"	"	"
V8 PU (8,000 GVW)	-	4.88	-
Six PU (5,000 GVW)	4.27 (4.88)	4.27 (4.88)	4.27 (4.88)
Six PU (6,000 GVW)	"	"	"
Six PU (7,000 GVW)	4.88	4.88	4.27
Six PU (8,600 GVW)	-	4.88	-

Dimensions & Capacities

Wheelbase	110in (SW)
	120 or 126in (PU)
LxWxH	186.6x75.6x64.2 (SW)
	183.75x75.6x71in (120in WB PU)
	195.75x75.6x71in (126in WB PU)
Shipping wt.	3,689 (4dr SW)
	3,759 (120in WB PU)
GVW	4,500 (SW)
	5,000, 6,000, 7,000, 8,600lb (PU)
Fuel capacity	20gal(SW)
	18gal (PU)

Engine

Type	4-cyl, F-head (std '67–71)
	V6, OHV (opt '67–71)
	6-cyl, OHV (std '72–73)
	6-cyl, OHV (opt '72–73)
	V8, OHV (opt '72–73)
Displacement	134cid
	225cid
	232cid
	258cid
	304cid
Power	75hp @ 4,000rpm
	160hp @ 4,200rpm
	100hp @ 3,600rpm (net)
	110hp @ 3,500rpm (net)
	150hp @ 4,200rpm (net)
Torque	118lbs-ft @ 2,000rpm (net)
	235lbs-ft @ 2,400rpm (net)
	185lbs-ft @ 1,800rpm (net)
	195lbs-ft @ 2,000rpm (net)
	245lbs-ft @ 2,500rpm (net)
Comp. ratio	7.4:1
	9.0:1
	8.0:1
	8.0:1
	8.4:1

Drivetrain

Trans type	3-speed, Warner T-86CC (std '67–71)
	3-speed, Warner T-14A (std '72–73)
	3-speed automatic, GM TH-400
T-Case type	2-speed, Spicer Model 20
Front axle	Spicer 27AF ('67–71)
	Spicer 30 ('72–74)
Rear axle	Spicer 44, semi-floating
Axle ratios	4.27 (5.38) 4-cyl
	3.73 (4.27) V6
	3.73 (4.27) ('72–73)

Dimensions & Capacities

Wheelbase	101in ('67–71)
	104in ('72–73)
LxWxH	168.4x65.2x64.2in ('67–71)
	174x65.2x64.2in ('72–73)
Shipping height	2,673lbs ('67–71 SW)
	3,010lbs ('72–73 SW)
GVW	3,550 (4,200) ('67–71)
	3,900 (4,700) ('72–73)
Fuel capacity	15gal (9.5gal aux) ('67–71)
	16.5gal ('72–73)

Chapter 5

International Harvester—from Farm Machines to 4x4s

International Harvester is a popular name that goes way back in American history. The company itself dates back to 1831, when Cyrus McCormick started building horse-drawn, mechanized grain harvesters. Called the McCormick Harvesting Machine Company for many years, the company changed to the more familiar International Harvester in 1902.

In 1907, IHC brought its first motor vehicles to the market and called them the Auto-Buggy and Auto-Wagon. The Auto-Buggy was primarily a passenger carrying conveyance, while the Auto-Wagon was for cargo. These rigs sold well in the fledgling days of the car and truck markets, and one reason was the conservative approach IHC took in design. They resembled, more than anything, a horseless wagon. Those people who grew up with horses and had trouble with "new-fangled" devices were more at home. It didn't hurt that these were reliable contraptions and easy to maintain.

Not to say that International's designers were backward types—they did their share of playing with advanced designs—they just knew that there was an "acceptance curve" in the marketplace and they were careful never to step out of this curve in a major way. This philosophy carried the company successfully for many years. IHC continued to market farm machinery but trucks also proved to be a lucrative business all through the teens, 1920s, and 1930s. Throughout that time, however, they didn't give much thought to all-wheel drive.

Binders for War

International finally got into the 4x4 business as war loomed in 1940. While the company had little experience in the all-wheel drive area, IHC trucks themselves were not complete strangers to four-wheel drive. In the late 1930s, Marmon-Herrington converted a number of IHC model D-1 1/2-ton trucks to 4x4 configuration for use as Coast Guard beach patrol vehicles. The trucks proved a near ideal platform for the conversion.

These conversions may have provided inspiration because IHC had its first 4x4 1/2 ton up and running in time for the rearmament scramble of 1940. Their first prototypes were odd looking units that appeared to use body parts from every sort and size of IHC truck. Development was obviously focused on the adaptation to four-wheel drive. The drivetrain was all business and used many of IHC's existing HD pieces when possible. Soon after, the M-2-4 1 ton was developed from the bones of the first prototypes. Development of the M-1-4 1/2 ton followed the 1 ton very closely. In fact, they were nearly identical trucks and shared similar mechanical characteristics. IHC also built the medium duty 1 1/2-ton M-3-4 4x4 and heavy-duty 2 1/2-ton M-

5-6 6x6. All these trucks shared the same, or similar, body features and even some mechanical parts.

Virtually all of IHC's 1942–1945 M-series production went to the Marines and the Navy. The trucks saw combat in most theaters of the war, though primarily in the Pacific, where the Navy and Marines had their hardest work. They earned the enviable reputation of being able to grind up sandy beachheads under fire, carrying an over-capacity load, and then spend months slogging though jungle mud without complaint.

The M-series IHC trucks were Spartan, even by military standards. Seldom seen with any sort of weather protection, the M-1-4 and M-2-4 trucks used an open, doorless cab with a heavy, welded steel box. They operated primarily in a weapons carrier role but were also used extensively for cargo and as a prime mover for light artillery. There was also an ambulance body that was most often fitted to the M-1-4. Some mounted 4.5-inch automatic rocket launcher racks carrying upwards of 40 rockets that could be fired in about a minute.

Both trucks were powered by versions of IHC overhead-valve sixes. Most M-1-4s used the "Green Diamond" 213-cid, 85-horsepower version and the M-2-4 had the 233-cid, 95-horsepower variant that was normally fitted to medium duty trucks. Some late M-1-4s were apparently also so equipped. Four-speed transmissions were combined with two-speed T-cases and 4.89 gears to give fabulous off-road performance. The major difference between the two rated capacities were springs, tire, and the engines. Many were fitted with winches. The M-1-4 sat on a 113-inch wheelbase while the M-2-4 was stretched to 125 inches.

The bigger M-series trucks are very common, many having been used in Stateside roles. The 1/2 and 1 tons are scarce but not all that popular among the military vehicle collectors. Less than 10,000 M-2-4s were manufactured and even fewer M-1-4s. Many were used (or used up) overseas, though the marines, always first on government budget-cutter's lists, brought many of their trucks back in case they had to wait for new equipment. Some parts are available for them but can be difficult to obtain. Fortunately, there is carryover from the prewar civilian trucks, though parts for these are not particularly plentiful either. As it stands now, these trucks have limited value growth potential, but like many trucks in this category, they still make a great collectable.

Binders in Civvies
R-Series Trucks, 1953–Mid-1955

There was quite a delay in International Harvester offering a postwar four-wheel drive in their civilian truck lines. It finally debuted, on paper at least, in the 1953 R-series trucks. The R trucks were little more than slightly restyled L-series rigs that dated back to 1950. The R-series 4x4 option was only available in the R-120 (3/4-ton) models. The trucks could be ordered in four wheelbase lengths, 115, 122, 127 and 134 inches, offering 6 1/2-

The first factory-made International 4x4 was this military prototype built in 1940. By all appearances, it used bits and pieces from every IHC truck then in production. It was powered by IHC's 213-cid engine that made 78 horsepower at 3,400 rpm. The wheelbase was listed at 115 inches and it used 7.50-16 traction type tires. *U.S. Army*

The M-1-4 was rated as a 1/2 ton in military service but you can see by the chassis and running gear that it would be a 1-ton or larger by any other standard. This is how the M-series trucks looked after they rolled off the line, prior to being fitted with whatever specialty body had been selected. *Navistar International*

The M-2-4 was rated as a 1-ton but, again, the unit was somewhat underrated. This prototype is fitted with dual wheels, which was not normally the case in actual service. These transverse troop seats were also not the norm in actual service, but the heavy, welded steel body is close to the production style. *Navistar International*

Could this be one of only two R-120 4x4s produced? An often seen factory photo shows the distinctive nose of the R-120 4x4 in a staged "at work" shot. According to factory production information, only two trucks like this were built, along with just under 2,000 heavier rated trucks.

foot, 8-foot and 9-foot pickup beds, as well as a stake bed or specialty bodies. The 4x4s were built on the R-130 (1-ton) 4x2 chassis for strength. This setup had a 5.03-inch section width rails and had five crossmembers. Three engine choices were offered, the standard 220-cid, 108-horsepower "Silver Diamond"; the 240-cid, 131-horsepower "Black Diamond" mill; and another 240 converted to run on LPG. This option did not include the LPG tank, however.

The drivetrain was typical heavy-duty binder stuff with a lot of choices available to suit just about any need. A three-speed IHC model HNS transmission was standard but a Warner T-98 four-speed was optional, as well as a Warner T-9 model that featured access for a PTO on both sides. The transfer case was called an "NP-91,000" on the sales brochures and had a 1.98:1 low range. Axle ratios came standard as 4.11:1 but could be ordered in 4.77:1. The front axle and much of the rest of the drivetrain was shared with the R-130 4x4, making the R-120 extra durable within its weight classification. The R-series also offered a wide selection of tires. The standard tire was a 6.50x16, but the options book shows 7.50x16, 9.00x16, and 7.00x18 as available.

A sales and engineering bulletin from the era touted the R-120's ability to outcarry the Jeep trucks of the era, outclimb both the Jeep and the Dodge Power Wagon at load capacity, to be more economical than the Power Wagon, and cheaper to purchase than the conversions then being offered.

The R-120 was quite a package. Many popular resources show that the R-120 4x4 was available from 1953 to mid-1955. On the face of things, this seems doubtful. IHC records show only two (count 'em) R-120 4x4 pickups were built. Whether it's true or not remains to be seen but the records from IHC are very specific. Much of the period R-120 literature, including a Sales & Engineering Bulletin, is dated 1955. International went to a great deal of trouble to publish literature on R-series 4x4s so the low figure is doubly perplexing. The figures show nearly 2,000 medium-duty R-140 and R-160 trucks produced.

Given the apparent rarity of R-120 4x4s, it's doubtful that any have survived. One R-120 truck has been seen in a variety of poses in period literature. Is this truck half the total production? The bottom line is that extremely rare trucks are not always extremely valuable but wouldn't it be grand to find one of the two R-120s built!

S-Line Trucks, Mid-1955–Early 1957

The most likely answer to the R-series 4x4 truck question posed above is that after an initial announcement, perhaps as early as 1953, development took longer than expected. The effort did not go to waste when the S-series 4x4 trucks debuted toward the end of 1955. These short-lived trucks shared most of the R-series mechanical features. Cosmetically, it was also very close, though the front end was restyled by placing the headlights in the fenders instead of the grille. A larger rear window was fitted and there were a few other very minor detail differences.

From the technical standpoint, there was very little difference to talk about. The "Silver Diamond" 220-cid was dropped as the standard engine for the trucks in favor of the 240-cid unit. An LPG fueled 240-cid variant was still offered. The drivetrain was essentially the same as the R-series.

The big news was that the S-120 4x4 chassis was available with the capacious Travelall body on it, as well as the 6 1/2-, 8- and 9-foot pickup boxes, a stakebed, and a Panel. The Travelall peoplemover and the Panel were offered only on the 115-inch wheelbase.

The Travelall was not a new idea. The concept went back to the now immortal Chevy Suburban that dated back to the 1930s era. International's version of the idea was prototyped in 1952 on an L-series chassis and introduced for the 1953 model year. Actually the story goes back even further to 1949, when the General Body Company of Chicago built a one-off Travelall type rig for use in the Philippines. Apparently, there were a few other conversions as well.

The S-series 4x4 trucks were virtual twins of the R-series, with the exception of the new front end. These trucks are relatively common but not usually in this exceptional original condition. Rob Schillinger's 1956 is carrying its original paint, despite the fact that it's still hard at work. Whether or not it would ever achieve a valuable "classic" status, it would still be a great truck to own.

Though no R-series 4x4 Travelalls were constructed, there were apparently a few among the 10,000 S-120 4x4 chassis built. The production numbers from International do not differentiate between body styles. The Travelall proved a popular unit for those folks who liked International products and needed passenger capacity. The Travelall could carry nine people plus a little luggage and a case or two of beer. Best of all, it was built on exactly the same chassis as the trucks so the unit was up to a good job of work. They found niches as mini school busses, hauling crews to remote construction sites, and as family haulers.

It's doubtful that very many S-series 4x4 Travelalls were constructed. The two-wheel drive models are difficult to find these days and a 4x4 model would be a real coup. S-series pickups are relatively common, though not popular except among the IHC collectors that are interested in 4x4 trucks. Like the R-Line, they are great trucks, but the general collectability issue is iffy. A Travelall could well be a few notches above the pickups in potential.

IHC's Golden Anniversary—The A-Series

In 1957, IHC celebrated 50 years of truck building by introducing the A-Line, or "Anniversary Line," as the period spin doctors put it. As was typical for International, they were not stylishly elaborate, despite their "Action-Styling" ad slogan—especially when compared to the flash, fins, and foo-foo-ra that was appearing on other motor vehicles in those days—even trucks! They were, however, sturdy and reliable and equipped with a common sense array of features. They did gain a few "styling points" by introducing curve-around windshields and two-tone paint. These new A-Line trucks were introduced mid-year, leaving the S-series trucks to become first series 1957s. IHC didn't have a big image to promote, so the races the Big-Three engaged in to introduce new models had little meaning in those days.

When the IHC overhead valve engines debuted in the late 1930s, it was a very advanced design. By the time 1956, the year of this 240, rolled around, the 241-cid was showing its age. The engine was still in service well into the 1960s. This basic design was first produced for light-duty rigs in a 213-cid, 78-horsepower version, then (by displacement, not by year), 220-cid, 108-horsepower; 233-cid, 93-horsepower; 241-cid, 131-horsepower; and 264-cid, 153-horsepower.

IHC did break a little new ground with the introduction of the Travelette. The Travelette was a three-door, six-person truck with a 6-foot bed and was built upon a 129-inch wheelbase. According to IHC, this was the first such offering from a production truck manufacturer. Like the Travelall, the Travelette had two doors on the passenger side but only one on the driver's side. It sounds like a great idea but IHC didn't sell many, even in 4x2 form. The records show that a mere 17 A-Line Travelette trucks were built in 4x4 livery.

The four-wheel drive Travelall was pushed a bit harder than before but sales were modest. A little more effort went into promoting the Travelall as a family vehicle. In its Custom Cab trim, the Travelall could seat up to eight in its foam-cushioned, nylon-covered seats. The comfort and practicality of a station wagon and the guts of a truck.

Mechanically, the changes were few on the new trucks. One new addition to the options list was the 264-cid six. V-8s were still a few years away at that time but this engine developed 154 horsepower and 248 pound-feet of torque. The standard engine remained the 240-cid six. Both engines were available converted to run on LPG fuel. The old standard three-speed and optional four-speed, in addition to the rest of the 4x4 drivetrain, were the same proven goodies from the R and S Lines. A power brake option was introduced, a Bendix Hydrovac, as an option in the light-duty 4x4s and power steering was also available.

The paint had hardly dried on the 1957 A-Line trucks when the 1958s were introduced. IHC was not much on delineating model years! The 1958s were virtually identical. The only real change was a slight increase in prices. A total of 8,873 A-Line 4x4 trucks were built in 1957 and 1958. There is, at present, no movement toward the A-series trucks as collectables. Like as not, only the Travelall and the Travelette, all 17 of them, will garner any interest at all. Parts are not easy to procure but the trucks themselves are not hard to find. They are tough trucks and have stood the years well. That is, perhaps, a better testimonial than value as a classic.

Into the 1960s: The B-Line

The 1959 B-Line IHC trucks were touted as a "New Look" in trucks but as before, with regards to styling, all you could say about the Binder trucks was, "much ado about nothing." Dual headlights were introduced, as well as a new aluminum mesh-type grille. A new "Bonus-Load" pickup body was also added to the line, with either 7- or 8-1/2-foot beds. This was essentially a smooth side bed, similar to the Chevy Fleetside, Dodge Sweptline, or Ford Styleside.

There was more to talk about on the mechanical side of things. IHC introduced its first light-duty V-8 engine, the 266-cid. It made 154 horsepower and 227 pound-feet of torque—actually the same power as the 264 six but less torque. Still, it was a V-8 and it gave the company the bragging rights to say that they had beaten Chevrolet in offering a V-8 in a 4x4 chassis. The V-8 became standard in the B-120 after July 1959 and remained as the standard powerplant in 1960. The 304-cid and 345-cid engines were introduced also, but these were used only in the medium and heavy-duty trucks at this time.

The A-Line trucks were considerably restyled, but the R- and S-series trucks could still be seen behind the new front end and windshield. This A-120 4x4 is a 115-inch wheelbase variety and is a fairly common truck nowadays. *Navistar International*

One IHC innovation that emerged in the 1957 A-Line trucks was the Travelette. Built with a three-door crew cab, it also had a 6-foot cargo box. It was an ideal go-to-work truck for small crews. The 129-inch wheelbase didn't hamper the truck's off-highway capabilities much. According to available production figures from IHC, only 17 were made in 4x4 configuration. *Navistar International*

The 1959–1960 B-Line was the same truck as the previous A-series but with a new grille and the dual headlights that were popular in that era. Shown here is a Travelall that has been modified for use as a fire department squad car. Note that the Travelalls were three-doors, like the Travelette, having two passenger doors on the right and one on the left. The 1960–1972 Chevy Suburbans shared this feature. *Navistar International*

The 1961 model IHC trucks looked completely new at first glance, but if you look more closely, you can see the older body has just been moved lower onto the chassis. This 1961 models the eight-foot Bonus Load bed on a 130-inch wheelbase chassis. The doors on the sides of the bed are not original.

Art Martinez's 1968 1100 4x4 1/2 ton shows that the old standard bed, dating back to the 1950s, was still in use. It was still used in the 1969–1975 era trucks.

Travelalls and Travelettes, as well as panels, were available in the B-120 4x4 chassis. Five wheelbase choices were offered, 110, 114, 117, 126, and 129 inches. Only the 114 and 126-inch chassis were fitted with standard pickup beds. The 129-inch chassis were used with stake and platform bodies and the Travelette. The Travelall was on the 114-inch chassis. The 4x4s got a slight lift with springs that were arched higher.

The B-Line was carried through the 1960 model year for light-duty trucks, but survived until 1962 for some of the medium-duty rigs. As with the other early IHC trucks, collector value is essentially nil, but the trucks are worth owning just for the sake of a good old truck that doesn't cost much.

The 1961–1968 Travelall 4x4s are very popular. This 1964 model is in showroom condition and showing only 33,000 miles on the odometer. The C1100 4x4 was equipped with the biggest engine available that year, the 304 V-8, a four-speed transmission and a dealer-installed air conditioning system. Roger Knight is the proud original owner.

A Modicum of Style: The A, B, C, and Ds

In the early 1960s, IHC got a little more fervent with their marketing. Not only did they introduce the new C-Line trucks in 1961, their most stylish rigs to date, they brought the ground-breaking Scout to market. The hoopla over the Scout almost overshadowed the new trucks. The new rigs looked longer, lower, and wider, but in reality, the old bodies were given some new features and lowered on the chassis to give the impression of a whole new truck. The wheelbases got a slight stretch (the range ran from 115 to 140 inches) which added to the effect. Though they did not have the flash of some other makes, they were actually pretty modern looking trucks.

While IHC had had a general policy not to introduce new models yearly, they began to get caught up more and more in the Detroit "badge re-engineering" game. In 1963, they adopted new designations to denote weight classifications. The 1/2 tons became 1100s (from 110), the 3/4-ton 1200 (from 120), and the 1 ton became a 1300 (from 130). Incidentally, until 1964, IHC had not carried a 1/2-ton 4x4 in the lineup. In 1965, though they were essentially the same trucks, they reverted to a new designation and called these the D-Line trucks—the second time this designation had been used in IHC's history. In 1966, they became the A-line, in 1967 the "B," and in 1968 they reverted to "C" again.

Under the skin, changes were relatively few. The 266 V-8 remained as the standard powerplant until 1963, when a new V-8 was added to the light line. That year, the 240 became standard, the 266 became the mid-range option, and the 304 (a bigger bore version of the 266) became the top dog option. From 1961 through 1965, the 264 disappeared, only to reappear for 1966 to give the line a fourth engine option. In the final year of this body style, 1968, the 345-cid V-8 was added to the options list.

The drivetrain finally underwent some evolution in the C-Line era. The old IHC three-speed (a variation of an old Clark design) was replaced by a Warner T-87 that IHC dubbed the T-7. An upgraded version of the T-98 went into service and in 1966, a Borg-Warner automatic was added to the options list. The line of axles gradually reverted to Spicer units from the old IHC designs, with the Models 44 and 60 being common in the light line.

The Travelall got some upgrading in this era. With the automatic and an air conditioning option, along with the previously available power steering and brakes, the old Travelall really did live up to its "Family Wagon" ad hype. As with the rest of the truck industry, IHC's rigs were finally adding some comfort and dress-up features to satisfy the recreational users of trucks.

With regard to the new usages of trucks in having fun, IHC was in a difficult position. Their clientele was different than the other truck makers. A Chevy truck buyer might have bought his recreational pickup at the same dealership from which he had purchased a car. More than likely, this dealership was on "Main Street" just up from the Ford dealer and he drove past it three times a day.

Historically, IHC dealers were far fewer in number and sited to service farm, ranch, or commercial customers. You came in to buy a tractor and got a pickup at the same time. The IHC dealer got few walk-in customers from the Ford-Chevy-Dodge crowd, so his products, arguably as good or better than the competition, stayed relatively unknown. This was a problem that was never fully rectified.

Nineteen sixty-one to nineteen sixty-eight IHC trucks were built in large numbers and in a wide variety of styles and specialist applications. The military was fond of these Binders, so ex-GI versions are commonly found. This era of truck has attracted slightly more interest than the earlier rigs. Perhaps wide availability has something to do with it or maybe it's the long, low look. The parts are a little easier to find than those of previous eras. There is little chance of them becoming really valuable but they are collectable and practical.

Last of the Breed: 1969–1975 D-Line

In 1969, IHC introduced a truly new body style. The new styling has a direct tie-in to the vastly successful Scout II that followed. The new bodies were more angular and this actually followed the current styles. With the truck market booming, IHC worked hard to bring their products more into the public eye and get a bigger share of the sales. This was not to be—but it wasn't from the lack of a quality product.

The new rigs were almost ground-up revisions. Nothing escaped scrutiny, and the result was a line of 4x4 trucks that were quieter, rode better, and were more comfortable than ever before. The pickup, Travelall, and

Cecil Winder's 1968 1100 Travelall was built for the military and equipped with the 241-cid six, three-speed transmission and 4.88 gears. The front-mounted winch is also an army addition. *Cecil Winders*

The 1969–1975 pickups and Travelalls bore a striking resemblance to the later Scout lines. This was no accident. A late model Travelall, like Gip Machette's 1975, is a popular addition to many IHC collectors fleets. This rig mounts a 392-cid IHC torquer, 3.54 gears, and an automatic. Gip reports that it's a great road vehicle and a good off-roader.

The D-Line trucks are not dated looking despite the 20-plus years since they were last built.

Travelette continued alongside the new Camper Special Package. Bucket seats, wood-grain exterior trim, AM-FM radios, eight-track players, and oversized chrome mirrors snazzed up the trucks more than just a bit. Mechanically a lot of new goodies surfaced and a few went bye-bye.

In the engine line, the venerable "Diamond" OHV sixes, a relic of the 1930s, finally left the light line in favor of a 232-cid, seven-main bearing six from AMC. Even this engine was dropped in 1974. The 266 was dropped as the base 4x4 V-8 to be replaced by the 304 (not the AMC 304, by the way). The 345-cid carried the mid-range V-8 title and the monster 392, four-barrel V-8, formerly available in only medium- and heavy-duty trucks, took the high ground. This big, slow-turning, 235-horsepower, 354-pounds-feet engine provided the awesome grunt needed for heavy loads and with its big truck design features (high nickel content block, among other things), it was nearly a forever engine in light-duty applications.

In the 1974 model year only, a new engine entered the lineup, the 210-horsepower AMC 401-cid. While not as torquey as the big IHC mill at low rpms, it was a much snappier performer overall, due to its higher rpm capability.

The drivetrain lineup changed to reflect the availability of new and better pieces. In 1973, the venerable Borg-Warner Model 11 automatic was replaced by a Mopar Torqueflite, and the T-18 and T-19 four-speed manuals replaced the old T-98. Open-knuckle front axles replaced the old closed designs and a better turning radius was the result. Front disc brakes replaced drums in 1974.

Safety and emission controls began to dictate some of IHC's policies. The safety items, like dual circuit brakes, padded dash and sun visor, seat belts, and a collapsible steering column became federally mandated items. In the last year of truck production, the 1/2-ton models were upgraded in capacity to escape new emissions regulations for light-duty trucks.

In 1974, the designations were changed one last time and reverted back to three digits. The 1/2 ton became the 100 (150 for 1975), the 3/4-ton became the 200. An "official" 1 ton was not offered for 1974 and 1975, but a 9,000-pound GVW was optional for the 200, in effect making it a 1 ton.

IHC light trucks went out with a whimper in 1975, the company producing only 6,329 units, total, according to published reports. This was not due to low sales but to the decision to stop production. Why stop production on a relatively successful and highly respected truck line? The bottom line—resources and politics.

It began at the dealers, where ag equipment and bigger trucks were the mainstay. The little stuff was a sideline and for some, a barely tolerated annoyance. At the corporate level, the big and small truck execs were constantly vying for resources—development money, ad money, and production space.

The 1961 Scouts were bare-bones creatures with sliding windows, but at least the heater was standard equipment. On the left is the full-length Traveltop and on the right a roadster with the windshield folded down and the doors removed. The Traveltop was the top of the line, and the roadsters were the bare-bones unit. In between was the pickup (not shown). *Four Wheeler*

IHC never was a huge company and to fight against the Big Three in the big truck arena was difficult enough. Fighting a two-front "war" that included light trucks stretched company resources to the limit. In the end, the big truck guys won and the light truck line was dropped, though the Scout stayed in production a while longer.

The last of the IHC trucks are quite popular, though not particularly valuable. 1975 models are scarce and considered collectable by those interested in IHC trucks. There is more interest, club activity, and expertise in the D-series 4x4 trucks than in any other. The resemblance to the highly popular Scout models probably accounts for this. As with the other IHC light-duty products, parts are scarce compared to other makes. A little extra creative work is required of the IHC collector.

The First Sport Ute? Scout 80

The Scout has been touted as the first American sport utility vehicle. That is debatable and depends on how you define "sport utility." You can go into other chapters and find examples that predate the Scout. It could be that these folks are referring to the "spirit and focus" of the development that makes the Scout America's first Sport Utility. Regardless of your opinion on that issue, it can be agreed that the Scout played a big role in the development of the sport utility and that it helped create the market we enjoy today.

The idea for the Scout hatched in the minds of IHC engineers in the late 1950s. No doubt this was inspired by the growing interest in the recreational use of trucks and 4x4s, and also the success of companies like Jeep and Land Rover. Once the market analysis was done, engineer Ted Ornas was given a clean sheet of paper to work with and by November 1960, the first Scouts were hitting the streets.

The Scout was designed to be adaptable and useful in a variety of roles. The basic structure was on a 100-inch wheelbase. A slab-sided body maximized interior space and minimized production headaches. Many of the first Scouts rolled off the line as pickups. It was predicted that these would

Few changes had been made by the end of the Scout 80 model in 1964. One of the few was the addition of roll-up windows. By the time this 1964 was built, the Traveltop was outselling all the other options by a wide margin. Chris Willsey's 1964 is an extremely original unit that's equipped with Powr-Lok limited slips front and rear, a PTO winch, bucket seats, dual fuel tanks, and a roof rack.

Few exterior changes were notable in the Scouts from 1965 to early 1971. Shown here is one of the very rare and highly collectable Aristocrat specials. Only 2,500 Scout Aristocrats were built in 1969. This restored version, belonging to Leonard Harrison, mounts a 304-cid V-8 and automatic transmission. When Leonard found this Aristocrat, it was a mouse-eaten derelict at the back of a feedlot. Now it's a show winner.

The Sportop special editions were available from 1966 through 1968 in two styles. The fiberglass hardtop version shown here was the lower price model and a convertible style was about $33 more. With the tailgate-mounted spare (this one is missing the tire) and the special bumpers, it was a pseudo-Continental kit. These rigs are very rare and collectable.

be the most popular model. Later, they rolled out in a variety of configurations. A full length "Traveltop" was available, but you could also go open air and remove both top and doors (or just the sliding window door tops), fold down the windshield and pick bugs from your teeth.

The front and rear compartments were divided by a bulkhead and the little Scout, though classed as a 1/4-ton, was rated to carry a 900-pound payload—not quite a 1/2 ton. The Scout was popular in commercial roles but there were a surprising number of recreational buyers. IHC's timing was just about perfect to get a reputation in the opening days of what would later be called the sport utility era.

Under the hood, Scout was a bit on the unique side. The 152-cid four-cylinder "Comanche" engine was actually half of IHC's 304 V-8. It churned out 93.4 horsepower (gross) and 135 pound-feetand was capable of high-teens, low-20s fuel economy. With the engine slanted over at a 45-degree angle, a low hood was possible. The "slant four" was a novel idea that made good use of company resources and gave customers a powerful, reliable four-cylinder unit.

The drivetrain was made up from high quality products like Warner Gear's proven T-90 three-speed, Spicer's Model 18 T-case, and Spicer 27 axles. Gearing was 4.27:1 and a Powr-Lok limited-slip was available for the rear. The suspension was a typical leaf spring setup that was noted for a ride quality that was at least tolerable and better than the immediate competition.

The Scout earned high marks from the press, except for the guy at *Car Life* who got thoroughly soaked after the hardtop leaked on him! The public also gave it praise in the form of buying them like crazy. By the standards of the day, it narrowed the gap between the utility rigs and a useful "mini-pickup," or day-to-day driver. It was capable of running down the freeway comfortably at 65 miles per hour and had a top speed of about 80 miles per hour. It was not comfortable in any real sense, but testers regarded it as more comfortable than the rigs in its class.

Initially, the Fort Wayne IHC plant built Scouts to the tune of 50 per day. This didn't come close to meeting demand, so production was doubled in February 1961 and then bumped again to 133 per day in March. According to published news reports, IHC was destined to build more than 35,000 units that first year, 80 percent of them 4x4 and most of those being the full-length Traveltops. It became the largest selling IHC model ever. The success of the Scout directly inspired Ford to start work on its Bronco and probably made Chevy think about a similar unit as well.

The first generation Scouts were called the Scout 80, and they were virtually unchanged from 1961 to 1964. Well, not quite. In late 1962, an option to the sliding windows was offered in the form of roll-up windows. At the same time, the bulkhead was eliminated in all but dedicated pickup models. A rear seat also went on the options list as well as a ragtop. An optional 10-gallon auxiliary fuel tank drew high praise from *Four Wheeler's* testers.

Though the Scouts as a whole are very hot items, the 80s seem to draw the least amount of general attention. Perhaps this is due to their bare-bones, low-power approach. Despite large numbers having been produced (some 100,000), Scout 80s have not survived in huge numbers. Rust is their biggest enemy, and they were particularly vulnerable. As Scout popularity works backwards along the timeline, look for the earliest 80s to rise in value, especially those that are fitted with the best of the period accessories.

First Upgrades: Scout 800

In 1965, the Scout got its first facelift and big engineering upgrades. The improved model was called the 800 and it embodied a large number of refinements. The 800 model continued though 1968. While the body remained essentially the same as the 80, a few readily visible styling changes were made. The fold-down windshield was replaced by a fixed unit, eliminating many of the "wet driver" complaints. The old wire mesh grille with an "I.H." in the center was replaced with an anodized flat grille that said "International." A new I.H. emblem was added to the leading edge of the hood.

The chrome bumpers, mirrors, and wheel trim rigs added to the options list highlighted IHC's focus on appealing more to general market customers. So did standard roll-up windows with vents, and tops with better drip rails. The metal tops were also fitted with sound-deadening material that reduced oil canning and reflected noise from the powertrain. Many smaller features were added that included a revised tailgate latch, improved door locks, and hanging pedal assemblies. New contoured, champagne-colored seats, with extra padding, and vinyl covered door panels were quantum improvements in comfort.

The most attention-getting new goody package that came to the Scout 800 line was the Sportop. This was a stylish variation of the Scout that turned it into a coupe via a removable fiberglass top or a fold-down convertible top. Both tops sloped stylishly in the rear and stopped just short of the rear end, leaving a ledge that was dressed with chrome. A rear bumper that split along either side of the tailgate-mounted spare tire gave the appearance of a Continental kit. Inside, the normally plain instrument panel was dressed up with vinyl padding, chrome, and a complete set of gauges. This dash design was adopted for all the later models. The floor was carpeted and the seats plushed and padded with high grade vinyl. The lowest priced Sportop, the fiberglass topped version, sold for just under $3,000, with the convertible only $33 more. The Sportop option was available from 1966 though 1967. This model came in direct response to the hot selling Bronco that had debuted in late 1965.

The V-8 was first available in 1966 Scout 800s in a 266-cid form. Later the 304 was hitched up to the little Scout. Shown here is a 304 in an 800A. These engines were powerful enough to scoot the Scout down the road pretty well. Some owners have fitted 345 and 392 powerplants into the smaller rigs.

In 1969, IHC started installing AMC-built inline sixes into the Scout 800 line. The 232 fit nicely under the hood and provided a nice alternative between the four-banger and the V-8.

Here's dual purpose for you! This 1971 factory photo shows a 1971 Scout II in a common recreational pose with the inset showing one of the Scouts that was raced in Baja races. The Scout II did a good job at both tasks! *Four Wheeler*

Nineteen seventy-seven to nineteen seventy-nine Scouts are pretty hard to tell apart, but it's obvious from this ad to whom the gauntlet was thrown!

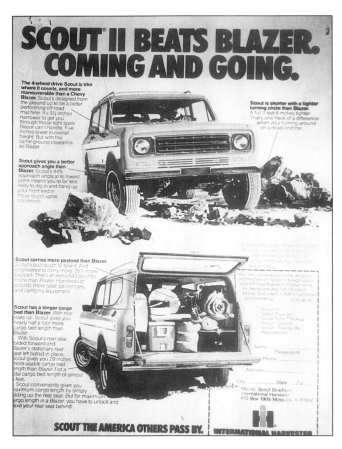

Under the skin, the initial changes were less dramatic—but inspired. A turbocharged version of the 152 was offered. With 111-horsepower and 166 pound-feet of torque, it added a fair bit of snap to the little Scout, especially on the highway. This engine was available only from 1965 through 1967. For 1966, mechanical changes became even more dramatic with the introduction of the 266 V-8 and the bigger 196-cid four (half of the 392-cid V-8), offering a four-engine lineup. The 152-cid was finally dropped after 1967.

After some improvements to the front axle, a Powr-Lok limited-slip was made available in the front as well as the rear. A four-speed transmission, a Warner T-18 close ratio, was added to the options list as well as a heavy duty, Spicer 44 rear axle. The axle ratio choices were expanded from 4.27:1 to include 3.73 and 4.88. The V-8 models had 3.31 axle ratios available. In 1968, the model 18 transfer case (IHC TC-144) was upgraded to the Model 20 (IHC TC-145).

The Scout 800s are quite popular, especially the V-8. The turbo models are very rare, partly due to low production but also due to the fact that the turbo was not as reliable (turbo technology was not what it is today) as the normally aspirated drive-it-and-for-get-it engines. The V-8s should prove very collectable and an original turbo four-cylinder is rare enough to attract a little attention and extra value. Sportops, both the glass version and the convertible, are already high on the collectable list.

Refinement: Scout 800A

The old Scout was revamped yet again for 1969 with the introduction of the 800A models. The 800A was produced only in 1969 and 1970. They are identified by an anodized grille, with a bright aluminum border, which utilized a smaller "International" offset to the drivers side. The headlights were surrounded by a black bezel and the front marker/turn signal lights were larger and recessed into the body. The "I.H." emblem stayed on the hood. Round side reflectors were added, amber up front and red in back. The rear side window glass area was increased for better visibility.

Mechanical upgrades abounded. The 266 was replaced with the 193-horsepower, 304-cid V-8 and a 232-cid inline six (from AMC) was added to the list. The 196 remained as the baseline powerplant. The T-39 automatic (a Borg-Warner 11), previously available on the trucks, was an option for V-8s and the new six.

Another special model debuted for 1969 in a run limited to 2,500 copies. The Aristocrat was decked out with a silver body and gunmetal blue top and hood. It used 7-inch Rallye style chrome wheels, roof rack, bumpers, mirrors, gas cap, and window trim. The interior used full carpeting, high-grade pleated seats, and lots of snazzy chrome-trimmed and upholstered pieces. According to available information, the Aristocrats came standard with the new inline six and limited-slip rear axle. They could be ordered with the new 304 V-8. Both the six and V-8 were available with the autobox.

In 1970, another special package was offered, the SR-2. While the target was 2,500 copies, many sources doubt that number was reached. The 1970 SR-2 came in a bright red color under a white top. A white racing stripe on the rocker panel proclaimed "SR-2" and the hood sported two big, wide hood stripes. Two white accent stripes ran front to back, just below the level of the door handle. The chrome wheels, interior accoutrements, and general trim and equipment levels were identical to the Aristocrat of the previous year models

800A models probably run about equal on the collectability scale with the prior 800s, with the exception of the Aristocrat and SR-2 rigs. These are the ones to watch out for.

The "Fridge's" Last Gasp: 800B

International was working on a completely redone Scout (the Scout II) when the 1971 800B debuted with little fanfare. The 800B was essentially an 800A and few resources were utilized in its construction and promotion. So few that it didn't even have sales literature devoted to it. A big strike early in the year had delayed the arrival of the new Scout, so IHC took the old "refrigerator" just a bit farther to carry them along.

Two very small features mark the 1971 models. One is the rectangular side marker lights, though these appeared on some 1970 Scouts. The other was the "I.H." emblem being moved to the right side of the grille from the hood and the "International" badge being eliminated. Don't count on a 1971 being outfitted this way, because documented 1971s have been seen in 1970 trim. The SR-2 was also produced in 1971 and beginning late in 1970 was available in white and bronze, as well as red and perhaps some other colors.

The SSII Scout was a bare-bones unit that was built for the dirt. The fiberglass door inserts and the roll bar were standard. You had to order the top, wheels, tires, and graphics. This unit, tested in 1978 by *Four Wheeler* magazine, was equipped with a 196-cid, four-speed, and 3.73 gears. *Four Wheeler*

The long-wheelbase Traveler was an ideal family wagon with gobs of room and lots of potential in a variety of roles. This was a practical rig that could have helped keep the Scout line running in the black had they chosen to work at it. Well, you can benefit from the same practical attributes today and own a classic to boot. The only downside is the poor fuel mileage delivered by these heavy rigs. According to owners, even the four-cylinder can barely break the 15-miles-per-gallon barrier. The diesel can manage to get mileage in the low 20s but is not overly powerful and, well, you gotta like a diesel to want to run one. *Four Wheeler*

The Scout Terra replaced the IHC trucks that went bye-bye in 1975. It was strictly light-duty but that was enough for most people. Rated for about a 1/2 ton, it could be outfitted to tow a considerable load. *Four Wheeler*

The 800B was really a carryover to get the new Scout IIs on line. They are equivalent in value to the 800As, though one could pick nits about them being a very low-production unit and the last of the old body style. Don't count on 800Bs bringing a higher price. Only the SR-2 models hold any real promise valuewise.

The New Breed: Scout II

The Scout II was introduced in the fall of 1971 and though they bore a resemblance to the old slab-sided rig, it was a pretty new machine all the way. It was no coincidence that the styling was very similar to the pickup line that had debuted in 1969. The Scout II sat on the same 100-inch wheelbase as previous, but it was made 11 inches longer and nearly an inch and a half wider. The extra length was mostly on the tail. This was a mixed blessing, of course, with the extra overhang increasing the departure angle somewhat.

All in all, the new Scout was a more people-friendly machine. Roomy and comfortable, it more truly fit the "family car" image than had the older unit. The passenger cabin had 6 inches of extra length, and it had an extra 5 cubic feet of cargo space. The longer chassis allowed the use of longer and wider leaf springs that resulted in a smoother ride and better stability. The wider track also resulted in a machine that was more carlike than ever (always a good sales feature) without a huge sacrifice in off-highway performance. The new 'Binder could be ordered as an open top, a pickup or in the popular Traveltop. Well, at least until the debut of the Terra and Traveler in 1976, when the short cab was eliminated on the 100-inch Scout.

Under the hood, the 196-cid four remained standard, with the 232 six and 304 V-8 as options, but a new engine, the 345-cid, took over as the high and mighty option. A direct transplant from the light- and medium-duty truck lines, it was a longer stroked version of the 304 and offered good torque characteristics. High rpm performance and fuel economy were not strong points, however.

During 1971 and 1972, emission controls started changing the options lists. For 1972, the four-cylinder was not available in California and the 232 six was replaced by the 258 six, also an AMC transplant. The four-cylinder was dropped after 1972 but reappeared after 1974 when the AMC-built six-cylinders were dropped. It stayed in the lineup (except for California) to the end of the Scout line. A six-cylinder, normally aspirated diesel was introduced in 1976. This engine was turbocharged in the latter part of 1979.

The Chrysler Torqueflite automatic was introduced as an option on the 1971 and 1972, but at first on the 345 only. The BW slushbox remained the automatic option for the six and the 304 V-8 but was finally dropped in 1973. The old T-90 remained as the baseline three-speed manual through 1974 when it was replaced by a Warner T-15D. The four-speeds were an option all the way through the Scout II era. Either a Warner Gear T-18 close ratio (4.02 first gear) or a T-19 wide ratio (6.32 first gear) was used.

The new Scout was quite a bit heavier than the old one, so new axles were in order. Up front, the open-knuckle Dana 30 replaced the old closed-knuckle 27. This resulted in a tighter turning radius. In the back, the Dana 44 semifloater became the only available axle, with or without a Powr-Lok or the later Trac-Lok limited-slips. With the V-8s being the common choice, the 3.31 and 3.73 axle ratios were most often seen in the early days of the Scout II. The 4.27 was available only with the four or the six cylinders. Later a 4.10 became the lowest ratio, with 3.07 and 3.54 being the norm for V-8s. Toward the later 1970s, the available rear axle ratio depended upon which engine and trans were installed.

In 1973 a single speed chain-drive transfer case was standard. The two-speed Dana 20 was optional. The single-speed case, though plenty durable, is pretty universally disliked these days, especially by folks who want to off-road their Scouts. Front disc brakes became standard on 1974 Scouts.

From the beginning, Scout IIs benefited from options that included air conditioning, deluxe interior, custom interior trim, tinted glass, bucket seats with a lockable center console, and the list went on. By ordering the right pieces, Scout could rival cars in most of the important areas, and though it was the equal of the Broncos, Ramchargers, and Blazers being sold, it was still a distant third in sales.

When the pickups were killed off in 1975, IHC devoted more resources to the Scout lines and produced a light pickup and long-wheelbase station

1980 Scouts can be quickly identified by their rectangular headlights. Don Evan's Traveler is a diesel-powered unit well-equipped with a winch, four-speed, 3.07 gears, and air conditioning. Don reports mileage in the mid-20s on the road.

wagon based on this design. The Terra pickup was essentially a standard Scout stretched to 118 inches, with a bulkhead and pickup cab added. It really was a masterful use of resources, because the Terra was a wonderful combination of 1/2-ton pickup and Sport Ute. The facts were (and still are) that a 1/2-ton pickup is the weapon of choice for many families. The Terra offered a 6,200 GVW and a 6-foot bed in a package that was more compact than the exciting 1/2 tons from other companies. The Terra remained in production to the end of the Scout in 1980.

The other adaptation on the long-wheelbase chassis was the Traveler. Instead of a bulkhead and short cab, the Traveler had a full-length top, a one-piece hatchback, and lots of open space. You could think of it as a two-door, Suburban-style vehicle or as a panel truck. It proved to be an extremely useful and relatively popular version of the Scout.

In 1977, IHC fielded another variant of the Scout they called the SSII. Conceived as a stripped down sport model, the SSII came without doors (with fiberglass inserts installed in their places), and had a special grille. The stripped out interior was perfect for the rigors of off-roading. It came without a top (an optional extra) so the SSII was also equipped with a roll bar as standard. The 196 four-cylinder and three-speed manual was the standard powerplant/transmission combo, though most SSIIs seen these days are V-8 models with automatics or four-speeds. The SSII was offered in the same nine colors as the other Scouts but special black and gold applique was optional. The SSII special was one of the few truly good off-highway capable options packages offered by any 4x4 manufacturer.

In the Scout era, IHC was fond of offering dress-up packages designed to attract more customers without spending money on new designs. The packages consisted mostly of lurid paint schemes or graphics and special combinations of standard options. In some cases, specialty packages were custom built by outside manufacturers but sold through the dealer network. Some of the names you might run across are Rallye, Family Cruiser, Midas, CVI, Midnight Star, Suntanner, and Terrastar. There were others. Some of these are quite rare and valuable; to wit, the CVI, Midnight Star, and Suntanner. The Midas was an interior package that, if in good shape, will bring extra money to any rig so equipped. The Family Cruiser is nothing special and the Rallye is very common. A great variety of optional graphics were applied to Scouts in the later years—some tasteful, some hideous. Well, it was the 1970s after all! Some folks enjoy finding and documenting these variations but they won't bring much extra money.

IHC dropped the Scout after 1980. The design was still marketable. Certainly the idea was. A Scout III design was worked up but never went beyond the prototype stage. As with the pickups, it was an issue of resources. There wasn't money to develop a new line of Sport Utes, and the company focused on a market in which it still had some dominance—tractors and big trucks. No doubt the management at IHC has had some cause to regret their action in the face of the now ballooning 4x4 and Sport Utility markets. Rumors have abounded regarding IHC's re-entering the ring but don't hold your breath.

IHC Drivetrain Component Designations

As a note to gearheads, remember that IHC liked to hide the fact that they sourced drivetrain parts outside the company. The tradition was to redesignate this equipment with an IHC term. The system listed below started about 1955 in the S-series trucks. Some of the stuff was manufactured especially to IHC specs and some was generic. It can be useful to be able to translate the IHC number over to more common Spicer, New Process, Warner Gear, or Borg Warner terms. Many times a similar brand-name component that was used on another make can be substituted for the IHC installed piece. Some internal parts can also be mixed and matched if you have the key. A partial list appears on the following pages.

The Scout II is the most popular and marketable breed of Scout. They are all collectable to a degree but only the specials bring big bucks. These would include some SSII models, the CVI, Midnight Star, and Suntanner. Combinations of hot options (variable according to the prevailing taste) can also bring a higher price. A diesel engine usually lowers the price and you will find a lot of 1979s and 1980s so equipped.

There is a vital, knowledgeable enthusiast group out there to support the IHC family. While parts can be rough to find, reproduction pieces are being made by aftermarket sources. The Scout IIs were woefully underprotected from the ravages of rust, so care must be taken in finding a good body and avoiding a "bondo-bucket." Ironically, the 1980 models featured some extra protection in that area! The Scout crowd is divided between rabid four-wheelers, who modify for performance, and the purists who restore to OE specs. The restorers seem to be slightly ahead of the four-wheelers in numbers but they are amicable to each other and get along well.

Another very rare Scout II special is the Midnight Star. Modified by Good Times of Midland, Texas, only about 120 units were sold in 1979. According to Scout expert Mark Drake, of Scout Madness, most of the Midnight Stars were black or bronze. Only one or two were done in blue. This rig, owned by Tom Drake (Mark's Dad) was recently restored by Scout Madness. It's all original and features a 345 four-barrel engine, 727 automatic and 3.07 gears with a Trac-Loc in the rear. The Good Times additions included the special paint and striping, cowl induction, special interior, body molding and fender flares, plus a hi-zoot stereo with an eight-track.

IHC Part Number	Type, Component Mfr and Number	IHC Application
13001 or T-1	3-speed man., IHC built to Clark design	R series S-series A-series B-series C-series thru '62
13005 or T-5	3-speed man., Warner Gear T-87 column shift	C-series frm '63 D-series
13007 or T-7	3-speed man., Warner Gear T-87 floor shift	C-series frm '63 D-series
13009 or T-9	4-speed man., Warner Gear T-9 w/dual PTO outlets	R-series S-series
13010 or T-10	4-speed man.,Warner Gear no PTO outlets B-series trucks	S-series trucks A-series trucks
13014 or T-14	3-speed man., Warner Gear T-90AA	Scout 80 Scout 800 Scout II thru '74
13016 or T-15	4-speed man.,Warner Gear T-98 Rt. PTO outlet	R-series (as WT-98) S-series trucks A-series trucks B-series trucks
13024 or T-16	4-speed man., Warner Gear T-98 Lt. PTO outlet	C-series frm '63
13024 or T-24	3-speed man., Warner Gear T-85	D-series
13034 or T-34	5-speed man. OD, IHC built to Fuller 5A35 design	D series
13035 or T-35	5-speed man., direct, wide ratio IHC built to Fuller 5A35 design	D-series
13036 or T-36	5-speed man., close ratio IHC built to Fuller 5A35 design	D series frm '73
13039 or T-39	3-speed auto., Borg-Warner 11 Similar to Ford Cruis-o-Matic	Scout 800B Scout II thru '72 D-series thru '72
13045 or T-45	4-speed man., Warner Gear T-181B Lt PTO	Scout 800 frm '67 Scout 800A Scout II thru '75
13332 or T-332	3-speed man., Warner Gear T-15D	Scout II, '75 up
13407 or T-407	3-speed auto., Chrysler 727	Scout II frm '73 D-series frm '73
13419 or T-419	4-speed man., T-181B	D-series
13427 or T-427	4-speed man, Warner Gear T-19 close ratio	Scout II frm '75 D-series frm '73
13428 or T-428	4-speed man., Warner Gear T-19A wide ratio	Scout II frm '75 D-series frm '75
13445 or T-445	4-speed man., Warner Gear T-181B R. PTO	D-series

TRANSFER CASES-

IHC Part Number	Type, Component Mfr and Number	IHC Application
13140 or TC-140	2-speed, 1.98: 1 low	S-series A-series B-series
13141 or TC-141	2-speed, Dana 20, divorced 1.96:1 low	C-series D-series
13143 or TC-143	IHC built single-speed	Scout II frm '73 D-series frm '73
?	2-speed, NP-250	D-series frm '73
13144 or TC-144	2-speed, Spicer 18 2.46:1 low	Scout 80 Scout 800 thru '66
13145 or TC-145	2-speed, Spicer 20 2.03:1 low	Scout 800 frm '67 Scout 800A Scout II thru '79
13146 or TC-146	2-speed, Spicer 300	'80 Scout II

FRONT AXLES-

FA-11	2,000lb, CK, Spicer 27 4.27–4.88 ratios	Scout 80 Scout 800 Scout 800A-B
FA-13	2,500lb, OK, Spicer 30 w/drum brakes	Scout 800B Scout II to mid '74
FA-14	2,100lb,CK, Spicer 27, 4.27–4.88 ratios	Scout 800 frm '67 Scout 800A
FA-15	2,800lb, CK. Spicer 44 4.11–4.77 ratios, 6-lug	S-series A-series B-series D-series
FA-16	3,500lb, CK, Spicer 44 "Orchard Model" wide axle	D-series
FA-18	3,500lb, CK, Spicer 44 3/4 ton	D-series
FA-21	2,000lb, CK, Spicer 27, 4.27–4.88 w/Powr-Lok limited slip	Scout 80
FA-24	2,500lb, OK, Spicer 27 4.27–4.88 ratios	Scout 800 frm '67 Scout 800A-B
FA-43	2,500lb, OK, Spicer 30 w/disc brakes	Scout II frm mid-'74
FA-44	3,200lb, OK, Spicer 44	Scout II frm late '74
FA-45	3,200lb, OK Spicer 44	Scout II frm late '74
FA-52	4,000lb, CK, Spicer 60	C-series

REAR AXLES-

RA-9	semi-floating, 3,500lb, Spicer 27	Scout 80 800 to '67
RA-10	full-floating, 4,500lb	S-series A-series B-series
RA-11	full-floating, 4,500lb with Powr-Lok limited slip	B-series
RA-14	semi-floating, Spicer 44 Rt. offset w/Powr-Lok	Scout 800

IHC Part Number	Type, Component Mfr and Number	IHC Application
RA-15	full-floating Eaton, 6,000lb, 1-ton, 8-lug	B-series D-series
RA-16	full-floating, 5,500lb, Spicer 60 1-ton, 8-lug	D-series
RA-18	semi-floating, 3,500lb, Spicer 44	D-series Scout 800A
RA-19	semi-floating, Spicer 44 w/Detroit No-Spin differential	D-series
RA-23	semi-floating, 2,300lb, Spicer 44	Scout 800A-B Scout II to '73
RA-24	semi-floating, 2,300lb, Spicer 44 w/Trac-Lok	Scout 800A-B Scout II to '73
RA-28	semi-floating, 3,500lb, Spicer 44 w/Trac-Lok limited slip	D-series Scout 800A
RA-53	semi-floating, 3,700lb, Spicer 60	D-series
RA-54	semi-floating, 3,700lb, Spicer 60 w/Trac-Lok limited slip	D-series
RA-83	full floating, 6,000lb, Spicer 60	D-series
RA-84	full-floating, 6,000lb, Spicer 60 w/Trac-Lok	D-series

Abbreviations-
CK= Closed knuckle, OK= Open knuckle
Notes:The multi-designations of the 1961–1968 era have been condensed to "C-series" to avoid confusion with the earlier trucks. The 1969–1975 era has been condensed to "D-series" for the purposes of the list.

4X4 TRUCK PRODUCTION
(1961–1975 NOT AVAILABLE)

	1953–1955	1955–1956	1957–1958
R-120	2		
S-120		10,941	
A-120			8,873
A-120 Travelette	17		

	1959–1960
B-120	6,770

SCOUT & SCOUT II PRODUCTION
(INCOMPLETE)

1961: 35,000 (as/per period literature)
1961–1965: 140,000 (as/per period literature)
1966–1973: NA
1974: 29,657
1975: 25,904
1976: 41,572 total (15,732 Terra and Traveler, 1,602 diesel)
1977: 39,191 total (2,688 Terra, 9,620 Traveler, 1,038 diesel)
1978: 39,191 total (2,966 Terra, 9,856 Traveler, 1,045 diesel)
1979: 44,343 total (2,437 Terra, 6,620 Traveler, 537 diesel, 1,108 turbo diesel)
1980: 30,059 total (5,389 diesel)

SCOUT 80 (1961–1964)

Engine
Type	4-cyl OHV
Displacement	151.8cid
Power	93.4 @ 4,000rpm
Torque	142.7lbs-ft @ 2,400rpm
Comp. ratio	8.19-1
Carb. type	1-bbl, Holly 1904

Drivetrain
Trans. type	3-speed,Warner T-90A-1 (IHC# T-14)
T-Case type	2-speed, Spicer 18 (IHC#T-144)
Front axle	Spicer 27 (IHC# FA-11)
Rear axle	Spicer 27 (IHC# RA-9)
Axle ratios	4.27-1

Dimensions & Capacities
Wheelbase	100in
LxWxH	154x68.6x67in
Shipping wt.	3,000lbs
GVW	3,900
Fuel capacity	9gal(10galx2 opt.)
Tires	6.50-15
App./Dep.	47/35 degrees

SCOUT 800 (1965-MID-1969)

Engine
Type	4-cyl OHV (std./opt.)
	4-cyl OHV Turbo (opt. '65–67)
	V8 OHV (opt. '66–69)
Displacement	151.8cid (std.to '68/opt. Turbo)
	196cid (opt. '66–67, std. '68-69)
	266.7cid (opt. '66–69)
Power	93.4 @ 4,000rpm (std.)
	110.8 @ 4,000rpm (std. 196)
	111.3 @ 4,000rpm (opt. Turbo to '67)
	154.8hp @ 4,400rpm (opt. V8)
Torque	142.7lbs-ft @ 2,400rpm (std.)
	153lbs-ft @ 2,000rpm (196)
	166.5lbs-ft @ 3,200rpm (opt. Turbo)
	227.1lbs-ft @ 2,800rpm (opt. V8)
Comp. ratio	8.19-1 (std. & opt. 4-cyl) 8.4-1 (V8)
Carb. type	1-bbl, Holley 1904 (151 &196)
	2-bbl, Holley 2300 (V8)

Drivetrain
Trans. type	3-speed,Warner T-90A-1 (std.- IHC# T-14)
	4-speed, Warner T-18 (opt.- IHC# T-45)
T-Case type	2-speed, Spicer 18 (to '67- IHC#TC-144)
	2-speed, Spicer 20 (IHC# TC-145)
Front axle	Spicer 27 (to '71- IHC# FA-11 or FA-14)
Rear axle	Spicer 27 (to '68, IHC# RA-9)
	Spicer 44 ('68–on, IHC# RA-14)
Axle ratios	4.27-1 or 4.88-1

Dimensions & Capacities
Wheelbase	100in
LxWxH	154x68.25x65.5in
Shipping wt.	3,465–3,615lbs (depending on model)
GVW	4,000lbs
Fuel capacity	9gal (10gal x2 opt.)
Tires	6.00-15 (std.) 8.45-15 (opt.)
App./Dep.	47/35 degrees

SCOUT 800A (MID-1969–MID-1971)
SCOUT 800B(1971)

Engine:
Type	4-cyl OHV
	6-cyl OHV
	V8
Displacement	196cid
	232cid
	304cid
Power	110.8 @ 4,000
	145 @ 4,300
	193 @ 4,400
Torque	180.2 @ 2,800
	215 @ 1,600
	272 @ 2,800
Comp. ratio	8.19-1
	8.5-1
	8.19-1
Carb. type	1-bbl, Holly 1904
	1-bbl.
	2-bbl, Holly 2300G

Drivetrain
Trans. type	3-speed, Warner T-90 (std.- IHC# T-14)
	4-speed, Warner T-18 (opt.- IHC# T-45)
	3-speed auto, Borg Warner 11 (opt. '69–71- IHC# T-39)
T-Case type	2-speed, Spicer 20 (IHC#T-145)
Front axle	Spicer 27
Rear axle	Spicer 44 (IHC# RA-14, 18, 24)
Axle ratios	3.31-1 (auto), 3.73-1, 4.27-1

Dimensions & Capacities
Wheelbase	100in
LxWxH	154x68.6x69in
Shipping wt.	3,000–3,150lbs (depending on model)
GVW	3,900 (4,700 opt.)
Fuel capacity	11gal
	(10galx2 opt.)
Tires	7.35-15 (std.)
	8.55-15 (opt.)
App./Dep.	47/35 degrees

Engine:

Type	4-cyl OHV ('71–73, '74–80)		8.0:1
	6-cyl OHV gas ('71)		22:1
	6-cyl OHV gas ('72-74)		21:1
	6-cyl OHV diesel ('76–79)		8.19:1
	6-cyl OHV turbo diesel ('79–80)		8.05:1
	V8, OHV ('71–80)	*Drivetrain*	
Displacement	196cid (4-cyl)	Trans. type	3-speed Warner T-90 (std '71–73)
	232cid ('71 6-cyl)		3-speed Warner T-15 (std '74–on)
	258cid ('72–74 6-cyl)		4-speed Warner T-18, close ratio (opt)
	198cid (turbo & non-turbo)		4-speed Warner T-19, wide ratio (opt)
	304cid		3-speed auto, Torqueflite (opt)
	345cid	T-Case type	1-speed, chain drive (std)
Power	86hp @ 3,600 (79hp in CA)		2-speed, Spicer 20 (opt to '79)
	145hp @ 4,300 (gross)		2-speed, Spicer 300 (opt '80)
	113hp @ 4,000	Front axle	Spicer 30
	81hp @ 4,000 (non-turbo)	Rear axle	Spicer 44
	101hp @ 3,800 (turbo)	Axle ratios	3.07, 3,31, 3.73. 4.10. 4.27
	122hp @ 3,400	***Dimensions & Capacities***	
	150hp @ 3,600	Wheelbase	100in, Scout II
Torque	153lbs-ft @ 2,000		118in, Terra & Traveler
	243lbs-ft @ 2,400 (gross)	LxWxH	165.8x70x66.4in, Scout II
	191lbs-ft @ 2,000		184.2x70x66.2in, Terra & Traveler
	137lbs-ft @ 2,000	Shipping wt.	3,846lbs, Scout II
	178lbs-ft @ 2,200		3,861lbs, Terra
	247lbs-ft @ 2,400		4,201lbs, Traveler
	275lbs-ft @ 2,400	GVW	6,200lbs, all models
Comp. ratio	8.02:1	Fuel capacity	19gal
	8.5:1	Tires	H78-15

Chapter 6

Land Rover— The British Legend

Pound for pound, the American Land Rover enthusiasts are among the most dedicated in the 4x4 crowd. Perhaps that's because they are outnumbered by just about all the other 4x4 brand names. Despite this, the Land Rover enthusiast group is one of the best organized networks around. Despite the relative scarcity of the older Land Rovers, a budding enthusiast has a variety of clubs, repair shops, parts establishments, and technical expertise at his disposal.

If you want to see a Land Rover owner grind his teeth, just ask him, "Hey, what sort of Toyota is that?" If you really want to twist the knife, you could say, "Nice Jeep!" These are both old inside jokes with North American Land Rover owners that stem from years of driving rigs that most people didn't recognize. Until 1987, when the Range Rover was introduced here, Land Rover products had not been imported to North America for 13 years. From about 1949 to 1974, Land Rovers were sold here to the tune of about 14,000 total units. Small wonder that nobody recognized them!

In the Beginning . . .

Rover is a time-honored name in Britain. The company started in the late 1800s, when founder J. K. Starley started building sewing machines. He soon branched out into bicycles and engineered the famous Rover Safety Cycle. By 1904, the Rover Cycle Company jumped onto the automotive bandwagon and built its first car. It was offered in addition to their bicycles and a line of motorcycles. Just a year later, "cycle" was dropped from the company name and by 1926, the two-wheeled equipment had been dropped from the lineup.

From there to the beginning of World War II, Rover established itself as a major mover in the British car market by fielding cars that became known as "the Rolls Royce of the middle class." In the final days leading up to World War II, Rover was assigned a factory in the Midlands under the "Shadow Factory" scheme and charged with setting up to build aircraft engines for the coming war effort. Once the war began, Rover got involved in the development of the Allies' first viable jet engine, the Rover-Whittle B-26. A version of this engine powered the Allies' first jet fighter, the Gloster Meteor. Rover later went on to develop gas turbine-powered automobiles.

By the time World War II was over, Britain's economy was on the ropes. The war had just about bankrupted the country. Raw materials were in short supply and being doled out like vintage brandy. In order to fill the nation's empty coffers, the resounding national cry was export, export, export and companies with export products were given priority

Jeep fans will love this! The very first Land Rover prototype was built on a Willys MB chassis and used the Jeep's Spicer 25 axles and Model 18 transfer case. The engine was a pre-war Rover engine and a Rover four-speed was mated to the Jeep's Spicer T-case. You'll note that the seat is centralized, the idea being to eliminate the need for left- or right-hand drive tooling. As you look at more photos, you'll see that this idea was quietly dropped. *Land Rover*

Once a final design was approved, 48 preproduction units were built; here is one of the later ones, owned by Ken Wheelwright on the other side of the pond. Only a handful of the "preprods" remain and thus far, none have been brought over to the United States.

The production 80-inch was pure simplicity and all go. This 1951 is a recent import from England. Very few Series Is, especially nice ones like this, are in the United States. Since import regulations are lax on early vehicles, a few Americans are importing the ones they like, as Quintin Aspin did with his 1951.

on materials. In these conditions, Rover set out to market a new line of cars. They soon got a reality check. By 1947, their factory was only able to work four days in every two weeks due to shortages. Their grand plans for the future looked like they'd have to wait.

The inspiration for the Land Rover came from Maurice Wilks, head of Rover's technical department. While fooling around on his estate with a tired, war surplus Jeep, Maurice Wilks got the idea of building a Rover 4x4 as an agricultural/commercial vehicle—a sort of farmer's best friend that could plow, run equipment via PTOs, haul hay, and then take the family into town on Sunday. No doubt the idea was inspired by Jeeps' efforts here in the "colonies." The best part was that there was great export potential in the idea. He worked out the details while on holiday with his family and later presented the idea to his brother Spencer, who was the Managing Director at Rover.

The idea got a lukewarm response at the board meeting where it was presented, but the project was given the go-ahead under the provision that it was to be regarded as a stopgap to help keep the company on its feet. Their mandate was to use as much existing Rover componentry and tooling as possible and not to interfere with car development when it came back online.

The project was handed off to a team of five Rover engineers. A couple of war surplus Jeeps were purchased for study. They were carefully scrutinized but that wasn't quite enough. A prototype vehicle was built on one of the Jeep chassis to test some of the engineer's layout ideas before they committed them to the final design. A leftover prewar 1,389-cc, 48-horsepower Rover four-cylinder was fitted into the chassis, and a Rover four-speed gearbox was grafted onto the Jeep's Spicer 18 transfer case. An all-aluminum body was hand-built. Aluminum became the Land Rover trademark and, as it happens, this was only partly from choice.

Aircraft aluminum was plentiful and not rationed (though expensive) in those days. Aluminum was also easier to form, resisted corrosion, and was light. The easy-to-form part was important, since they didn't want to build specialized equipment for their "stopgap" vehicle. Also, since the company was familiar with the material from its wartime association with aircraft manufacture and also in some automotive applications, it was an easy choice.

Once completed, the hybrid rig was tested in a variety of conditions as development continued on more focused designs. One of the major flaws noted was the relative weakness of the C-section Jeep chassis design. They learned that the assembly was dependent on the stamped steel body for much of its structural integrity. After some brainstorming, Rover engineers found an elegantly simple idea. Their "four-plate" concept involved building a fully boxed chassis out of steel plates that were cut, assembled, and continuous welded at all seams with the crossmembers built in. This made for an amazingly strong but light assembly that didn't depend on the body for support. The four-plate chassis design was used well into the 1980s, when a less labor-intensive method was devised.

After the first prototype was built and evaluated, 48 updated models were put together to test the new layout. Beyond the 80-inch wheelbase, there was next to nothing similar on these rigs to the inspirational Jeep. It used an aluminum body with a steel bulkhead. On the preproduction rigs, all the steel pieces, including the chassis and bulkhead, were heavily galvanized (in production, only exterior pieces were galvanized). Twenty-two of the 48 were built with left-hand drive, attesting to the international concept.

The 13 remaining "PreProd" Land Rovers are highly prized and lovingly restored by Land Rover fans in England. In an amazing book by Tony Hutchings, *Land Rover —The Early Years*, the details and history of each of the prototypes is traced. Every once in a while, another preprod will resurface and cause a stir in the collector continuum. Unfortunately, the original prototype was scrapped a few months after Land Rover production began.

GO anywhere... DO anything

- **ENGINE.** High efficiency four-cylinder Capacity 1595 c.c. Develops more than 50 B.H.P. 25-27 m.p.g.
- **CHASSIS.** Side and cross members of box section. Light but exceptionally rigid.
- **BODYWORK.** High tensile non-corrodible aluminium sheet metal work.
- **POWER TAKE-OFF.** Gives a powerful pulley drive for generators, compressors or agricultural equipment.
- **ELECTRICAL SYSTEM.** 12-volt starting and lighting.

The versatility of the Land-Rover is really amazing. A four-wheel drive tractor, a delivery wagon, a mobile power plant and a fast economical vehicle on the road — the Land-Rover is all these things rolled into one. With its power take-off, that can be coupled up to any equipment needing pulley drive, it makes a direct appeal to farmers, field engineers, industrialists, in fact anyone who needs a fast, powerful, adaptable, utility vehicle. The Land-Rover is built for hard work and hard wear at low running costs and (note for the exporter) is supplied with right or left-hand drive as required. Ask your local dealer for particulars.

Price of vehicle only without additional equipment — £450.

LAND-ROVER

Britain's most versatile vehicle

Made by The Rover Company Limited, Solihull, Birmingham.

The, "go anywhere, do anything" slogan became a way of life to Land Rover engineers and customers. This was the first 1948 ad for the new Land Rover.

The 1.6-liter F-head four-cylinder powered the 80-inch Land Rovers until 1952, when the engine was enlarged to 2 liters. The 1.6-liter engine made 50 horsepower in detuned Land Rover form. When used in Rover cars, it was nearer 60 horsepower.

Series I—1948–1957

The Land Rover was introduced to the world at the Amsterdam Motor Show on April 30, 1948, but sales did not commence until much later in the year. The little Land Rovers soon became a hot item and long waiting lists were the norm. Rover had planned on building about 100 units a week. Before long, they doubled that number and added to it again. Still, they could not keep up with demand. Like it or not, Rover was in the 4x4 business. Before 1949 ended, Land Rover production had exceeded car production by three to one.

The 1948–1949 Land Rovers were all very much alike with their 80-inch wheelbase and ragtops. They also used a full-time four-wheel drive system with lockable dog clutch in the two-speed transfer case. Axle gearing was 4.88:1 and the rear axle was semifloating. The differentials were adapted from the car line. The engine was a 1.6-liter F-head four that had been developed for the postwar P3 sedan. In its detuned "off-road" form, it delivered 50 horsepower.

Almost immediately, the clamoring began for a more comfortable Land Rover. Rover answered with a limited production "Estate" version. These hand-built enclosed bodies came from Tickford, one of the best known coachbuilders in England. It used a mahogany frame with a pressed aluminum body. Though offered into the 1951 model year, these station wagons were very expensive and only a few hundred were built. They are extremely rare and prized. As far as this writer can determine, there are none of the factory-built Estate Land Rovers in the United States, but there is a one-off "Woody" conversion here that was specially built for an English Lord.

In 1950, a metal hardtop was offered for the standard 80-inch Land Rover, which answered many of the comfort needs. Before long, hardtops started outselling ragtops, especially in the rain-soaked British Isles. Also in 1950, the four-wheel-drive system was changed to a more user-friendly part-time setup. For 1952, a 2-liter engine replaced the 1.6, having about the same power but 21 pound-feet more torque. These short wheelbase rigs could generate 2,000 pounds of drawbar pull, which equalled many small tractors of the day. A rear PTO was available and after 1950, a front was optional.

In 1954, Land Rover stretched the wheelbase to 86 inches on the SWB models for more cargo capacity and introduced a long-wheelbase, 107-inch model that was offered initially only as a hardtopped pickup. By 1956, the 107s came as both pickup and four-door station wagons. These people-movers became a hit right away. Though the 107s had the same tiny 2-liter, 52-horsepower engine, the payload was increased by 50 percent to 1,500 pounds.

Another innovation of the 86-inch station wagon era was the "tropical roof." These were double-skinned roofs, the upper layer open at both ends, with just over an inch of airspace in between. The outer skin reflected the sun's heat and airflow cooled the inner skin. Also, vents were fitted to the inside roof to allow the cooler air to enter or heated air to escape. The tropical roof concept continued in production until the early 1980s. Another popular Land Rover roof accessory was the Alpine windows. Fitted over the rear pas-

One of the big breakthroughs for Land Rover sales and popularity was the introduction of the long-wheelbase model in 1954. The first versions were built as 107-inch pickups. This is actually a very early Series 107 PU. Built in 1953, the 107 spent its life working at a Canadian mine. It apparently outlasted the mine and is now owned by noted Canadian Land Rover collector Aart Vanderstar.

senger or cargo compartment, these elongated oval windows allowed light to enter the rear of the interior but they had a more practical purpose. On switchback roads, the windows allowed the driver to glance up at the road above the switchback for oncoming traffic.

In 1956, the wheelbases were stretched another two inches on each model, to 88 and 109 inches respectively. Where the 80-inch had been stretched aft of the bulkhead, the 88s and 109s had their two inches added to the front. This was done to fit a new OHV 2-liter diesel engine for 1957. This engine design became the basis for the 2.25-liter that came a bit later and the 2.5-liter four-cylinders that remain in production to this day.

The 1948–1958 Land Rover are known as "Series Is." This moniker appeared in 1958, when redesigned Land Rovers appeared and were dubbed "Series II." The Series II was introduced in April of 1958, so it's possible to find 1958 Series Is. The 107" Station Wagon was continued through most of 1958 until a Series II, 109" was developed.

Very few Series Is are found in the United States, and it's only recently that they have begun attracting any serious attention from American collectors. Much like the flat-fendered Jeep, they are fairly impractical for day-to-day use. Because of this, the prices have remained reasonable compared to the more popular Land Rover Series II or IIA models. This is quickly changing, so now is the time to buy a Series I before prices go for a home run.

Series II and IIA

For 1958, a major redesign brought the Series II 88 and 109-inch vehicles to market. The "slab-sided dumpster" look was gone and sills that have been called "modesty skirts" hid some of the chassis goodies. Aesthetically, the Series Is were strictly an engineer's dream of form following function. With the Series II, a styling department was created and utilized. Not that you could call the new Land Rovers stylish, they were just a little *more* stylish.

The 86-inch wheelbase Series I Land Rovers are a little more common here than the 80-inch. In the era of the 86 inch, Land Rovers were imported to the tune of 100, or so, per year. This 86 is using the half-cab normally fitted to the 107 PU; however, since Land Rovers were (and are) mix-and-match vehicles, it's possible this setup was fitted by the dealer at the time of purchase.

This Series IIA has had an impeccable restoration, even though it isn't 100 percent period accurate. That's okay most of the time. The few alterations that have been done, most notably the narrow sill panels, are within the acceptable range for most collectors. The Series IIA up to the period where the headlights moved into the fenders (1968) are the most popular.

The "beauty," however, was more than skin deep. A new 2.25-liter four-cylinder, OHV gasoline engine debuted that was based on the earlier 2,052-cc diesel engine. It made 77 horsepower and gave the new Rovers a 25-horsepower boost over the old ones. The traditional Rover full-floating axle appeared about this time as well. The chassis and suspension were revised to offer greater strength combined with an improved ride.

The Series IIA that debuted in1961 looked identical to the Series II, but hosted a few subtle mechanical improvements. The diesel engine was enlarged to match the displacement of the gas engine. After that, a bevy of improvements followed that included more efficient exhaust systems and a boost in compression ratio that raised power to 81 horsepower.

The 1960s could be called Land Rover's "age of specials." A 1-ton forward control variant, called the 109 FC, was introduced, as well as a variety of specialist military bodies. Military forces all over the world availed themselves of ambulances, armored cars and a lightweight air-portable version. Tracked Land Rovers and 6x6 conversions enhanced the Land Rover job description as a tough, go-anywhere customer. A plethora of other commercial conversions from mobile cranes to garbage trucks proved the basic adaptability of the chassis. In the mid-1960s, 150 different Land Rover variants were available. Most of them never saw our shores.

In 1966, a six-cylinder Land Rover was introduced in the long-wheelbase U.S. models (called NADA—North American Dollar Area), models to address the requests for more power. This 2.6-liter F-head engine used a specially designed aluminum Weslake head. Adapted from the 3-liter six used in

This 1964 military 88 is nearly 100 percent accurate except for the American-made Koenig PTO winch. This low-mileage NATO unit was brought over in the 1970s. Several hundred 1960s and 1970s era NATO rigs were imported in the late 1970s and early 1980s. Though many have been altered to civilian specs, some of the giveaways are the hood hold-downs, military headlights (24 volt), and the bridge plate on the passenger fender. Many of these NATO rigs were left-hand drive because they operated in countries that required it.

passenger cars, this engine produced 95 horsepower, in its 7.8-1 compression ratio form, and 134 pound-feet of torque at 1,750 rpm. This was more like it. While it didn't turn the LWB into an instant hotrod, it did allow it to cut about 10 seconds off its 0–60 times compared to the four-cylinder. While Land Rover continued with the six-cylinders in various markets to 1979, the high-compression NADA version was unique.

Unfortunately, the six-cylinder engine was only available from early 1966 through the 1967 model year. In 1968, Leyland Motor Sales made the marketing decision to discontinue importation of long-wheel-base models to the United States. A few found their way in via private efforts, but as emissions regs and importation restrictions increased, private importation practically ceased. The 109 was imported to Canada until 1972.

Available records are sketchy, but it appears that only about 811 six-cylinder 109s were imported during the 1966 and 1967 model years. The rigs all bore a special serial number that began with "343." Because the sixes were prone to internal engine problems and parts have been very scarce for many years, few examples remain that still bear their original engines. Many were converted to a Chevy six via a popular kit, a few had been retrofitted with four-cylinders, and a variety of other conversions from A to Z have been done.

The military ambulances were brought over in small numbers. Unfortunately, they are heavy, ungainly, and suitable for only a few uses beyond their designed one. Many had their ambulance bodies stripped off and were converted to standard 109 pickups.

The Series IIA seems to currently hold the most appeal to collectors. For a time, 109 Station Wagons were the hot ticket but now the mid-1960s 88-inch has taken the lead in popularity. In that era, quality control was at its best, and the headlights had not yet moved to the fenders. An original six-cylinder wagon is many people's dream and holds a high value. The 109 pickups are also highly sought after, though few are available.

The American Series III: 1972–1974

The Series III models were introduced late in 1971 and hosted a few improvements over the IIA, most notably a new padded dash and an all-syncro gearbox. With the new dash, they were a bit more quiet and civilized compared to the earlier rigs. The all-syncro gearbox allowed a downshift into first on the roll, but some of the durability of the older box was sacrificed for this feature. It took a few years for the bugs to be worked out.

Unfortunately, the British Leyland era brought with it a drop in quality. The Series IIIs seemed to suffer the most in the Land Rover family. By the time quality control caught up a little, Series IIIs were already a memory here. Warranty nightmares were common for Series III buyers.

While the Series III is the most civilized of the leaf spring Land Rovers, today it is the least sought after. It's not all that much different in spirit but many diehards regard them as "not as rugged" as the IIA. The plastic grille of the Series III seems to be the major bone of contention. Well, you certainly can't cook on it as you could with the IIA piece. More plastic in the dash and

A 109 regular can be fitted out with a canvas top as shown here, as a pickup with the addition of a short cab, or a full-length metal top, with or without windows. A 109 regular is a two door-and a station wagon is a four-door.

Oddly enough this is a Land Rover. The military air portable 88-inch Land Rovers, commonly known as Lightweights, are extremely popular but rare in the United States. To make a Land Rover that was transportable by the helicopters of the day, modular bodies were built onto a standard Land Rover SWB chassis that could be stripped easily for transport.

One of the rarest and most sought after Land Rovers are the Dormobile conversions. These pop-top campers were built in the late 1960s by the Martin Walter Company of Folkstone, Kent, England. They featured a pop-top camper addition with a built in set of bunks. Below, the front a rear seats folded into two more very comfortable bunks and in the rear, a water tank, sink, and stove was fitted in custom built cabinets. Some were imported to the United States semi-officially in 1966 and 1967, but John Hess' is a right-hand drive model brought over from the United Kingdom some years ago. *John Hess*

interior is the other complaint. Odd, nitpicky stuff, yes, but it has affected the current price to some degree. Series IIIs were sold in North America through 1974 (though imports stopped late in 1974) and into 1975. Elsewhere in the world, the Series III continued to be a strong seller. In nearly 14 years of production, at least 250,000 were sold worldwide making them the most numerous Land Rover by far.

The American Idea

The Series III became the springboard into a new era for Land Rover. In 1979, a 109 V-8 was introduced with detuned 3.5-liter, 91-horsepower V-8 under the hood. Though it was never seen in America, except as a gray market importation, it was an evolutionary vehicle that led to the later coil sprung 90 and 110 V-8 models. Had this rig been developed just a few years earlier and offered here, fate might have dealt American Land Rover nuts a much better hand.

The V-8 Land Rover was not a new concept. Knowing what was needed for this market and hoping to impress this onto the upper management back at Solihull, Rover Motor Company of North America (RMCNA) started building a one-off, V-8 powered 88-inch in 1966 and shipped it back to the United Kingdom for evaluation. Called the "Golden Rod," it featured a 215-cid, 155-horsepower aluminum V-8 from a 1963 Olds F85. Rover had recently acquired the patents and remaining tooling for the GM-designed aluminum V-8s. Golden Rod was modified by uprating the brakes, changing the gears to 3.54, and adding wide 15-inch wheels and tires. Even though the conversion was successful and the rig could blow the doors off most anything in England at the time, U.K. engineers turned up their noses. It may, however, have had an influence on the engineers then just beginning to design the Range Rover.

Coming to America

Land Rovers were sold virtually everywhere in the world outside the Iron Curtain. The earliest known importation of Land Rovers to America began about 1949. The first documented showing is reputed to be at a British Automobile and Motorcycle show in April of that year. The Rootes Group had established a small presence here, marketing some famous British names like Sunbeam, Hillman, and Humber. They entered into an agreement with Rover to market their products in North America. Land Rovers and Rover cars were thrown into the dealership pot as a bonus but were not fielded with any enthusiasm. Sales averaged about 100 Land Rovers per year into 1957.

In 1958, Rover got more serious and sent out H. Gordon Munro to oversee a new subsidiary, the Rover Motor Company of North America, to be headquartered in Toronto. A subsidiary office was set up in New York City and parts depots were established in San Francisco, New York, and Vancouver, Canada.

A restored British spec Series III, complete with tropical roof and Deluxe hood.

The first official U.S. dealer, Concours Motors of Springfield, Massachusetts, came aboard in 1959, and later that year, Rover created a presence at the New York Motor Show. Unfortunately, Rover cars were the major focus of sales. This was a mistake. Where the Rover cars were generally unsuited to the American market (sales don't lie), Land Rovers of the late 1950s and early 1960s were more on par with the other 4x4s being marketed here.

In 1962, leadership of RMCNA was handed off to an American, J. Bruce McWilliams. Under his guidance, things began moving—both for cars and Land Rovers. Some of the most memorable and innovative advertising appeared in this period. Success brought a little more slack in the reins for McWilliams. As the 1960s progressed, McWilliams kept a close watch on the competition and proposed changes to the Land Rover to make it more marketable. Some of these were adopted, including a more powerful six-cylinder engine. Others, like more creature comforts and larger fuel tanks, were ignored.

The late 1960s were probably the American heyday for Land Rover. When most of the ailing British motor industry was nationalized and put under the British Leyland flag, McWilliams was assigned to head the entire American branch in 1970 and had to manage virtually every British car name sold in America. Land Rover soon went to the back of the bus and so did further improvements to make it more suitable to the market. In the tight-budget British Leyland era, the development money simply wasn't available. They could barely stay ahead of the rapidly unfolding lists of new American emissions regulations. Leyland Sales announced its intention to drop the Land Rover from the lineup in mid-1974. By early 1975 the last had been sold.

Nobody here was anxious to apply life support to a dying horse, so dealer support disappeared quickly. Fairly rapidly, the world's most practical vehicle became decidedly impractical. Once warranties ran out, the aftermarket took over and the true enthusiasts were counted. Die-hard individualists endured "the great Land Rover depression" that lasted well into the 1980s. By then, the aftermarket parts suppliers had taken up the slack and the parts situation had stabilized.

Some gray market Land Rovers were brought over privately in this period as well as a whole lot of used parts. Official Land Rover products were

Telling Land Rovers apart is not always easy—even for the dedicated Roverphile. It doesn't help that many of the parts interchange so in 30 years, who knows what goodies have been swapped around to make your identification more difficult. Here are some visual clues to help you tell them apart.

Early Series I 80 Inch—1948 to mid–1950
-Headlights behind wire grille.
-Four air inlet holes in radiator support (behind grille).
-Body has flat sides.
-Instruments in centrally located, protruding pod.
-Door release handles on inside of door.
-Seatbacks rounded (clamshell look).

Series 1 80 Inch—Mid–1950 to Late 1953
-Larger headlights protruding through holes in grille. (1953 models had inverted "T" shaped grille).
-Four air inlet holes in radiator support (behind grille—1953 models had three holes).
-Body has flat sides.
-Instruments in centrally located, protruding pod.
-Door release handles on inside of door (late 1952 and on with exterior handles).
-2-liter engine 1951–1953.
-Rectangular seatbacks.

Series I 86 Inch—Late 1953 to 1956
-Large headlights in radiator support. Body color headlight trim rings.
-Inverted "T" grille.
-Three radiator air inlet holes (behind grille).
-Centrally located instruments on flat dash.
-Recessed external door handles.
-Flat sides on body.

Series I 107 Inch—1954–1956 Pickup, 1955–1958 Station Wagon
-Large headlights in radiator support. Body color headlight trim rings.
-Inverted "T" grille.
-Three radiator air inlet holes (behind grille).
-Centrally located instruments on flat dash.
-Recessed external door handles.
-Removable hardtop on PU.
-Station wagon, five-door with sliding windows on rear door.
-Flat sides on body.

Series I 88 and 109 Inch—1956–1958
-Large headlights in radiator support. Chrome headlight trim rings.
-Inverted "T" grille.
-One radiator air inlet hole (behind grille).
-Centrally located instruments on flat dash.

-Recessed external door handles.
-Extra wheelbase is fwd of firewall. Look for extra material on fender between wheel arch and door.
-2-liter OHV diesel available.
-109s available as pickup only.
-Flat sides on body.
-Windshield vents don't open.
-More interior insulation and padding than previous.

Series II—88 and 109 Inch—1958–1961
-Body sides bulge out at waist.
-4-inch "Modesty Skirt" sill panels.
-Dual vents under windshield. Some opened with cranks instead of the later levers.
-OHV 2.25-liter gas engine available.
-Three radiator air inlet holes (behind inverted "T" grille).
-Hood rounded at edges.
-109-inch available as pickup or five-door Station Wagon.
-Steering arms on top of swivel housings.
-Canadian versions have one piece doors and dual circular heaters.

Early Series IIA—88 and 109 Inch—1962 to Mid–1968 (for NAS)
-Early IIAs are generally regarded as units with the headlights between the fenders.
-Steering arms moved to bottom of swivel housings.
-Body sides bulge out at waist.
-Six-inch "Modesty Skirt" rocker panels.
-Dual vents under windshield.
-OHV 2.25-liter gas engine available.
-2.25-liter OHV diesel available.
-2.6L F-head six available mid-1966–1967.
-Three radiator air inlet holes (behind inverted "T" grille).
-Flat hood starting in 1968 (though rounded hood still seen).
-109-inch available as pickup or 5-door Station Wagon, 1962–1967.
-NAS spec 88-inch adopted for 1968. 109-inch dropped.
-15-inch wheels starting with 1968 models.
-Amber reflectors on four side corners of 1968 models. Red reflectors on rear.
-Four-inch amber turn signal lamps front and rear.
-Two-speed single wiper motor replaced dual single speed units.
-Electrical system changed from positive to negative ground for 1967. Negative ground models have a black painted center dash panel. Positive ground dash panels are painted body color.
-Sideview mirrors mounted to fenders.

Late Series IIA 88 Inch—Mid-1968–1971

-Late IIAs are generally regarded as those with the headlight in the fenders.
-Headlights moved to fenders about April 1968 for NAS. Early "Bugeyes" had light assembly attached to exterior of fender with chrome bezel. Early in 1969, a recessed arrangement was adopted.
-Body sides bulge out at waist.
-Four-inch "Modesty Skirts" rocker panels in 1969. About mid-1969, a narrower three-inch skirt was used.
-Dual vents under windshield.
-Three radiator air inlet holes (behind inverted "plus-sign" shaped grille).
-Flat-type hood.
-15-inch wheels.
-Dual circuit brakes.
-Sideview mirrors mounted to upper door hinges.

Series III 88 Inch—Late 1971–1974 (NAS) to 1983 for Commercial Markets, 1986 for Military

-Plastic grille.
-Revised padded dash with instrument pod at drivers station.
-Windshield hinged on front of bulkhead instead of sides.
-Flat door hinges on side doors.
-Hood hinges with plastic inserts.
-Plastic heater air inlet on passenger fender instead of galvanized metal.
-Significant emission controls (EGR and vacuum retard distributor).
-Side marker lights, yellow front, red rear.
-All-syncro gearbox.
-9.5-inch diaphragm-type clutch.
-Alternator instead of generator.
-Two-fuse fusebox replaced by four-fuse unit.

The 2.25-liter four-cylinder was one of Land Rover's better ideas. Introduced in 1958, this engine was produced almost unchanged into the late 1970s, when it was given a five main bearing crankshaft. Later it was stroked to 2.5 liters and is still in production in that displacement. Though not overly powerful, this is one ruff-tuff powerplant.

Series III 109s are very scarce in the United States. Sand Toler's gorgeous station wagon is complete with tropical roof, deluxe hood, and side steps.

Whats the Diff?

There were a number of differences between North American Dollar Area (NADA) and other world market Land Rovers, beyond the placement of the steering wheel. One very welcome item that was added about 1961 was the Kodiak heater. Where the original equipment heater was barely able to forestall frostbite, the Kodiak was capable of keeping all body parts toasty warm and the windshield relatively free of ice. These units were built in North America and installed at the dealership when they arrived. They weren't automatically installed everywhere in the United States, having been designed primarily for northern climates. In 1968, a new Smiths heater was added, and while it was an improvement over the old circular "ankle warmer" heaters, most Americans regarded it as a big step back. Kodiaks are still a popular option among Land Rover collectors.

After 1967, the NAS Land Rover lineup was standardized to one—the 88-inch. Despite upgrading the 109 with a special six-cylinder engine for 1966 and 1967, it was mysteriously dropped from the lineup. For 1968, a North American Spec (NAS) 88 was adopted. The specification was for an 88 Station Wagon (fitted with rear seats and a side swinging rear door as opposed to a cargo box with a tailgate) with sliding rear windows and a Deluxe interior but without the tropical roof or Deluxe hood that came with this package in Britain. Four colors were offered—limestone, pastel green, marine blue, and poppy red. The red was a NAS-only color.

The deluxe interior offered the most comfort available in the marque but the NAS deluxe interior differed from the UK version. They were alike in the headliner, rolled trim around the interior roof edge, door panels, pleated front seats, floor mats, and tunnel cover. They differed in that they didn't have a seat base cover and instead of four separate jump seats as in the rear of the UK deluxe, ours came with flat rear seats normally offered in the lower spec basic models. Other standard NAS interior features from 1967 on were emergency flashers and an electric oil pressure gauge. Seat belts were required by law.

Mechanically, it was more of the same. Subtle differences that grew into more significant differences as the years passed. In 1967, emission controls had appeared but had not yet taken a big bite into engine performance. The extent of emission control in that era was a "gulp" type PCV (positive crankcase ventilation) valve.

From 1968 to 1974, underhood emissions labels were standard. In 1969 a tamperproof cover was installed on the idle mixture screw and an electric fuel cutoff solenoid on the carb's idle circuit. This version of the Zenith 36 IV carburetor was called the 36 IVE.

In 1973, NAS Land Rovers got an EGR (exhaust gas recirculation) valve, a vacuum retard distributor, and various forms of vacuum devices to control and restrict ignition timing. Despite the common rumors to the contrary, none of these engines were particularly choked down powerwise. They were known to have an off-idle stumble and an erratic idle.

It is interesting to note that up to about 1967, most NAS engines were the 77-horsepower, low-compression 2.25-liter. The change to negative ground in 1967 generally marked the changeover to an 81-horsepower, 8.0-1 engine, though it's possible to see later engines in 7.0-1. The low-compression engines were referred to in period literature as "special export" engines and were designed to run on subgrade fuel.

One of the most noticeable NAS features was the 15-inch wheels. The USA vehicles were shod with minuscule 7.10-15, British-made Goodyear Ultra-Grips that were 27 inches tall mounted. Special speedometers were installed to compensate for the difference in tire size from the standard vehicles with 16-inch wheels.

One noteworthy fact is that all NAS vehicles were equipped with jaws-type tow hitches. This was normally one towing option among many in other markets. Most Americans were completely baffled by this setup and adapted the hitch to accept the common 1 7/8-or 2-inch tow balls.

Late in 1968, due to a Federal standard, Land Rover adopted the dual circuit master brake cylinder. This was supplemented with a vacuum brake booster. This proved to be a worthwhile improvement and the dual cylinder was adopted for worldwide use in 1970 or 1971. Prior to that, a CV-type cylinder was fitted to the booster in every market but North America.

The lighting arrangement differed on NAS Land Rovers, starting mainly in 1968, with the introduction of the fender-mounted headlights as opposed to the grille-mounted units that had been standard since 1948. Other differences were amber reflectors on all four corners of the vehicle and a pair of red reflectors low down on the rear. In 1972, the Series IIIs got side marker lights with yellow up front and red in the rear. Some very late Series IIAs saw them as well. Turn signal indicators front and rear from 1968 on were four-inch amber units, available nowhere else, and all vehicles were equipped with a pair of backup lamps that appear to be right off an MGB.

One nifty NAS lighting feature that appeared in Series III in 1973 was a hooded light on the left side of the fascia to illuminate the switch panel. Also appearing then was a Federally mandated dash light rheostat.

Daktari? Not quite, but this personalized Series IIA is loaded for bear.

not to reappear until 1987 with the introduction of the American-spec Range Rover. The utility type Land Rover did not reappear in the North American market until 1993 and the introduction of the Defender 110.

Range Rover—Bred for the USA

Well, the title isn't 100 percent true but our market helped get the slow-moving decision makers to commit to a new project. Though the American market was definitely in the minds of the Range Rover designers, ironically, it was not offered for sale here until 17 years after its intro. Because of its popularity and the fact that nearly a thousand gray-market Range Rovers were imported from 1970 to 1986, a few words on this popular and high zoot 4x4 are in order.

Before the British Leyland takeover, the American market was regarded as an important one to pursue. The introduction of the Scout in 1961, the Ford Bronco in 1965, and the Blazer in 1969 gave the Brits an indication of where the ever-growing North American 4x4 market was headed. The rest of the world was only a few steps behind. Gone were the days when a simple, basic 4x4 was the order of the day. Enter the days when folks used them for a variety of recreational pursuits. People are generally not thrilled with privation, so creature comforts were prime selling points.

From the first, Land Rover had been pressed by requests for more comfort. They had answered with the limited production Estate cars in the late 1940s and early 1950s. They had half-heartedly pursued a project called "Road Rover" in an effort to combine street comfort and manners with an off-highway machine. The new project finally got the nod in 1966, and the Land Rover development team was charged with producing a recreational 4x4 worthy of carrying the Rover name.

The first moniker for the new vehicle was "hundred-inch station wagon," following Land Rover tradition of naming the vehicles after their wheelbase lengths. The original plan called for fitting one of Rover's six-cylinder car engines, probably the 3-liter F-head, to an all-wheel drive two-door estate car. When the aluminum V-8 came available, it was quickly adopted for the project. A unique coil-spring suspension was designed and four-wheel disc brakes were engineered.

Owning Land Rovers is much like an incurable disease. The Miller family obviously has a very bad case. They own, from left to right, a late model Discovery, a Series III, and this genuine one of a kind, a 1952 Land Rover 80-inch with a Mulliner estate conversion body. This custom body was built for a British lord and installed on a 1949. When the larger engine was introduced, Lord Viner had the body moved to the 1952. This classic woody has appeared in several British TV shows and Michael Caine movies.

The first two prototypes used some "not quite there" styling that only hinted at the eventual result. The third prototype bore the now familiar lines the world has known and loved from 1970 to 1995. It wasn't until much later that the project acquired a name. The early preproduction Range Rovers bore the code name "Velar" to confuse observers. Popular belief, backed up by a few of the folks who were around then, says that the acronym stood for "Vee-Eight LAnd Rover." The official name of Range Rover was adopted in December of 1968 after toying with "Land Rover Ranger." One of the first six prototypes was a left-hand drive version with an approximation of current U.S. emission controls fitted to the engine. If this isn't an indication of intent, what is?

The new Range Rover was launched in June of 1970, with the first deliveries in September. It became the new European automotive rage. In 1971 a Range Rover was displayed at the Louvre in Paris as an example of automotive art. Unlike the Range Rovers of today, these first examples were not particularly luxurious. They didn't begin applying the glitz until about 1980. A special "In Vogue" edition was produced that became the basis for a very popular Vogue model that premiered in 1984. A four-door came available in 1981, answering the needs of many would-be customers, as did the three-speed automatic transmission that came a year later. A slick five-speed manual replaced the clunky four-speed in 1984. Late in 1985, the first fuel-injected Range Rover appeared and in 1986 a German-made four-speed automatic replaced the three-speed. unit. A high-revving Italian-made diesel became a Range Rover option late in 1986. When the U.S.-spec Range Rover debuted in 1986, it did so to rave reviews. Twenty-twenty hindsight tells us that the same thing would have occurred in 1970, had they chosen to market the vehicle here.

Build Your Own Land Rover

From the advent of the Series II in 1958 to the last Series IIIs built for civilian use in 1985, the major parts are interchangeable. Much is interchangeable with the Series Is as well. This means that many of the later upgrades can be retrofitted to early models. Or vice versa. Many owners will build a Land Rover out of what they regard as the "best" pieces. It's not unusual to find a Series III with a tropical roof, deluxe hood, and metal grille from an earlier unit. Early rigs originally fitted with upper and lower tailgates are often equipped with the later side-swinging rear door.

A five-main bearing engine debuted in the late 1970s and some owners will take the trouble to import one and retrofit it. Same goes for the more powerful, long-stroke 2.5-liter engines. The bugs were worked out of the all-syncro box, so later-suffix gearboxes (each box has a suffix indicating general characteristics—a suffix C gearbox has improvements over a suffix A box) are often swapped for earlier units.

In the early 1970s, a Salisbury-style axle was introduced as an option for 109-inch models. About 100 percent stronger than the standard Rover axle, it is a popular retrofit for owners desiring more beef for hard work.

When looking at a Land Rover, originality is an issue but certain changes often enhance value. A Series III with a tropical roof is worth more than one without, even though the roof was not an item offered on North American versions. Engine swaps usually decrease value. An especially well done conversion might hold its own, however.

The bottom line is that if the modifications carry the flavor of the original vehicle, they do not usually detract from the value. Poorly done adaptations using AMC Gremlin parts or cheap mail-order goodies will certainly knock the price down.

Useful items can add to value. One of the most popular items is an aftermarket overdrive. Two types are available, a Fairey/Superwinch or a Toro. The Toro is out of production. Winches, either PTO type or electric, are available. The PTOs can be divided by drum type and capstan type. The commonly seen drum styles are the American built Koenig (either transfer-case driven or engine driven) or a Fairey. The capstan winches are less common. Though quaint, they are not as useful in recovery situations as a drum and cable winch. Electric winches are more common and readily available.

Another common conversion is to install 16-inch wheels and 7.50-16 tires. The NAS Land Rovers from 1968-on used 15-inch wheels and dinky 7.10-15 tires. The bigger wheels are fitted to increase clearance and offer a slight overdrive effect for the highway. The speedometers must be recalibrated for the taller tires.

While a Land Rover can exist in rust-inducing conditions longer than the average all-steel vehicle (two to three times longer by most reports), they will eventually succumb as well. The steel plate chassis will be the first to go. It isn't unusual to find a Land Rover with a pristine body and a chassis like Swiss cheese. The rear crossmember is the first to go but a replacement can be installed *in situ*. Other chassis members are available for spot repairs as well as complete replacement chassis. In severe situations, even the aluminum skin can be damaged—especially where it is attached to a steel part.

New, used, and reproduction parts are readily available for all Land Rovers. Only with the most uncommon versions will a collector have parts trouble. You needn't send to England for parts, though many people do, because there are at least half a dozen good-sized parts houses here and a host of small outfits scattered around the country. Club activity is brisk, concentrated mainly in the coastal states. The Midwest is particularly devoid (gradually changing) but there are inland pockets, like Colorado, where activity rivals the coasts.

Prices for Land Rovers have been on the high side for a number of years and continue to steadily climb. Parts are not inexpensive. While they are very user friendly to the home restorer, they are not generally a budget restoration. Even with the relatively high prices a Land Rover commands, care must be taken that the cost of the resto does not exceed the value of the vehicle.

Rootes Group Era -
Series 1 80, 86 and 107 Models
1950–1957- 700 units (note 1)

Rover Motor Company North America Era -
Series 1 86 &107, Series II 88 & 109, Series IIA 88 & 109 Models
1958- NA (Note 2)
1959- NA
1960- NA
1961- NA
1962- NA
1963- NA
1964- 952
1965- 1,840
1966- 1,137
1967- 2,415 (includes 811 6-cylinder 109 for '66–67)
1968- NA

1969- 1,222
1970- 873
1971- 756 (incl. 30 Series III)
1972- 1,114
1973- 1,246
1974- 469 (Note 3)

Note 1 - There are no records to indicate exact numbers. An estimate shared by many experts in the field is an average of 100 units per year.
Note 2 - Records are unavailable and little evidence exists to make an educated guess. No doubt, the numbers increased by 1958 as RMCNA took charge of the marketing. This writer would estimate 1,500 units over the six year period from 1958 to 1964.
Note 3 - This is the number of NADA Series IIIs produced but some sources estimate as many as 1,200 were sold. This writer tends to disagree.

	Series 1 80in	Series 1 86/107in	Series 1 88/109in
Engine:			
Type-	4-cyl, F-head	4-cyl, F-head	4-cyl, F-head 4-cyl, OHV diesel
Displacement-	97.2cid	97.2cid('48–52) 121.8cid ('52–56)	121.8cid 125.1cid
Power-	50hp @ 4,000rpm	50hp @ 4,000rpm 52hp @ 4,000rpm	52hp @ 4,000rpm 51hp @ 3,500rpm
Torque-	80lbs-ft @ 2,000rpm	80lbs-ft @ 2,000rpm 101lbs-ft @ 1500rpm	101lbs-ft @ 1,500rpm 87lbs-ft @ 2,000rpm
B&S	2.7x4.13in	2.7x4.13in 3.06x4.13in	3.06x4.13in 3.37x3.5in
CR-	6.8:1	6.8:1	6.8:1 22.5:1
Carburetor-	1-bbl Solex	1-bbl Solex	1-bbl Solex
Transmission:			
Type-	4-speed manual	4-speed manual	4-speed manual
Ratios-	1=2.99,2=2.04 3=1.33,4=1.00 R=2.54	1=2.99,2=2.04 3=1.33,4=1.00 R=2.54	1=2.99,2=2.04 3=1.33.4=1.00 R=2.54
Transfer Case:			
Type-	2-speed, full-time (to '50 then part-time)	2-speed, part-time	2-speed part-time
Ratios-	1.14 high/2.88 low	1.14 high/2.88 low	1.14 high/2.88 low
Axles:			
Front type:	Full-floating	Full-floating	Full-floating
Rear type:	Semi-floating	Semi-floating	Semi-floating
Ratios:	4.88 (early) 4.7 (late)	4.7	4.7
Tires:			
Type-	Traction	Traction	Traction
Size-	6.00x16 7.00x16 (LWB)	6.00x16 (SWB) 7.00x16 (LWB)	6.00x15 (SWB)

Dimension & Capacities:

LxWxH-	132x60.5x72in	140.5x62.5x76in (86SW)	
		172x62.5x76in (107PU)	
		173x62.5x77.5in (107SW)	
Wheelbase-	80in	86/107in	88/109in
Curb weight-	2,490lbs	2,900/3,000/3,400	
Fuel capacity-	12gal	12gal	12gal
GVW-	3,500lbs	3,500/4,500/4,500lbs	

SPECIFICATIONS, SERIES II, IIA & III

	Series II 88/109in	Series IIA 88/107in	Series III 88/109in
Engine:			
Type-	4-cyl, OHV	4-cyl OHV	4-cyl, OHV
	4-cyl, OHV diesel	4-cyl, OHV diesel	4-cyl, OHV diesel
		6-cyl, F-head	
Displacement-	139.4cid	139.4cid(Gas/Diesel)	139.4cid
	125.1cid	160cid	
Power-	77hp @ 4,250rpm	77hp @ 4,250rpm	81hp @ 4,250rpm
	51hp @ 4000	62hp @ 4,000rpm (D)	
		81hp @ 4,250 (8.0)	
		95hp @ 4,500 (6-cyl)	
Torque-	124lbs-ft @ 2,500rpm	124lbs-ft @ 2,000rpm	127lbs-ft @ 1,500rpm
	87lbs-ft @ 2,000rpm	103lbs-ft @ 1,800rpm(D)	
		127lbs-ft @ 2,500rpm(8.0)	
		134lbs-ft @ 1,750rpm (6-cyl)	
B&S-	3.56x3.5in	3.56x3.5in (G&D)	3.65x3.5in
	3.37x3.5in (D)	3.06x3.62in (6-cyl)	
Carburetor-	1-bbl Solex	1-bbl Solex or Zenith	1-bbl Zenith
	CAV fuel injection	CAV fuel injection	
		1-bbl SU sidedraft	
Transmission:			
Type-	4-speed manual	4-speed manual	4-speed manual
Ratios-	1=2.99,2=2.04	1=3.60,2=2.22	1=3.68,2=2.22
	3=1.33,4=1.00	3=1.50,4=1.00	3=1.50.4=1.00
	R=2.54	R=3.02	R=4.02
Transfer Case:			
Type-	2-speed, part-time	2-speed, part-time	2-speed part-time
Ratios-	1.15 high/2.88 low	1.15 high/2.35 low	1.15 high/2.35 low
Axles:			
Front type:	Full-floating	Full-floating	Full-floating
Rear type:	Full-floating	Full-floating	Full-floating
Ratios:	4.7	4.7	4.7
Tires:			
Type-	Traction	Traction	Traction
Size-	7.00x16 (SWB)	7.00x16 (SWB)	7.10x15
	7.50x16 (LWB)	7.50x16 (LWB)	
Dimension & Capacities:			
LxWxH-	142.4x66x77.9 (88)	142.4x66x77.9 (88)	142.4x66x77.9 (88)
	175x66x81(109PU)	75x66x81(109 PU)	
	175x66x81.4 109SW)	175x66x81.4 (109SW)	
Wheelbase-	88/109in	88/109in	88in
Curb weight-	3,281lbs (88SW)	3,281lbs (88SW)	3,281lbs
	3,301lbs (109PU)	3,301lbs (109PU)	
	3,752lbs (109SW)	3,752lbs (109SW)	
Fuel capacity-	12gal (88)	12gal(88)	12gal
	16gal (109)	16gal (109)	
GVW-	4,300lbs (88)	4,300lbs (88)	4,300lbs
	5,800lbs (109)	5,800lbs (109)	

133

Chapter 7

Chevrolet and GMC— The GM Legacy

Chevrolet has a legacy in light trucks that goes back to 1918, the same year that Chevrolet joined William Durant's car empire, General Motors. The Chevrolet car was famous for offering great value for the dollar, and the trucks continued this strategy. One of the first of Chevrolet's many truck milestones was the introduction of their famous "stovebolt" six-cylinder engine in 1929. This powerful, economical engine helped Chevrolet to take the truck sales lead from the Ford juggernaut in 1933, 1934, and 1936 and finally hold it unbroken from 1938 until 1969. This writer will make no attempt to add fuel to the fires of rivalry between the Ford and Chevy camps by stating a preference.

And then there's GMC. Not as numerous as the Chevy but still a force to be reckoned with and probably more numerous than many of the other makes presented in this book. GMC goes back farther in trucks than Chevy, all the way back to 1902 and a gent named Max Grabowsky. Grabowsky built trucks with his brother under the Rapid Motor Vehicle Company nameplate until 1908, when he branched off into building the Grabowsky Power Wagon on his own. Rapid continued doing good business building trucks until 1909, when the fledgling General Motors purchased the company along with another well-known truck company, Reliance. These two large truck manufacturers were merged in 1912 to form GMC Truck.

Some "Jimmy" enthusiasts may resent GMCs being lumped in with Chevrolet. They must, however, realize that the development of the two makes, especially in the era we are discussing in this chapter, was very closely tied together. By the end of the 1960s, the line that had divided the two brands for many decades had blurred to the point of being almost nonexistent. By 1972, GM had blended the best of the two light-duty lines into nearly identical equipment.

In the Beginning

GMC beat Chevrolet to the light-duty 4x4 draw by a long time when it assembled a prototype 2-ton 4x4 truck in 1915. This development apparently went nowhere. In 1935, GMC fielded a 1 1/2-ton 4x4 that was unusual in that it used Chevrolet sheet metal with a "General Motors Truck" emblem on the hood. Called the model 4272, this hybrid "Jimmy" also used a Chevy 207-cid, 72-horsepower six instead of GMC's own 228-cid mill. The drivetrain was all GMC, however, and the truck had a very

The ACK 101 was GMC's attempt at a big army contract for 1/2-ton 4x4s. Built in 1939, the truck was basically a standard 1/2-ton "Jimmy" with the cab cut away, a military brush guard added up front and military bumperettes in the rear. The fuel tank was mounted under twin bucket seats. The ACK-101 was powered by GMC's 224-cid inline six (a pressure lubricated engine, as opposed to Chevy's splash-feed 216-cid) that made 80 horsepower at 3,200 rpm. With a 3.56x3.75 bore and stroke and 6.5:1 compression ratio, it made 175 pound-feet of torque at 1,600 rpm. The truck was built upon a 113.5-inch wheelbase and was designed for a GVW of about 4,400 pounds. Gearing was probably 4.11. The front axle and transfer case were probably Timken pieces. *U.S. Army*

high stance. This truck could be regarded as a direct ancestor of the Chevrolet G7100 series trucks of World War II.

GMC was also first with a light-duty rig when it assembled a 1/2-ton prototype truck in 1939. The ACK-101 was basically a civilian truck to which four-wheel drive had been added. The truck was militarized by having the cab sheet metal removed and a military canvas top added. A welded steel brush guard and heavy-duty bumper were added. The truck was built as a contender for the light-duty 4x4 military contracts in the late 1930s and early 1940s, but Dodge ended up with the brass ring here and GMC concentrated on building the big stuff—their specialty.

At nearly the same time, Chevrolet was debuting a 1 1/2-ton 4x4 truck, the G7107. While the truck exceeds this book's light-duty classification, it was a vital and pivotal truck for World War II. Based on the civilian trucks of the late 1930s, it was powered by one of the earliest versions of Chevy's 235-cid six. Using a civilian hard cab with militarized hood and fenders, the 1 1/2-ton Chevy was produced throughout the war to the tune of almost 150,000 trucks with a wide variety of specialty bodies. These rigs are still extant in fairly large numbers and make an interesting medium-duty collectable. Chevrolet played with some light 4x4 designs during the war but never got beyond the experimental stage.

After World War II, Chevrolet and GMC involvement in four-wheel drive was indirect. The conversion companies like NAPCO, discussed in

From 1941 to 1945, the Chevrolet G1701 1 1/2-ton truck was the standard medium-duty military truck. Chevrolet built more than 113,000 of them. Variants included a panel delivery, a dump truck, a tractor, a bomb service vehicle, and even a wrecker. Designated by Chevrolet as the G7100 series, power came from an 83-horse (net), 235-cid six. With 6.67:1 axle ratios, top speed was a governed 48 miles per hour. These trucks have a 32-inch fording depth, and 45- and 30-degree approach and departure angles. Their normal towed load was 4,000 pounds, and they were often equipped with a 10,000 pound PTO winch. *U.S. Army*

chapter 2, took care of most of this work. Both GMC and Chevrolet began installing NAPCO kits on the assembly lines in 1956 and 1957 respectively but for 1960, the pieces were sourced directly from Spicer or Rockwell and the era of the *real* factory-built GM 4x4 began.

Shark Nosed 4x4s: 1960–1966

The introduction of a new line of trucks complicated the four-wheel drive situation at GM. The 4x2 trucks got a new independent front torsion bar suspension (scrapped in 1963 for a cheaper coil spring setup) and coil spring rear suspension that necessitated a redesign of the chassis. This meant that separate chassis had to be made for each type of drive system. A great deal had been learned from the association with NAPCO and to save costs, GM began sourcing 4x4 parts directly from the manufacturers.

A variation of the G7107 series was this 1-1/2 ton low profile truck, designated the G7129. In 1942, the Army began a project to build trucks that were more concealable on the battlefield. Chevrolet built one of the better prototypes. The low profile was obtained by lowering the driver position and moving it outboard of the chassis rail. The truck was pretty standard Chevy stuff mechanically but the 235cid was replaced by a more powerful GMC 270cid and the four-speed trans by a Clark 5-speed. The truck proved to be a good performer but eventually, the Army's fetish for low-profile trucks waned when the costs were investigated and the Chevy prototype was relegated to history. *GM Media Archives*

With the new era, Chevrolet changed the designations of their trucks. The two-wheel drive trucks used a "C" prefix and the 4x4s a "K." Instead of 3100, 3600, 3800, etc. to designate load capacity, the new designation was "10" for 1/2 ton and "20" for 3/4 ton. From 1960–1966, only K10 and K20s were available. No 1-ton 4x4 Chevy trucks were offered. GMC used a "P" prefix for 4x2 and adopted Chevy's "K" for 4x4s. Their weight rating classifications were 1000 for 1/2 tons and 1500 for 3/4 tons. Like Chevy, no 1-ton 4x4s were offered in the 1960–1966 era.

Nineteen sixty marked the beginning of the recreational vehicle market boom, and this translated into a gradually increasing market for dual-purpose trucks. For the first time, trucks began to be marketed as "fun" vehicles. More people were going out to "play" in their trucks and as time went on, the brick simple, Spartan, and uncomfortable 4x4 pickup was replaced by trucks that tried to mimic cars for comfort features. It took a long while for the trucks to truly catch up, but through this era a custom-chrome appearance option dressed up the exteriors while custom and custom comfort options made the GM interior a nicer place to work or play. This was rela-

In 1962, a new hood and grille eliminated the "eyebrows" or "pods" on the hood and cleaned the lines up considerably. This K-10, model K1534, long-wheelbase Fleetside 1962 would have cost $2,678 with a 235 six-cylinder, three-speed transmission and 3.90 gears. For another $86 you could order an HD four-speed and $65 could get you a 261-cid, 150-horsepower six. For an outrageous $118, you could have the 283-cid V-8. Free-wheeling hubs would set you back another $79. *GM Media Archives*

tive, of course. Trucks of this era still had a lot of catching up to do.

The big Chevrolet news for 1960 was the availability of a V-8 engine, the 283-cid, in the 4x4s. In the middle and late 1950s, GMC had offered four-wheel drive in all of its trucks, including the V-8 models, but the Chevy line had stayed conservative and offered only its big seller, the six. The increased use of travel trailers and cab-over, slide-in campers led to "camper special" editions and the preponderance of V-8 engines in the lineup. Nope, the general public would not endure the long, slow six-cylinder grind up to the mountain campground. They had to do it faster, and the line of V-8s being offered gradually increased in displacement. By the end of 1966, Chevrolet had done a complete turnaround and was building more V-8 powered trucks than six-cylinders.

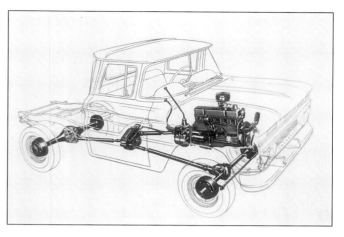

The drivetrain of the '60-66 Chevy and GMC trucks was very close in concept to the Napco trucks of the '56-59 era. They featured a divorced transfer case, a single stick Rockwell T-221, and a closed knuckle Dana 44 front axle. This truck is a pre-'63 model, as evidenced by it's removable carrier, Hotchkiss type rear axle.

GMC took a completely different tack in 1960 and began offering an all new engine, the 305-cid V-6. This was the first use of a V-6 powerplant in an American light truck. This big bore, slow-revving "industrial strength" V-6 had the guts of a V-8 but didn't sell well in the light-duty 4x2 platforms compared to the inline 270 six. 4x4 buyers had no choice in this era, the 305-cid V-6 being the only engine available.

The 305A engine was a real heavyweight, tipping the scales at nearly 1,000 pounds dry. It had a cooling system that could pump 135 gallons a minute and an oil pump that could pump 15 gallons a minute.

The Chevy 4x4s of the 1960–1966 era shared the same basic drivetrain. The setup was very "NAPCO" in appearance. Using a divorced Timken-Rockwell T-221 transfer case that was connected to either a three- or four-speed manual, the power was directed to a front Spicer 44 axle and either a semi-floating or full-floating GM Corporate rear axle. From 1960 to 1962, this was a Hotchkiss-type axle with a removable carrier and an inspection plate on the back of the axle housing. This axle is sometimes called the "old" 10-bolt. In 1963, the Salisbury style axle was adopted which featured an integral carrier.

B. F. Kissner, of Cederedge, Colorado, bought this 1964 Suburban K-10 model 1416 in 1969 and has used it as a hunting vehicle ever since. It's optioned out with a 283 V-8, four-speed, Posi-Traction rear differential and tailgates. Its still in regular use.

The GMC drivetrain was virtually identical in the light-duty realm, but the range of axle ratios offered was slightly different. Some confusion exists as to the transfer case used for 1960–1966 GMC trucks. Some sources quote the same Rockwell 221 as in the Chevy while others mention the Spicer 23. Others say they mixed them through the years. Both cases hung low and offered a convenient place for rocks to cause damage. The higher stance of the trucks partly compensated, but it makes these units less steady than later trucks. The addition of powerful "go fast" V-8 engines complicated this and a current owner should drive these rigs with respect, lest he end up on the roof.

One noteworthy addition was the hydraulic clutch. This assembly allowed for hanging pedals, a feature that eliminated pedal holes

Some of the most stylish of the 1960–1966 Chevies are these short-bed 1/2 tons. With a 115-inch wheelbase, they would be potent on the trail. Shown here is a 1964 model 1404 Stepside 1/2 ton that would have had a base price of $2,660. *GM Media Archives*

The 1960–1966 Suburbans were all two-door models and used this pivoting right-hand seat for passenger access to the back seats. The Suburbans could be outfitted to carry up to nine passengers with an optional third bench seat. Also optional were side-swinging rear doors.

in the floor (read lots of dust) and clutch problems due to frame flex in rough terrain.

Terminology differed between Chevy and GMC models. Chevy called their flush-sided pickups Fleetsides while GMCs were Widesides. The Chevy Stepside was called the Fenderside in GMC parlance. Forces within GMC were still resisting the Chevrolet influence as much as they could.

Running mechanical changes in the 1960–1966 era included replacement of the old, heavy, four-main bearing "Stovebolt" sixes in 1963 with a new seven-main bearing engine that was much lighter and more powerful. It also used pistons, rods, bearings, rocker arms, and pushrods from the V-8. The famous Delcotron alternator was standard in 1963, replacing the generator for good. Factory installed air conditioning became available in 1965, though an add-on system had been available in 1961.

So far, the 1960–1966 GM trucks have not generated a great deal of collector enthusiasm. They were built in fairly large numbers but it could be a "style kinda thing" and as we all know, beauty is in the eye of the beholder. Look for this to change as people look past the more popular Chevy trucks and recognize the attractive qualities of this era. These were stylish 4x4s and with their tall stance, they really look the part. Most mechanical parts are easily obtained, but body parts are getting tougher to find. The Rockwell transfer cases are expensive to rebuild, as are the closed-knuckle Dana front axles. Suburbans from this era are very scarce and may be the first "up-and-comer."

Low and Sleek: 1967–1972

When the new Chevy trucks debuted in September of 1966, GM had high hopes that this new line would bolster their shrinking lead in the ever growing truck market. This was not to be, but nonetheless, GM fielded a line of 4x4 trucks that made pivotal changes in the market. This was also the era where Chevrolet and GMC 4x4s became more or less the same under the skin.

The new trucks were built with a low, sleek look. This was accomplished by integrating the transmission and transfer case into a single unit, thereby decreasing driveshaft angles. This eliminated the low-hanging transfer case and made ingress and egress much easier for driver and passengers. The new front suspension used reversed arch leaf springs that combined a fantastic ride (relative, of course) with good articulation off-highway and car-like manners on the highway.

The 283 was one of the best of the Chevy V-8s. The High Torque version was common in the 4x4s through 1966. It made 175 gross horsepower at 4,400 (145 net at 4,200), 275 gross pound-feet of torque at 2,400 rpm (245 net at 2,000) and had a 9:1 compression ratio. Bore and stroke were 3.875x3.00 and the engine was offered only as a two-barrel in the 4x4 trucks. The engine shown is a 1962 version, complete with oil bath air filter and generator. Note the hydraulic clutch on rear of the engine. *GM Media Archives*

Chevrolet jumped into the recreation market with both feet by offering a comfort package they called the CST, for Custom Sport Truck, option. The CST package consisted of some snazzy exterior trim that included chrome bumpers, a cushy full-width seat, interior trim, carpeting, and insulation, in addition to a cigarette lighter and a door-operated dome lamp.

The CST package was one of the earliest options packages to be applied to the truck line. A small percentage of trucks were built with them (just 3 percent of all trucks in 1967) and they could be special ordered. As the era progressed, more and more trucks were fitted with the CST package and later, other options groups were offered, such as the Cheyenne super package. Other goodies were available singly, such as tilt steering columns, bucket seats, and a host of little things like tachometers, mirrors. and such.

Some mechanicals transferred from the old line, such as axles, but there were many new additions. The "horsepower race," long running in cars and 4x2 trucks, was taken seriously for the first time in the 4x4s. The first entrant from GM in that race was the mighty 327-cid V-8, made famous in the early 1960s hi-po cars and later in 4x2 trucks. The 327 was optional alongside the 283 and

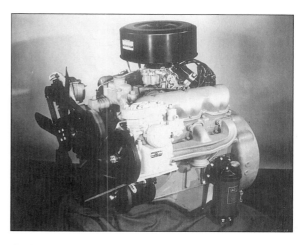

GMC's 305-cid V-6 was a true heavy duty powerplant. This was the only engine available in the 4x4s and was one of two in the 4x2s. The engine weighs 1,000 pounds, so the GMC used a much heavier set of front springs to carry it. Parts are a bit more expensive for the 305 V6s than for your average Chevy, but the engine is known for a very long service life.

The 235-cid "stovebolt" six of 1962 was a far cry from the 235 that appeared in some 1950 light-duty trucks. The engine was actually available in larger trucks in the late 1930s. The first 235 used a splash feed on the poured-babbitt rod bearings. This later 235 was an upgraded unit with a fully pressurized lubrication system and, at 135 horsepower, was considerably more powerful than the 92 horsepower babbitt engine. The 235 had a cousin, the 261, that was offered as an intermediate between the 235 and the V-8. It was even more powerful, cranking out 150 horsepower. Both these six cylinders were replaced in 1963 by the 230 and 292-cid sixes that used many V-8 parts in their constructions. *GM Media Archives*

The 1967–1972 Chevy and GMC trucks were long and sleek in appearance but at the time, they didn't sell very well. Today, they are a hot number. Tom Noble wouldn't sell his restored 1971 GMC K20 for anything less than top dollar.

The 1967–1972 Chevy and GMCs were alike in the three-door configuration. This layout was shared in the 1960–1966 Suburbans also. John Konkis' 1971 GMC is ready for another 26 years of work!

On the left is a factory photo celebrating the debut of the 1969 Blazer. On the right is Ed Fortson's recently resurrected 1969 that's well on its way to a new life. Many new and reproduction parts, including some body parts installed in Ed's Blazer, are available via an enthusiastic aftermarket. *GM Media Archives*

the 292-six. Also, the NP205 transfer case debuted. This unit has proven to be one of the toughest units ever to spin four wheels and was used for many years.

The debut year models are somewhat different than the 1968-on rigs. For one item, they are missing the side marker lamps that were a federally mandated item from 1968-on. Also, 1967 was the last year for the 283 in trucks. For 1968, the 307 took over as the low-option V-8 and featured a 1/4-inch longer stroke than the 283. For 1970, Chevrolet offered its first automatic in a 4x4. The TH-350 made the Chevys even more carlike with little sacrifice in work or off-highway capacity. Front disc brakes appeared in 1971 as standard equipment.

In the midst of an industry rife with labor troubles, GM fielded a totally new entrant into the 4x4 realm, the Blazer. Though the successful Ford Bronco preceded it by three years, and the Scout by seven years, the Blazer became in instant sensation. The Blazer is generally acknowledged as the rig that waved the green flag in the sport utility race. While this term did not exist in 1969, the powerful, comfortable Blazer stressed "sport" over "utility."

The Blazer was larger than either the IHC Scout or the Ford Bronco and, as a result, far more comfortable. It also had a more impressive list of options that included a class-beating 350-cid V-8, automatic, air conditioning and a variety of comfort and glitz items. Based on the K10 truck line, the Blazers sat on a 104-inch wheelbase and featured a removable fiberglass hardtop. They could be ordered as plush or as Spartan as you liked. The CST Package was a popular option but you can find Blazers in all levels of trim.

The Blazers shared the mechanical options with the K10 trucks. A 250-six and a three-on-the-tree was standard. The 307 V-8 was next up the line, with the 350 as the top-dog. Besides the standard SM-330 three-speed and the bulletproof SM-465, the truck-duty version of the TH-350 automatic was an option. The manual trans rigs got Spicer 20 transfer cases whereas the automatics were fitted with the NP-205 box. All the 1969–1972 Blazers used a front Dana 44 axle (open-knuckle type) with a 12-bolt semifloating rear axle in the rear. In the compact Blazer, these drivetrains made for a very durable combination.

Only 4,935 1969 Blazers were sold, making them something to look for. Of these, some 290 came with black-painted tops, instead of the more common white paint. This fact is passed along as something of interest to a collector. While a 1969 Blazer might be worth marginally more than a 1970 or later due to its relative scarcity, it's doubtful the black-topped version is any more valuable.

The 1967–1972 Chevy and GMC trucks have become very popular of late. Sales were a bit off during the era when they were marketed but in the early 1990s, they began to get popular as collectables, both in 4x2 and 4x4 circles. They make a very stylish, practical 4x4 that is easily usable as a day-to-day vehicle as well as a four-wheeler or even as a hauler. These trucks are easily repaired and most parts are still available for restoration.

	1965	1966	1967	1968	1969*	1970	1971	1972
K-5 Blazer	-	-	-	-	4,935	11,527	17,220	44,266
K-10 PU Stepside (SWB)	1,127	1,123	1,229	1,706	1,698	1,629	1,438	1,736
K-10 PU, Stepside (LWB)	513	?	500	552	521	464	364	407
K-10 PU, Fleetside (SWB)	633	678	1,046	1,449	1,849	2,554	3,068	6,069
K-10 PU, Fleetside (LWB	1,459	?	2,715	3,625	4.937	7,328	9,417	18,431
K-10 Suburban (doors)	444	530	509	1,143	697	926	631	991
K-10 Suburban (gates)	433	418	-	-	-	-	-	2,145
K-10 Panel	103	170	30	59	-	287	256	503
K-20 Suburban (doors)	-	-	120	299	289	254	353	879
K-20 Suburban (gates)	-	-	-	-	256	953	674	755
K-20 Panel	-	-	8	68	-	-	10,006	-
K-20 PU, Stepside	889	923	872	1,047	1,071			
K-20 PU, Fleetside	1,459	1,796	2,773	3,625	6,124			

SPECIFICATIONS
1960–1966 CHEVROLET   1960–1966 GMC

Engine:

	1960–1966 CHEVROLET	1960–1966 GMC
Type-	6-cyl, Inline (std.) V8, OHV (opt.)	V6, OHV (std)
Displacement-	235.5cid, std. ('60–62) 230cid, std. ('63–66) 261cid, opt. ('62) 292cid, opt., ('63–66) 283cid, opt., ('60–66)	304.7cid
Power-	135hp @ 4,000rpm 140hp @ 4,000rpm 150hp @ 4,000rpm 165hp @ 4,400rpm 175hp @ 4,400rpm	165hp @ 3,500
Torque-	217lbs-ft @ 2,000rpm 220lbs-ft @ 1,600rpm 235lbs-ft @ 2,000rpm 280lbs-ft @ 1,600rpm 275lbs-ft @ 2,400rpm	280lbs-ft @ 1,600rpm
B&S-	3.56x3.93in 3.87x3.25in 3.75x3.93in 3.87x4.12in 3.87x3.00in	4.25x3.58in
CR-	8.00:1 8.50:1 8.50:1 8.00:1 8.00:1 9.00:1	7.75:1

Transmission:

Type-	3-speed manual (std.) 4-speed manual (std.)
Ratios-	1=2.94, 2=1.68, 3=1.0, R=3.14 1=7.06, 2=3.58, 3=1.71, 4=1.0 R=6.78

Transfer Case:

	1960–1966 CHEVROLET	1960–1966 GMC
Type-	2-speed, Rockwell T-221	2-speed Spicer 23
Ratios-	Low= 1.94, High= 1.0 or 2-speed Rockwell T-221 Low =1.94, High= 1.0	Low= 1.87, High =1.0

Axles:

Front type-	Full-floating	Full-floating
Rear type-	Semi-floating (K10) Full-floating (K20)	Semi-Floating (K1000) Full-floating (K1500)
Ratios-	3.90 (K10) 4.57 (K20)	3.54 (K1000) 4.56 (K1500)

Tires (Typical):

Type-	Various non-directional	Various non-directional
Size-	6.50-15 (K10) 7.00-17.5 (K20)	6.70-15 (K-1000) 7.00-17.5 (K-1500)

Dimensions & Capacities (Typical):

LxWxH-	186.75x78.75x77.12in (SWB PU) 201x78.75x80.5in (Suburban) 206x78.75x78.26in (LWB PU)	186.75x78.75x77.12in (SWB PU) 201x78.75x80.5in(Suburban) 206x78.75x78.26in (LWB PU)
Wheelbase-	115 or 127in	115 or 127in
Curb weight-	3,450lbs (K10 SWB PU) 4,080 (K10 Suburban) 3,840 (K10 LWB PU) 4,225 (K20 PU)	4,360lbs (K1000 SWB PU) 4,950lbs (K1000 Suburban) 4,460lbs (K1000 LWB PU) 4,725lbs (K1500 LWB PU)
Fuel capacity-	18.5gal (PU) 20.5gal opt. (PU, '61–66) 17.0gal (Suburban and Panel)	17.5gal (PU) 17.0gal (Suburban & Panel)
GVW-	5,600 (K10 all) 7,200 (K20)	5,600 (K1000 all) 8,100 (K1500 all)

Custom appearance, custom chrome, custom comfort, custom side moulding, two-tone paint, air conditioning (1963–1966), 283-cid V8, four-speed manual, locking front hubs, rear Posi-Traction differential, 20.5gallon fuel tank, side-mounted spare tire, 11-inch clutch, tachometer (V8), full instrumentation, Soft-Ray glass, third seat (Suburban), two-speed wipers and washer.

1960–1966 GMC-

Deluxe cab, 16.5gallon auxiliary fuel tank, Custom seat, Chrome front and rear bumpers, two-tone paint, locking hubs, maximum traction rear differential, third seat (Suburban), air conditioning (1965–1966), windshield washer, Braden PTO winch.

SPECIFICATIONS: 1967–1972

	Chevrolet	GMC
Engine:		
Type-	6-cyl, Inline (std)	V6 (std. '67–69)
	V8, OHV (opt)	6-cyl, Inline (std. '70–72)
	V8 (opt.'68–72)	
Displacement-	250cid, std'	304.7cid V6, std. ('67–69)
	292cid, opt., ('67–70)	250cid, std. ('70–72)
	283cid, opt., ('67)	292cid, opt. ('70–72)
	307cid, opt. ('68–72)	307cid, opt. ('68–72)
	327cid, opt. ('67–69)	327cid, opt. ('68)
	350cid, opt. ('70–72)	350cid, opt. ('69–72)
Power-	155hp @ 4,000rpm	165hp @ 3,800rpm
	170hp @ 4,200rpm	155hp @ 4,000rpm
	175hp @ 4,400rpm	170hp @ 4,200rpm
	200hp @ 4,800rpm	200hp @ 4,800rpm
	220hp @ 4,400rpm	220hp @ 4,400rpm
	250hp @ 4,400rpm	250hp @ 4,400rpm
Torque-	235lbs-ft @ 1,600rpm	280lbs-ft @ 1,600rpm
	275lbs-ft @ 1,600rpm	235lbs-ft @ 1,600rpm
	275lbs-ft @ 2,400rpm	275lbs-ft @ 1,600rpm
	300lbs-ft @ 2,400rpm	300lbs-ft @ 2,400rpm
	320lbs-ft @ 2,800rpm	320lbs-ft @ 2,800rpm
	355lbs-ft @ 3,000rpm	355lbs-ft @ 3,000rpm
B&S-	3.87x3.53in	4.25x3.58in
	3.87x4.12in	3.87x3.53in
	3.87x3.00in	3.87x4.12in
	3.87x3.25in	3.87x3.25in
	4.00x3.25in	4.00x3.25in
	4.00x3.50in	4.00x3.50in
CR-	8.50:1	7.75:1
	8.50:1	8.50:1
	9.00:1	8.50:1
	9.00:1	9.00:1
	9.00:1	9.00:1
	8.50:1	8.50:1

Transmission:

Type-	3-speed manual SM-330 (std.)
	4-speed manual SM-465 (opt.)
	4-speed manual NP-435CR (opt. '70–72, close ratio)
	3-speed automatic TH-350 (opt.)
Ratios-	1=3.03, 2=1.75, 3=1.0, R=3.02
	1=6.55, 2=3.58, 3=1.70, 4=1.0
	R=6.09
	1=4.45, 2=
	1=2.52, 2=1.52, 3=1.00, R=

Transfer Case:

Type-	2-speed, NP-205 (auto trans)	2-speed, Timken T-223('67–69)
	2-speed, Dana 20 (man. trans)	2-speed, NP-205 ('70–72)
Ratios-	low= 1.96, High= 1.0	low=1.94, high=1.0
	low=2.03, high 1.0	low=1.96, high=1.0

Axles:

Front type-	Full-floating
Rear type-	Semi-floating (K10)
	Full-floating (K20)
Ratios-	3.73 (K10, manual trans, exc. 350 V8)
	3.07 (K10, w/350 V8)
	4.57 (K20, K15, except with 350 V8)
	4.10 (K20, K15, w/350 V8)

Tires (Typical):

Type-	Various non-directional
Size-	G-78-15 (K10), std.
	H-78-15 (K-10) opt.
	8.00-16.5 (K20) std.
	9.50-16.5 (K20) opt.

Dimensions & Capacities (Typical):

LxWxH-	188.75x79x72.5in (SWB PU)
	208x75x74.5in (LWB Suburban)
	208x75x73.25in (LWB PU)
Wheelbase-	115 or 127in
Curb weight-	3,8240lbs (K10 SWB PU)**(check no.)**
	4,191 (K10 Suburban)
	3,836 (K10 LWB PU)
	4,131 (K15,20 PU)
Fuel capacity-	21.5gal (PU)
	23.5gal (Suburuban & Panel)
	20.5gal aux. (K20 Fleetside only)
GVW-	5,200 (K10 all)
	6,400 (K20)

CST package, Cheyenne Super package, Custom Appearance, bucket seats and console, two-tone paint, 350V8, TH-350 automatic, four-speed manual, locking front hubs, power steering, tilt steering column, air conditioning, Special Instrumentation, limited slip rear differential, HD front axle (K20), auxiliary battery, auxiliary fuel tank.

Chapter 8

Ford—Blue Oval 4x4s

Beyond reaping the sales benefits of Marmon-Herrington's Ford 4x4 conversions, FoMoCo's earliest factory excursions in all-terrain design began about 1940. Prior to that, there was little interest by upper management. Henry Ford's handshake agreement with Marmon-Herrington gave both companies what they wanted; Ford had another sales outlet for trucks and Marmon-Herrington got the benefit of "good-guy" prices on trucks and a big market for their conversions.

The rearmament push of 1939 and 1940 offered the American auto and truck manufacturers a veritable cornucopia of contracts. The Allies overseas, many with their industries under assault, were clamoring even more stridently for military vehicles. If you translate the business opportunities of that time into military terms, you could call the situation "a target-rich environment."

In the light-duty 4x4 area, Ford got involved on two levels; one in competition for the 1/4-ton 4x4 and another for the 1/2-ton 4x4. With regards to the 1/4-ton, Ford, along with 134 other motor vehicle manufacturers, got a packet from the U.S. Government containing design specs and rough blueprints for a four-wheel drive scout car. These specifications had been drawn up by the Quartermaster Corps and the American Bantam Car Company in the summer of 1940.

At first, Ford was lukewarm on the idea but gradually Henry Ford and the rest of the ruling body realized the potential gold mine in the project. Due to the company's vast production capability, Ford was blatantly courted by several involved government officials and eventually dove in with both feet. Ford not only built several thousand "Jeeps" to its own design, but ended up producing 277,896 1/4-ton 4x4s built to the standard Willys design, itself an amalgamation of all the best features of each of the prototypes. Called the GPW (G=government, P= 80-inch wheelbase reconnaissance car, W= Willys pattern), there were just a few subtle differences from the Willys. Ford also contracted for 12,778 GPA amphibians (GP the same as GPW, the A=amphibian) that were basically a Ford jeep chassis with a waterproof hull. The 1/4-ton story is told in more detail in chapter 3.

The First 4x4 Trucks

Concurrent with the 1/4-ton developments in 1940 and 1941, Ford pursued the 1/2-ton contracts by building several prototypes. Designated the GC series, these V-8 powered 1/2-ton trucks were a halfhearted stab at the market already dominated by Dodge's VC and WC series trucks. A 1 1/2-ton prototype was also built utilizing the same basic design but again, this

Ford's GC program also produced some 1/2-ton pickups. The general resemblance to Dodge's 1/2-ton WC-12 model pickup is striking. Apparently more than one Ford GC was built. Some were evidently fitted with the new 226-cid inline six as well as the quintessential Ford flathead V-8. This GC has also had a PTO winch added. *U.S. Army*

The Ford GTB was an unusual design that placed the driver outboard of the engine by a large distance and very low. The passenger was placed way to the right but faced inboard. The GTB was powered by Ford's G8T L-head six that displaced 226 cubic inches and pumped out an honest 90 horsepower. The front differential was by Timken, the rear from Ford, and the gear ratio was 6.61. The truck carried a large 49-gallon fuel supply, so a 440-mile range was possible at the truck's 45-mile per hour top speed. Wheelbase was 115 inches, but the truck was capable of a 3,350 pound payload. *Jeff Bombay*

was too little and too late to stop the Chevrolet G-1700 trucks that already ruled the genre. Ford had been a little bit slow off the starting line.

The 1941 prototypes were built in three configurations, as a 1/2-ton command car, a 1/2-ton pickup, and a 1 1/2-ton cargo truck. The command car utilized a body that was very similar in execution to the Dodge WC series command car. In fact, it's almost certain that the Ford's body was built by Budd, who was also building the bodies for the Dodge command cars. The front sheet metal was all new and unique and was shared by the other two trucks.

The 1/2-ton pickup and its big brother both shared a closed cab that was nothing more than the 1941 civilian cab with a few adaptations. The rear body of the 1/2 tons was a modified version of the light-duty beds Ford had in production at the time while the single "buck-and-a-half" built used a Galion dump body. Both the 1/2 tons shared a 115-inch wheelbase while the 1 1/2 ton stretched out to 158 inches.

Mechanically, the trucks were very similar. Reportedly, the three or four prototypes mounted a mix of Ford's venerable 221-cid, 95-horsepower V-8

Fred Scharff's 1959 1/2 ton, a daily driver that has been fitted with a later model flatbed, is used on the Scharff's farm. If this isn't proof that old trucks can work as well today as they could yesterday, what is? *Fred Scharff*

A very popular option was the mighty 292 V-8, a durable power plant in the Y-block family that included 239, 270, 292, and 312 displacements. The trucks were all fitted with two-barrel carbs. The exhaust crossover at the front of the engine is a Y-block trademark, but the hydro-vac power brake unit is an add-on from later years.

This 1960 F-250 Styleside is optioned out with a Custom Cab and 17.5-inch wheels. Note the difference in grille design from the 1959 model photos. Note also that the identification badge on each side of the hood has changed. If you wanted a heater/defroster, it was an extra-cost item, as were outside mirrors and windshield washers. Differences between 1959 and 1960 were minor, consisting mainly of uprated springs, a standard 11-inch clutch, and a steering box ratio change from 18.2:1 to 24:1. Base price for the 1960 F-250 Styleside was $2,697. *Ford Motor Company*

They don't get any nicer than this! Colin Hutto's pristine 1965 F-250 is all original and showing but 39,000 on the clock. It is decked out with a 352 V-8 and a four-speed tranny. Note that rear body doesn't quite match the cab. After the integral body fiasco, the 1959–1960 beds were resurrected for 4x4 use. The 4x2 F-350 box was similar.

This is a 100 percent correct and original 1965 engine compartment. Colin Hutto's fantastic 1965 is a real time machine. The rig represents the year when the 352 FE replaced the 292 for a boost in power. The other engines in the FE family, 332, 360, and 428 all interchange. Though Ford didn't trust the public with Hi-Po engines in 4x4s, don't be surprised to find that something a bit warmer has been swapped under the hood of a vintage Ford of the FE engine era.

or the newly introduced 226-cid, 90-horsepower L-head six in an effort to determine the ideal powerplant for the purpose. The rest of the drivetrain was sourced from the Ford truck parts bin. Timken supplied the front axle and probably the t-case.

The final variant of the GC development was a low-profile 1/2-tonner that used a very military looking body resembling, more than anything, an enlarged jeep. The welded steel grille and stamped hood were very similar to the Ford GP 1/4 tons, but the fold-down windshield was virtually the same part. The GC program ended in 1941 after Ford realized it had been aced out of the competition by Dodge and Chevy in both areas.

Ford's Low Riders

One of the unexpected benefits to the GC program was a heads-up for Ford on another army development that began in 1942 and wrapped up about 1944. The low-silhouette project took note of the fact that many of the newer tactical vehicles, primarily the 1/4-ton and 3/4-ton, were more easily concealed on the battlefield due to their removable tops and fold-down windshields. Field commanders wondered if the same could be done for the larger rigs, many of which still used tall, closed cabs.

The low-silhouette program was one in which Ford could compete on even footing with the other seven companies involved. Ford had entries in two of the weight classes, 3/4 ton and 1 1/2 ton. In the lighter class, Ford submitted three prototypes. The GCA featured a conventional driving position and was built on a 103-inch wheelbase. It was very similar to the last of the GC models. The GLJ put the driver beside the engine and shortened the wheelbase to 92 inches. The GAJ hung the driver way, way outboard and was also built upon a 92-inch wheelbase.

The GTB was Ford's entrant in the 1 1/2-ton category and oddly enough, this was the only design in the low-silhouette competition to go into production. The low-silhouette idea was eventually dropped as being impractical within reasonable standardized production limits; however, the GTB proved itself able beyond the parameters of the tests. Eventually a contract was drawn up and Ford built 6,000 of them, all out of their Edgewater, New Jersey, factory. Most went to the navy as bomb service trucks for remote Pacific airstrips, where their low profile was useful in getting under aircraft and their all-wheel drive allowed them to negotiate the notorious monsoon mud. Some were used by the army in the Far East, most notably India and Burma. It is here that they probably acquired the nickname, "Burma Jeep."

The GTBs are very few in number. They have attracted interest from military collectors due to their unusual design but are not as popular as the more famous rigs of World War II, despite their relative scarcity. Their value has stabilized at a reasonable level but does not appear to be on the rise. Parts are moderately difficult to obtain.

Ford Factory Built 4x4s: 1959–1960

There was a 14-year gap between the last of Ford's World War II 4x4 developments and the first factory-built light-duty trucks. In between, Ford spent time developing the M-151 MUTT (Mobile-Utility-Tactical-Transport), an innovative, independently suspended replacement for the standard jeep. You'll find this story detailed in chapter 10.

The 1961–1966 Ford trucks shared a similar interior. This is the plain Jane version of a 1965 F-250 interior.

Between the end of the war and 1959, Ford relied on Marmon-Herrington to convert their trucks into all-wheel drive configuration as needed. When the end of the 1950s hovered into sight, as well as a big jump in 4x4 popularity, Ford decided to cash in on the market. Companies like Borg Warner and Spicer were offering a variety of four-wheel drive hardware and Ford, like the other truck builders, saw no reason why they couldn't eliminate the middleman and source the parts themselves. In 1958 (they probably got the phone call earlier), Marmon-Herrington was given an "adios" from the Ford light-duty realm, though they continued "officially" converting Ford's larger rigs for some years.

The 1959 Ford 4x4s were based upon the boxy "rolling refrigerator" truck designs that had debuted for the 1957 model year. The new four-wheel drive trucks were offered in two weight classifications, 1/2 and 3/4 ton and in one wheelbase length, 118 inches. Boxes could be ordered in the Styleside or Flareside configurations. A Custom Cab option was available but this was little more than a two-tone instrument panel, candy-striped nylon seat covers, and a white steering wheel with a chrome horn ring. The front bumper also had an indent for the license plate.

Standard power came from a 223 OHV six that pumped out an honest 139 horsepower. Optional was Ford's famous Y-block 292-cid that boasted a 186-horsepower output with the two-barrel carb that was fitted for trucks. A "three-on-the-tree" was standard with a Warner Gear T-98A floor shift four-speed being the optional gearbox. The rear axle was a Ford piece, a semifloating 9-inch for the 1/2 ton and a full-floating Spicer 60 in the rear of the 3/4 ton. Axle ratios depended on weight category, with the F-100 being at 3.89:1 and the F-250 at 4.56. A Spicer 44-4F front axle and two-speed Spicer 24 divorced transfer case completed the drivetrain.

Along with a few frilly options like two-tone paint and chrome mirrors, there were some practical four-wheeling options as well. The Equa-Lock lim-

The first short-wheelbase 4x4 Ford truck came in 1966; here is the Styleside version. The base price of a 1966 F-100 Styleside like this was $2,803. This rig was purchased new with the optional 352-cid V-8 and the standard NP435 4-speed with 3.50 gearing and a single speed Spicer 21 transfer case. Gary Anderson bought this truck as a derelict and has been steadily putting it into top shape.

This 1966 F-250, nicely restored by Joseph Mims, features a custom-built flatbed that replaced the original flatbed. The 1966 3/4-tons came standard with a T-89F three-speed, but could be ordered with an NP-435 four speed. Delivered in the last year for this body style, this truck came equipped with the 240-cid six, the standard engine for the truck line.

ited-slip rear axle, front tow hooks, and a grille guard were available for those with more off-road oriented needs. The aftermarket offered items like winches, snowplows, hydraulics, free-wheeling hubs, and so on, which could be dealer installed.

The 1960 trucks were nearly identical to the 1959s, with just a few cosmetic changes, such as the obligatory yearly grille change. The brakes got improved and the heavy duty suspension option for 1959 was added to the standard 1960 list. The 292 V-8 saw a few upgrades in the form of new cylinder heads with improved combustion chambers, smaller valves, and relocated spark plugs. An improved lubrication system with a higher capacity oil pump and a two stage oil filter was also added. Power outputs, however, remained the same.

The 1959–1960 Ford trucks are beginning to attract attention from the collector crowd because of their relative scarcity and good looks. They're modern enough to be useful as a practical day-to-day hauler but old enough to have that "funky" flair that makes you want to show it off. Parts are reasonably easy to obtain and a good number have survived the years, though this appears to be a regional phenomenon. The Pacific Northwest, by all reports, is infested with them. The Fords of this era were a little more resistant to rust than the same era Chevy or Dodge but a good body is the most important requirement. Prices are still reasonable at this writing but look for them to gradually climb in the coming years.

The 240-six evolved from the old 223. It featured seven main bearings instead of four and was a much stronger powerplant. The 300-cid six was a stroked version of the 240. Both engines, especially the 300-cid, have earned a nearly untarnished reliability record and can be hot-rodded to the point where they can give many V-8s a run for their money.

The Ford 4x4 Grows Up: 1961–1966

In 1961, Ford did a complete makeover of the entire truck line, though the 4x2s received most of the benefits. The much vaunted integral Styleside body debuted, though only for the two-wheelers. The 4x4s needed the extra flex that a separate cab and cargo box offered. The integral body was dropped in the 4x2s by 1964 for the same reason—heavy loads and chassis flex was tearing the bodies apart. The Styleside 4-bys used the 1959–1960 style bed that didn't quite match the new cab. This continued right through 1966 on the 4x4s (except the 1966 F-100s) as well as the F-350 4x2 with a similar 9-foot bed. The round taillights are a giveaway visual feature to watch for, since the 4x2s used a "D" shaped light. Oddly, according to published production figures, 1961 Flareside pickups outnumbered the Stylesides by about 10 to one, making the 1961 Styleside a rare item. This trend gradually reversed, making the Flaresides the rare number from 1962-on.

The front wrap and the cabs of course, were completely restyled. The change was popular and Ford started to seriously chip away at Chevrolet's truck sales lead. The available options increased to reflect, in part, the public's recreational use of the 4x4 truck. This included a gradual softening up of the interior. Factory-installed stake and platform trucks made it to the options list. A wraparound rear window was an option, as was tinted glass. An all new chassis design for the 4x4 beefed up the side rails and lengthened the wheelbase from 118 to 120 inches. Mechanical items for 1961, however, changed very little from the 1960 models.

This 1967 3/4-ton flatbed has survived many years as a ranch truck and is likely to last another generation. The new 1967s were a big departure stylewise for Ford, and the gamble paid off. They finally broke the Chevrolet sales lead with this body style. Base price on an F-250 stake like this was $3,013 with a six and a three-speed. Original flatbeds are very uncommon.

This clean 1971 F-100 truck is factory original with an optional contractor's box, 360 V-8, full instrumentation, and free-running front hubs. Examples like these are still common enough to go out and look for with a reasonable expectation of finding one. This is a truck you can live with day to day, as Ken Frazier does. Ken has taken good care of the vintage 4x4 and uses it as a daily driver.

The Bronco Roadster was available until 1968. This 1966 is shown with the correct hubcaps that were available only that year. For a vintage restorer wanting 100 percent, these hubcaps can be hard to find.

The 1967 Broncos were essentially identical to the 1966 models with the exception of the new T-handle transfer case shifter, Sport Bronco package, and a few safety goodies that included a padded dash, seat belts, backup lights, electric windshield wipers, and dual circuit, self-adjusting brakes. It was still missing the side marker lights and rear reflectors that marked the 1968 models. This rare Model U14 pickup belongs to Jeff Lyon and is nearly stock. It does not carry the original hubcaps but it still has the half-cab, fold-down windshield and 170-cid engine. Pickup cabs are becoming quite popular but good examples are hard to find—and expensive.

Other than the essential grille change every year, the Fords continued with only minor styling changes through 1966. The options list continued to grow but major mechanical changes were slow in coming. Free-running front hubs were added to the factory options list in 1964, but 1965 brought a whole new line of engines to the lineup. Ford had been offering its durable 223 six for 12 years as a baseline plant. In the face of Chevy's bigger 261-cid six-cylinders as intermediate offerings, the 223 was beginning to look the wimp. Ford had opened the 223 up to 262 inches in 1964 but didn't offer it in 4x4s. Ford's new 240 and 300-cid sixes took up the challenge as base and intermediate engines. The 300-cid was an especially popular option, because it combined the torque and economy characteristics of a six with some of the oomph of a V-8. Both the new engines were based on the old 223 but had seven main bearings instead of four and a whole passel of other advancements.

By 1973, the Bronco line had narrowed to one model. The roof was no longer easily removed and the windshield no longer folded down. Many of the hard work goodies had left the options list but with power steering, automatic, the Ranger package, and a number of other features, it had become a very civilized machine. You could still order it with trail-beating 4.10 gears, front and rear limited-slip differentials, auxiliary fuel tanks, and skid plates. This extremely original 1973 belongs to George Wright, a.k.a. the Bronco Man, and has only 55,000 miles on it. It has the Ranger trim package, V-8, automatic, and power steering. This is an extremely valuable find.

The old 292-cid was finally dropped in 1965 in favor of the 352 FE block. The Y and FE blocks shared similar roots. The 332 and 352-cid FE engines had been introduced in cars for the 1958 model year and were a development of the Y-block 239, 270, 292, and 312-cid powerplants. Ten years later, the 352 was far from the top-o-the-line position it had held in 1958 but was still a big jump in power compared to the 292. Improvement or not, the 4-bys were still getting the low-power options in these years. The 4x2 trucks were benefiting from the big 390 FE in two and four-barrel configuration.

Nineteen sixty-six saw the introduction of the shortbed 4x4 Styleside and Flareside F-100 in 115-inch wheelbase. This is the only year in which these were made, though short two-wheel versions had been around since 1961. The Monobeam coil spring front suspension debuted in the F-100 short- and long-wheelbase models, which coincided with the introduction of the the same setup in the first Broncos. A shorty F-100 4x4 is a highly stylish item. It has only one failing and that's the ridiculous single-speed Spicer 21 transfer case. It's only redeeming characteristic is the fact that it's a married case, which did eliminate the low-hanging aspect of the earlier Spicer 24. Fortunately, a later two-speed is an easy swap that retains an original flair but offers better off-pavement performance.

The 1966 long wheelbase 4x4s got stretched from 120 to 129 inches, two years after the two-wheelers got the longer ride. The Styleside F-100 4x4s finally got the fancy bed instead of the old mismatched box of previous years. These were available with storage boxes built into the side of the bed. The F-250 4-by hung on that last year with the old style bed.

Mechanically, the vaunted New Process 435 four-speed, with its extra-low 6.69-1 first gear, saw its first service with Ford in 1966, replacing the dated T-98A. There were still no automatics available. Power steering had been an option in two-wheel drive trucks since 1965 but remained a much wished for option in the all-terrain rigs.

The 1966s are probably the best of the breed in terms of features, options and, arguably, looks. They embodied many of the new goodies Ford had in mind for the new rigs they were set to debut for 1967. They

In the last year of production, the Bronco was very refined but the options list was very narrow. You were also likely to find odd assemblages of parts and options packages as Ford used up as much of its stockpile as possible. Some experts have said that the Bronco's usually good fit and finish slipped quite a bit in 1977. Still, a 1977 is the most popular year because it is the most refined. This is George Wright's 1977, which he has owned since new. Though it is a Ranger, George has left the striping off.

Would you buy this Bronco? In every way but one, it's a perfect specimen of a 1977, but those cut rear fenders would drop the value to a collector wanting originality. On the other hand, some owners want to run larger tires, and a nicely done "fenderectomy" is a plus. What you do with your Bronco is really nobody else's business, but a small group of Bronco owners from both camps were polled on the "to cut, or not to cut" question. The consensus was that an uncut good example should remain uncut for history's sake. Especially since there are so many cut examples out there to be found.

are currently the most popular year for this era of Ford truck, with the short F-100 heading the list for desirability. Parts are relatively easy to obtain and good examples are not terribly difficult to find. Prices are very slowly rising but it may be a long while before these trucks get into the high buck area. Now is the time to buy and enjoy!

Taking the Lead: 1967–1972

1967 was a time for big changes in the Ford truck line. As 4x4 popularity rose to then unheard of heights, the options list on them began to rival the 4x2 trucks in many ways. The 1967s were completely redesigned in more than just a cosmetic sense. Along with the fresh, angular look came comfort and convenience, features never before seen in the Ford truck line. Three trim levels were offered, Standard, Custom, and Ranger. The Ranger package had a deep cushion seat, carpeting, padded door panels, and lots of chrome trim. Interior dimensions were increased and the familiar double-sided Ford ignition key appeared. The short-wheelbase trucks stayed at the 115-inch wheelbase but the long F-100 and 250s stretched to 131 inches.

Initially, the mechanical lineup stayed pretty much the same but by 1968 a few changes began to creep in. That year, the 360 FE replaced the 352-cid as the V-8 option, which upped the power from 208 to 215 horsepower. Ford still steadfastly refused to offer four-barrel or larger displacement engines in the 4x4 line. The front axle underwent some evolution when the closed-knuckle style Spicer 44 was replaced in mid-1968 with a more serviceable open-knuckle type.

Other than minor trim changes, not much happened until 1970, when the Ranger XLT package debuted. Along with the color-keyed, pleated cloth seats, wood grain dash inserts, improved mirrors, and extra interior lighting, the XLT package featured a much more comfortable seat, a double ration of sound deadening material, and wall-to-wall carpets. Things were beginning to get nice inside the new Ford 4x4s.

Also offered in 1970 were a variety of special packages aimed right at the working man. The Contractor Special included a locking toolbox, rear step bumper, and extended mirrors. The Farm and Ranch Special included sideboards, the step bumper, and the mirrors. A Heavy Duty Special came with uprated springs, larger alternator and battery, the step bumper, and extended mirrors.

Factory-installed air conditioning finally came into the option package for the 4x4 trucks in 1971, but this style of truck was destined to end its days without an automatic transmission or power steering option. The 240-cid was dropped this year as standard fare for the F-250 and the three-speed followed. The 300, NP-435 became SOP for F-250s.

The 1967–1971 Ford pickups are seeing an upswing in popularity, though not to the degree that the 1967–1972 Chevy trucks have experienced. This is a little strange, since these Fords are the ones that finally broke Chevy's hold on the truck sales lead in 1969. Prices are still very reasonable and a big selection awaits the shopper. They are practical in every sense and easy to restore or repair. Parts are easy to find. The lack of power steering makes these Fords a bit of a struggle to drive for those lacking upper body strength, though later PS systems can be adapted in with some effort.

The Pony That Started the Sport-Ute Stampede: Bronco 1966–1977

While the introduction of the Bronco can't really be called the beginning of the sport utility era, it was certainly one of the milestones that helped shape public opinion in that direction. From the outset, the Bronco was marketed as a day-to-day and recreational vehicle as well as a worker. It was designed to be comfortable enough to used as "the family car," yet tough enough to be used as a light truck and four-wheeler. In 1960, the total market for light-duty 4x4 utilities was about 11,000 units. By 1965, this market had grown to over 35,000 units, consisting of IHC Scouts, Jeeps of various types and the few Land Rovers, Toyotas, and Nissans that were imported. Ford analysts looked at the market and predicted a jump to at least 70,000 units in just five years. Yep, the time was right for the Bronco!

The Bronco was introduced in August of 1965 in three variations, a doorless, open-topped roadster, a pickup, and a fully enclosed station wagon. Prophetically, the pickup was called the "sports utility" model. The Bronco body was constructed so that any of the three styles could be converted into any of the others by switching parts. A station wagon, for example, could be converted to a sports utility pickup by removing the full-length top, installing a bolted-in bulkhead behind the seats, and topping off with the pickup cab.

While the Bronco was not a huge station wagon, it had more room than the competing short-wheelbase 4x4 rigs. With a 92-inch wheelbase and 152-inch overall length, it was one of those vehicles that was a "just right" compromise between size on the trail and day-to-day usefulness elsewhere. It was aimed directly at sportsmen and working folks who needed the 4x4 utility but needed a second means of day-to-day transport.

The Bronco had a few mechanical firsts. It was the first nonmilitary production utility rig to use coil springs. The Monobeam front axle used a pair of soft coils for a good ride (by utility standards anyway) and more car-like road manners. Coils have remained a big part of 4x4 development to this day. Bronco was also the first short-wheelbase utility to offer a V-8, countering an industry trend to deliberately underpower 4x4s. In March of 1966, the famous 289-cid Ford smallblock was announced as an option to the standard 170-cid six. The 289's 200 horsepower almost doubled the 105 ponies of the six.

The Bronco was a little short of luxury features at first, but an astounding variety of practical goodies were available. One of the most striking, at least to dedicated four-wheelers, was the availability of limited-slips front and rear. True four-wheel drive was possible! Other goodies included skid plates, an auxiliary fuel tank, front and rear PTOs, snowplow, tow

Until 1975, when the 302 became the standard powerplant, a six-cylinder was the baseline engine. The 170-cid (1966–1971) and 200-cid (1972–1974) sixes were originally designed for the Falcon cars and Econoline vans of earlier years. They were very light in weight, economical, and reliable as gravity. Power was another matter. At low speeds, they were adequate, but highway running was not a forte. When you look at power specs, you will note the 105-horsepower rating for the 170 and an 84-horsepower rating for the 200. What? Emission controls did take a bite but the major drop was on paper. About 1972, the automotive industry adopted the more accurate SAE net power and torque measurements and they were roughly 30 percent lower. A 170 measured the same way still had an edge, making 89 SAE net horsepower.

The 289/302 engines were very similar in appearance and power output. Again, the SAE net measurements took the power listings down on paper but emission controls brought the 302 down to an abysmal low of 125 horsepower in 1976. The 289, by comparison, pumped out an honest 150 net horsepower in 1968. The hottest of the 302s were the 1969–1973 models that made 139 net horsepower. Torque, however, was very close for both engines at 241 and 237 pound-feet respectively.

The early models were often plain in appearance. This 1967 has the bench seat and rubber floormats and is missing the radio. It does have a heater and the new to the year padded dash and seat belts, as well as the new chrome-plated T-handle transfer case shifter.

Compared to a 1967, this 1973 is the lap-o-luxury. This rig is bone stock down to the AM radio and the period aftermarket air conditioning unit. The then-new Ranger package nicely plushed out the interior. Three interior colors were available that year—ginger, blue, and avocado. This one is the attractive blue.

hooks, winch, free-wheeling hubs, compass, two-way radio, tach, and a 4,700 GVW package. Ford certainly went whole hog on the practicality aspect.

The Bronco had a good sales year in 1966, with 20,176 units being sold. Ford entered 1967 with a new Sport Bronco package that included bright instrument panel molding, chrome horn ring, vinyl door panels with bright trim, a hardboard headliner with bright trim, armrests, and a lighter for the inside. Outside trim included chrome bumpers with bumperguards plus bright metal trim on the driprails, grille, headlights, and taillights. Further dress-up included a chrome tailgate release handle, a chrome "Sport Bronco" emblem, and bright wheel covers.

Once the momentum started, a variety of changes came to the Bronco. Some of these were probably market driven, such as the elimination of the roadster model from the lineup after the 1968 model year. The pickup hung on through 1972 but was finally discontinued due to lack of sales. As time went by, Ford gradually adopted many of the commonly ordered options as standard equipment. Many of the practical items that were noteworthy in the early models disappeared from the options lists.

Introduced in 1973, the Ranger package proved to be the most popular option package for the Bronco. This luxo outfit came with unique exterior paint schemes and white striping on the lower body, as well as a special "Ranger" spare tire cover. Inside, three color choices, with cloth houndstooth inserts, full carpeting, and woodgrain trim on the doors. The new automatic transmission and power steering options blended nicely with the new luxury options.

Throughout its 11-year run, the Bronco received relatively minor mechanical refinements and most of those came well behind the competition. The Broncos chief sales rival, the Chevy Blazer, was introduced in 1969 with power steering and automatic transmission. The Bronco didn't get these upgrades until 1973. Disc brakes appeared on the Blazer in 1971. The Bronco was held back until 1976. These sorts of overlooked items, and others, lend credence to the common belief that after the initial developmental push, Ford management regarded the Bronco as a "back burner" product. Despite this, the Bronco sold well even though the automotive press was less than kind.

The early Bronco was replaced with a new version after 1977. Since then, they have become immensely popular with avid four-wheelers and collectors alike. As a trail brawler, they have the dimensions and adaptability to be the ideal base for a variety of modifications to enhance their already considerable trail prowess. A big part of the aftermarket is geared towards building hop-up pieces for the Bronco.

From the stock outlook, many replacement parts are being reproduced for restoration. This includes body parts, interior trim, and mechanical parts. Some of the shortcomings noted during production years can be sorted out using re-engineered parts from the aftermarket, and improvements like front disc brakes and power steering can be installed via aftermarket kits.

Popularity tends to bring the aftermarket producers into the game but it also brings up the prices. Depending on where you live, you may have to shell out upwards of $10,000 for a decently restored Bronco. Generally the later rigs are the most popular, particularly the 1977s. The 1966–1968 roadsters are almost unheard of and pickups are seldom seen. These low production early units may one day become hot collectors items.

Many Broncos have had their rear wheelwells cut out for larger tires. This generally decreases the value for collectors. The Ranger package adds a bit to the price. Nobody seems to want the six-cylinder rigs and the three-speed manuals are often replaced with four-speed NP-435 truck trannies or automatics. If the conversion is well done, it need not detract much from the value.

Hot-Rod Four Wheeler: 1971–1975 Stroppe Bronco

From the collectability standpoint, the most spectacular versions of the Bronco were the ones built by Bill Stroppe & Associates starting in 1971 and ending sometime in 1974. Stroppe had been actively desert racing the Broncos since 1966, when he had been given six crash-tested 1966 models, "to see what he could do with them." Stroppe had an illustrious racing career that went back into the 1930s and included some of the early 1950s Pan-American Races. Once he had hauled the Broncos to his shop, he was able to put together one good racer and a backup.

Desert racing was in its infancy then. Most of it was done in the deserts east of Los Angeles. The big Baja desert races were still a few years away. Among the first of the desert races was one that was organized by Brian Chuchua, later a big-time Jeep dealer and racer, in a Riverside, California, dry wash. Stroppe was prepared to race one of his newly refurbished V-8 rigs when a Ford rep asked if he wouldn't mind running one of the six-cylinder rigs instead of a V-8. Stroppe agreed. He took a 6-cylinder Ford demonstrator, a roadster model, added a roll bar, stripped it of anything not vital and went a-racin'. Stroppe competed against his own V-8s in the race and against all the odds, the six-banger won easily.

When the Baja races got started in the late 1960s, Stroppe actively campaigned the Broncos. He was reputedly the first builder to install power steering and automatic transmissions in the desert racers. The Broncos did well. With Stroppe building and Parnelli Jones driving, the succession of Stroppe Broncos was hard to beat. The most famous of these was "Big Oly."

Stroppe was doing prep work on a variety of race cars when he was approached to do a limited production street version of his red, white and blue "Baja Bronco" for sale through the Ford dealer network. Starting in 1971, the Broncos arrived from Ford in stock mechanical condition but with a particular set of options and painted in the Stroppe colors. When they arrived, each vehicle was equipped with the Bronco Sport package, a bench rear seat, swing-away tire carrier, 302 V-8 with the heavy duty 11-inch clutch, 800- pound/inch front springs, the extra cooling package, the auxiliary fuel tank and skid plate, and the 4,700-pound GVW package (which included the 3,300-pound rear axle). This basic setup cost you $5,434 before Bill got hold of it.

When Stroppe finished, the Bronco emerged with a three-speed automatic transmission (not available from Ford until 1973), a Saginaw power steering conversion (also not available till 1973), a roll bar, dual shocks front and rear, 8.5x15 wheels with gates 10.00x15 Commando tires installed (some came with 9.15x15 tires), a class two trailer hitch, a rubberized steering wheel, cut out rear fenderwells with fender flares, and special trim which included the "Baja Bronco" nameplate. This was the basic package.

To this you could add a beefed up 302 equipped with a four-barrel carburetor (never offered from the factory) that pumped out 158 horsepower at 5,000 rpm and 242 pound-feet at 2,000 rpm (stock output was 139 horsepower and 237 pound-feet). A much stronger and more positive Detroit Locker could be installed in the rear axle. Air conditioning, a tach,

Major Bronco Changes- 1966-1977

March 1966- -289 V8 introduced

1967-
- Sport Bronco package introduced.
- seat belts introduced
- electric wipers standard
- dual brake system introduced
- self-adjusting brakes introduced
- optional wheel cover design changed
- T-handle transfer case shifter introduced

1968-
- side marker lights on lower fenders added
- swinging 270 degree tire carrier introduced
- 302 V8 replaces 289 late in year
- heater and defroster made standard
- emission controls introduced

1969-
- roadster model eliminated
- fold-down windshield eliminated
- removable hardtop eliminated on station wagon
- body strengthened
- amber lenses replace clear on front marker lamps
- "302" emblem appears on front fender above marker light for V8 models
- reflectors appear in rear below taillights
- 9.375in clutch made standard on 6-cyl

1970-
- flush-mounted marker lamps installed higher up replace previous protruding lights
- shoulder seat belt harness introduced
- main and auxiliary fuel tank capacities reduced from 14.5 and 11.5gal to 12.7 and 10.3gal to contain evaporative control apparatus
- padded dash introduced

1971-
- Dana 44 front axle replaces Dana 30
- remote control outside driver mirror introduced
- mid-year, front bucket seats made standard
- mid-year, freewheeling hubs made standard
- high performance Stroppe Bronco made available

1972-
- 170 six not available in California
- standard GVW uprated from 3,900 to 4,300lbs
- two optional GVW available, 4,500lbs and 4,900lbs
- main fuel tank reduced in capacity to 12.2gal
- auxiliary fuel tank reduced in capacity to 7.5gal
"302" emblem disappears from front fender of V8s

1973-
- pickup discontinued
- power steering option available (V8 only)
- 3-speed automatic option available (V8 only)
- 200cid six replaces 170cid
- Ranger package introduced

1974-
- T-handle transfer case shifter replaced with stick
- solid state ignition introduced in some models
- dome light replaces map light

1975-
- 200cid six eliminated
- catalytic converter introduced

1976-
- non-power front disc brakes introduced
- rear brake size increased from 10x2.50 to 11x2.25
- rear wheel bearing size increases
- quick ratio power steering introduced
- front sway bar introduced
- stronger triangulated rear axle housing introduced
- front limited slip option deleted
- Special Decor option introduced

1977-
- fuel fillers located behind doors
- 14.4gal plastic fuel tank introduced
- rear side marker moves to vertical position
- power assist added to front disc brakes
- V8 compression ratio raised from 8.0 to 8.4:1, power increases from 125 to 133 hp
- Dura Spark ignition introduced

and full carpeting were available to enhance the interior. This whole zoot package brought the price up to $7,663. Also, since Stroppe modified the rigs on an individual basis, many custom modifications could be made by prior arrangement.

An original Stoppe Baja Bronco is a very valuable item. Valuable enough that copies are beginning to emerge, produced and sold at very high prices by profiteers. Since many of the records at Stroppe have been lost in the years since they were produced, it may be difficult to verify a Stroppe. Especially a restored one. Obviously, original paperwork from Ford and Stroppe that verify the serial number is a good first step. An unrestored vehicle, still in original livery, that's obviously had the wear and tear of 25 years is a fairly safe bet as well. An original Stroppe Bronco is the Bronco buff's No. 1 dream. Don't expect to pick one up very cheap.

FORD 4X4 TRUCK PRODUCTION: 1959–1977

	Styleside	Flareside	Platform/Stake	Chassis/Cab
1959 F-100	NA	NA	NA	NA
1959 F-250	NA	NA	NA	NA
1960 F-100	4,334	964	-	442
1960 F-250	1,806	828	98	411
1961 F-100	255	2,468	-	180
1961 F-250	149	1,621	78	359
1962 F-100	NA	NA	NA	NA
1962 F-250	NA	NA	NA	NA
1963 F-100	2,809	967	-	179
1963 F-250	1,835	865	89	348
1964 F-100	2,922	802	-	330
1964 F-250	2,232	1,028	68	410
1965 F-100	NA	NA	NA	NA
1965 F-250	NA	NA	NA	NA
1966 F-100	4,493	839	-	145
1966 F-250	3,559	1,595	29	644
1967 F-100	3,445	481	-	135
1967 F-250	3,836	915	29	426
1968 F-100	NA	NA	NA	NA
1968 F-250	NA	NA	NA	NA
1969 F-100	7,950	465	-	56
1969 F-250	10,286	973	30	641
1970 F-100	NA	NA	ANA	NA
1970 F-250	NA	NA	NA	NA
1971 F-100	12,870	591	-	96
1971 F-250	16,164	635	23	649
1972 F-100	18,323	492	-	96
1972 F-250	21,654	538	-	-

BRONCO SALES: 1966–1977

	Roadster (U130)	Pickup (U140)	Station Wagon (U150)
1966	4,090	6,930	12,756
1967	698	2,602	10, 930
1968	NA	2,210	NA
1969	-	2,317	18,639
1970	-	1,700	16,750
1971	-	1,503	18,281
1972	-	NA	NA
1973	-	-	21,894
1974	-	-	18,786
1975	-	-	11,273
1976	-	-	13,625
1977	-	-	13,335

Stroppe Bronco: 1971–1974

Total number-   552 units

1959–1960 SPECIFICATIONS

Engines:
Type-	6-cyl, inline OHV (STD)
	V8,OHV, (OPT)
Displacement-	223cid
	292cid
Power-	139hp @ 4,200rpm
	186hp @ 4,000rpm
Torque-	207lbs-ft @ 1,800–2,700rpm
	269lbs-ft @ 2,200–2,700rpm
B&S	
	3.62x3.60in
	3.75x3.30in
CR-	8.3:1

Transmissions:
Type-	3 speed, T-87 (STD)
	4-speed, T-98A (OPT)
Ratios-	1=2.79, 2=1.70, 3=1.00, R=2.87 (6-cyl)
	1=2.59, 2=1.58, 3=1.00, R=2.66 (V8)
	1=6.40, 2=3.09, 3=1.68, 4=1.00, R=7.82

Transfer Box:
Type-	2-speed, Spicer 24 divorced
Ratio-	High range: 1.00-1
	Low range: 1.86-1

Axles:
Front type-	Spicer 44-4F, full-floating
Rear type-	Ford 9-inch, semi-floating (F-100)
	Spicer 60, full-floating (F-250)
Ratios-	3.89 (F-100)
	4.56 (F-250)

Tires (Typical):
Type:	various highway and non-directional
Size:	6.70x15 (F-100 STD)
	7.10x15 (F-100 OPT)
	6.50x16 (F-250 STD)
	7.00x17.5 (F-250 OPT)

Dimensions & Capacities:
LxWxH-	NA
Wheelbase-	118in
Curb weight-	3563 (F-100)
	3853 (F-250)
Fuel capacity-	18gal
GVW-	5,600 (F-100)
	6,400 (F-250)

DESIRABLE OPTIONS: 1959–1960

292 V8, four-speed trans, two-tone paint, flareside bed, Custom Cab, Equa-Lock limited slip rear axle, front grille guard, aftermarket locking hubs, radio, tow hooks.

1961–1966 SPECIFICATIONS

Engines:

Type-	6-cyl, inline OHV (STD)
	V8, OHV (OPT)
Displacement-	223cid (STD '61–64)
	240cid (STD '65–66)
	300cid (OPT '65–66)
	292cid (OPT '61–64)
	352cid (OPT '65–66)
Power-	139hp @ 4,200rpm
	150hp @ 4,000rpm
	170hp @ 3,600rpm
	186hp @ 4,000rpm
	208hp @ 4,400rpm
Torque-	207lbs-ft @ 1,800–2,700rpm
	234lbs-ft @ 2,200rpm
	283lbs-ft @ 2,200rpm
	269lbs-ft @ 2,200–2,700rpm
	315lbs-ft @ 2,400rpm
B&S-	3.62x3.60in
	4.00x3.18in
	4.00x3.98in
	3.75x3.30in
	4.00x3.50in
CR-	8.3:1
	9.2:1
	8.4:1
	8.0:1
	8.9:1

Transmissions:

Type-	3-speed, T-87 (STD '61–65)
	3-speed, T-89F (STD '66)
	4-speed, T-98A (OPT '61–65)
	4-speed, NP-435 (OPT '66)
Ratios-	1=2.79, 2=1.70, 3=1.00, R=2.87 (6-cyl)
	1=2.59, 2=1.58, 3=1.00, R=2.66 (V8)
	1=2.99, 2=1.55, 3=1.00, R= NA (T-89)
	1=6.39, 2=3.09, 3=1.68, 4=1.00, R=7.82 (T-98)
	1=6.69, 2=3.34, 3=1.66, 4=1.00, R=8.26 (NP-435)

Transfer Box:

Type-	2-speed, Spicer 24 divorced
	Single-Speed, Spicer 21 married ('66 F-100)
Ratio-	High range: 1.00-1
	Low range: 1.86-1
Ratio-	1:1

Axles:

Front type-	Spicer 44-4F, full-floating
Rear type-	Ford 9-inch, semi-floating (F-100)
	Spicer 60, ful- floating (F-250)
Ratios-	3.89 (F-100)
	4.56 (F-250)

Tires (Typical):

Type:	various highway and non-directional
Size:	6.70x15 (F-100 STD)
	7.10x15 (F-100 OPT)
	6.50x16 (F-250 STD)
	7.00x17.5 (F-250 OPT)

Dimensions & Capacities:

LxWxH-	NA
Wheelbase-	118in
Curb weight-	3563 (F-100)
	3853 (F-250)
Fuel capacity-	18gal
GVW-	5,600 (F-100)
	6,400 (F-250)

DESIRABLE OPTIONS: 1961–1966

292 or 352 V8. Four-speed trans, Equa-Lock limited slip rear differential, Custom Cab, two-tone paint, wrap-around rear window (Styleside only), padded dash, tinted glass, front grille guard, chrome bumpers, freewheeling hubs, alternator, short wheelbase F-100 (1966).

1967–1972 SPECIFICATIONS

Engines:

Type-	6-cyl, inline OHV (STD)
	V8,OHV (OPT)
Displacement-	240cid
	300cid (OPT)
	352cid (OPT '67)
	360cid (OPT '67–72)
Power-	150hp @ 4,000rpm
	165hp @ 3,600rpm
	208hp @ 4,400rpm (352)
	215hp @ 4,400rpm (360)
Torque-	234lbs-ft @ 2,200rpm
	294lbs-ft @ 2,200rpm
	315lbs-ft @ 2,400rpm (352)
	327lbs-ft @ 2,600rpm (360)
B&S-	4.00x3.18in
	4.00x3.98in
	4.00x3.50in (352)
	4.00x3.50in (360)
CR-	9.2:1
	8.8:1
	8.9:1
	8.4:1

Transmissions:

Type-	3-speed, T-89F (STD '67–71)
	4-speed, NP-435 (STD '72, OPT '67–71)
Ratios-	1=2.99, 2=1.55, 3=1.00, R= NA
	1=6.69, 2=3.34, 3=1.66, 4=1.00, R=8.26

Transfer Box:

Type-	2-speed, Spicer 24 divorced (F-250)
	1-Speed, Spicer 21 married (F-100)
Ratio-	High range: 1.00-1
	Low range: 1.86-1
Ratio-	1.00:1

Axles:

Front type-	Spicer 44, full-floating
Rear type-	Ford 9-inch, semi-floating (F-100)
	Spicer 60, full-floating (F-250)

Ratios-	3.70 (STD F-100)
	3.50, 4.10 (OPT F-100)
	4.10 (F-250)

Tires (Typical):

Type:	various highway and non-directional
Size:	G-78x15 (F-100 STD)
	6.70x15 (F-100 OPT)
	6.50x16 (F-250 STD)
	8.00x17.5 (F-250 OPT)

Dimensions & Capacities:

LxWxH-	188.9x79.8x75in (F-100 SWB)
	204.3x79.9x77.5in (F-100-250 LWB)
Wheelbase-	115in
	131in
Curb weight-	3,750 (F-100 SWB)
	3,805 (F-100 LWB)
	4,110 (F-250)
Fuel capacity-	18gal
GVW-	4,600 (F-100 STD)
	5,600 (F-100 OPT)
	6,300 (F-250 STD)
	7,700 (F-250 OPT)

DESIRABLE OPTIONS: 1967–1972

300cid six, 352 or 360 V8, four-speed transmission, Equa-Lock limited slip rear differential, front tow hooks, two-tone paint, Ranger package, Ranger XLT package, Custom package, Contractors Special, Camper Special, Farm & Ranch Special, Heavy Duty Special, free-wheeling hubs, grille guard, air conditioning, under-bed toolboxes, power brakes, auxiliary fuel tank.

BRONCO SPECIFICATIONS: 1966–1972

Engines:

Type-	6-cyl, inline OHV (STD)
	V8, OHV (OPT)
Displacement-	
	170cid (STD '66–72)
	200cid (STD '73–74)
	289cid (OPT '66–68)
	302cid (OPT '69–74, STD '75–77)
Power-	105hp @ 4,400rpm
	84hp @ 3,800rpm (net)
	200hp @ 4,400rpm
	139hp @ 4,400rpm (net '73)
	158hp @ 5,000rpm (net Stroppe)
Torque-	158lbs-ft @ 2,400rpm
	131lbs-ft @ 2,400rpm (net)
	300lbs-ft @ 2,400rpm
	237lbs-ft @ 2,400rpm (net '73)
	242lbs-ft @ 2,000rpm (net Stroppe)

B&S-	3.50x2.94in
	3.68x3.13in
	4.00x2.87in
	4.00x3.00
CR-	9.1:1
	8.3:1
	9.3:1
	8.6:1 ('73)

Transmissions:

Type-	3-speed, Ford Model 303 (STD)
	3-speed, automatic C-4 (OPT '73–77)
Ratios-	1=3.41, 2=1.86, 3=1.00, R=
	1=2.46, 2=1.46. 3=1.00, R=

Transfer Box:

Type-	2-speed, Spicer 20
Ratio-	High range: 1.00-1
	Low range: 2.46-1

Axles:

Front type-	Spicer 30, full-floating ('66–70)
	Spicer 44, full-floating ('71–77)
Rear type-	Ford 9-inch, semi-floating
Ratios-	4.10 (STD 6-cyl))
	3.50 (OPT V8, STD '76–77)
	4.56 (OPT '66–68)

Tires (Typical):

Type:	various highway and non-directional
Size:	7.35x15 (STD '69)
	E78x15 (STD '77)
	6.50x16 (OPT '69)
	L-78x15 (OPT '77)

Dimensions & Capacities:

LxWxH-	152.1x68.8x71.4in ('66 Station Wagon)
Wheelbase-	92in
Curb weight-	3,025 ('66 SW)
	3,490 ('77 SW)
Fuel capacity-	14.5/12.7gal '66–67
	12.2/7.5gal '72–76
	14.4/7.5gal '77
GVW-	3,900 (STD '68)
	4,400 (STD '77)
	4,900 (OPT '77)

DESIRABLE OPTIONS: 1966-1977 BRONCO

V8 engine, automatic transmission, power brakes, power steering, limited slip front or rear axles, Bronco Sport Package, Ranger Package, Custom Appearance Package, bucket seats, Convenience Group, hand throttle, skid plates, auxiliary fuel tanks, GVW package, free-wheeling front hubs, front tow hooks, swing-away spare tire carrier, tachometer.

Chapter 9

Toyota and Nissan— The Japanese Connection

Japanese-built 4x4s play a major role in the current American market. Their efforts here began in the late 1950s as Nissan and Toyota analyzed the market and began importing high-quality utility vehicles that often beat the American and British built 4-bys at their own games. In a humble, understated but utterly unstoppable way, the Japanese carved out a niche for themselves in the American 4x4 market.

Nissan Patrol

The Nissan Motor Company can trace its origins back to 1911. First known as the Kwaishinsha Company, then the DAT Motor Car Company and the Jidosha Seizo Company, they finally became the familiar Nissan Motor Company in 1934. Along the way, they marketed a line of popular and practical cars that became known as the "Datsun," a name that would later help them gain a marketing foothold in America.

By 1938, Nissan had ceased building cars and devoted 100 percent of its output to commercial and military vehicles. They continued building large numbers of 4x2 trucks, most notably the Nissan 180, which was arguably the Japanese army's best truck, and aircraft engines during World War II.

Nissan got into the 4x4 game in the early 1950s by marketing a jeep-like utility vehicle they called the 4W-60. By the late 1950s, this unit had evolved into the Patrol models that became much less a jeep clone and more a unique, world-class 4x4. Patrols were marketed all over the world, earning a fabulous reputation, and finally arrived in the United States in late 1961 for the 1962 model year.

Where the 4W-60 had closely resembled the flat-fendered Jeep, the L-60 bore a strong resemblance to the British Land Rover. Under the skin, however, there was no similarity. One common complaint among the buyers of the more common short-wheelbase utilities was lack of power. Nissan answered with a powerful 242-cid (3,956-cc), OHV inline six that made 125 horsepower at 3,400 rpm and 210 pound-feet of torque at 1,600 rpm. This blew away all the American-built short-wheelbase utilities, the Land Rover 88, and was rivaled only by the six-cylinder Toyota Land Cruiser of the same vintage. This engine also had an optional waterproofing kit that took the standard 28-inch fording depth (very respectable in itself) to a whopping 40 inches.

The Patrol had a nearly bulletproof drivetrain that featured a three-speed manual transmission, beefy axles with 4.10 gears, and a two-speed transfer case with a reasonably low 2.26-1 low range. Period road tests by *Four Wheeler* magazine touted the Patrol's on and off-highway competence and questioned the low numbers of vehicles being imported. The suspension was highly praised for ride comfort and flexibility. It featured a standard front anti-sway bar, which may have been the first such offering on a utility 4x4.

The only serious reservation, noted in some tests, was the lack of a four-speed transmission. The 2.90-1 first gear was regarded as a bit too high. Oddly, reverse gear was a "getting there" 4-1. By comparison, Jeeps from this general era could be ordered with an optional four-speed Warner Gear, T-98 transmission that featured a 6.3-1 first gear. In some ways the Patrol was like the Model T Ford, able to back up things it couldn't go up frontways!

That first year, only the soft top L-60 model was available in the United States. In 1963, the hardtop KL-60 went on sale that featured a steel top with a pair of side swinging rear doors that also split in the middle like Dutch doors. The vehicle came with a standard tool kit that was very complete, a swing away rear tire carrier and seating for seven. All in all, the Patrol was a darn nice package. Why then, does nobody remember it?

From late 1961 to late 1969, a total of 2,616 Patrols were imported. Not exactly record sales. After the glowing praise heaped upon it by magazines, one wonders why. While period magazines like *Four Wheeler* regularly featured Nissan Patrol ads or tests, it seems that Datsun cars and pickups had priority at the dealers, and the 4x4s were a back-o-the-lot afterthought. The sport-utility rage had only just begun. The small economy car rage was well on its way. Perhaps the cars were just cuter.

Other than some power upgrades, first to 135 and finally 145 ponies, the Patrol stayed pretty much the same throughout its short run in America. Like many of the Japanese vehicles of the era, rust protection is not a strong point. Mechanically, they are well built and strong, though they have an odd clutch arrangement that is particularly difficult to repair. Parts are the major difficulty. This writer could find few parts sources in the United States and no club activity at all.

A handful of Nissan Patrols remain, most of them sitting in the weeds awaiting spare parts. Despite their attributes, they have no current collector value or interest, except to a few diehards. Their future prospects are equally grim. If you dare to be different, perhaps a Patrol is in your future. As four-wheelers go, you could do lots worse, but collecting Patrols will certainly be a lonely hobby.

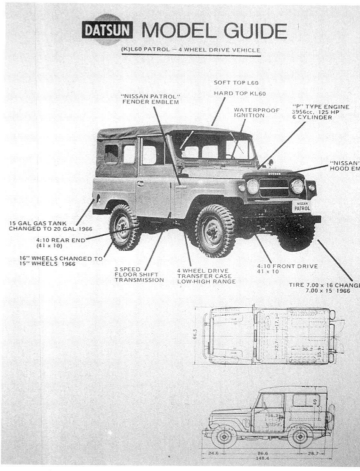

DATSUN MODEL GUIDE

(K)L60 PATROL — 4 WHEEL DRIVE VEHICLE

SOFT TOP L60
HARD TOP KL60
"NISSAN PATROL" FENDER EMBLEM
WATERPROOF IGNITION
"P" TYPE ENGINE 3956cc, 125 HP 6 CYLINDER
"NISSAN" HOOD EM
15 GAL GAS TANK CHANGED TO 20 GAL 1966
NISSAN PATROL
4:10 REAR END (41 x 10)
16" WHEELS CHANGED TO 15" WHEELS 1966
3 SPEED FLOOR SHIFT TRANSMISSION
4 WHEEL DRIVE TRANSFER CASE LOW-HIGH RANGE
4:10 FRONT DRIVE 41 x 10
TIRE 7.00 x 16 CHANGE 7.00 x 15 1966

The Nissan Patrol was in production from the mid-1950s all the way to 1980, essentially looking the same. Sold in the United States from 1962 to 1969 as the L60 (soft top) and KL-60 (hardtop), they sold for about $2,700. In other markets, both long- and short-wheelbase versions were available in two- and four-door styles, as well as a pickup. A total of 975 L60 soft-tops were sold in the seven-year run and 1,641 KL-60 hardtops. *Nissan Motor Corporation USA*

The AK-10 was Toyota's first light 4x4. Development began in 1942 with the capture of American 1/4-ton 4x4s. As crude as it appeared, the AK-10 was reputed to have much better off-pavement performance than the American jeeps it emulated. Assembled from bits and pieces from a variety of Toyota vehicles, the AK-10 featured a leading arm front suspension that enabled a vertical approach angle. The rear axle was mounted under the rear springs for ground clearance. Much of the bodywork (such as it was) was adapted from the KC truck line, as were the differentials and most of the rest of the running gear. It was powered by a 137.5-cid four-cylinder engine that made approximately 45 horsepower. *Toyota Motor Sales USA*

Few nonrusty Nissan Patrols remain. This is a pristine L-60 that's bone original right down to the paint. This unit may have some collectable value simply due to its extra fine condition. Nissan used a restored Patrol in some of its 1996 TV commercials.

Engine:

Type-	6-cyl, OHV
Displacement-	242cid
Power-	125hp @ 3,400rpm
	Late '62–65 - 135hp @ 3,400rpm
	'66–69 - 145hp @ 3,800rpm
Torque-	210lbs-ft @ 2,600rpm
	Late '62–65 - 225lbs-ft @ 2,000rpm
	'66–69- 235lbs-ft @ 2,000rpm
B&S-	3.375x4.5in
CR-	7.0-1
Transmission:	
Type-	3-speed manual
Ratios-	1=2.90, 2=1.56, 3=1.0, R=4.02
Transfer Case:	
Type-	Two-speed
Ratios-	High- 1-1
	Low-2.26-1
Axles:	
Rear type:	Semi-floating
Front type-	Full-floating
Ratios-	4.10-1
Tires:	
Size-	7.00-16 ('62–65)
	7.00-15 ('66–69)
Dimensions & Capacities	
LxWxH-	148.5x66.5x78
Wheelbase-	86.6in
Curb weight-	3,392lbs
Fuel capacity-	15gal ('62–65)
	20gal ('66–69)
GVW-	4,575lbs

Toyota Land Cruiser

The Toyota Land Cruiser story begins back in 1933, when Kiichiro Toyoda took over a section of his father's textile factory, the Toyoda Automatic Loom Works, Ltd., to build cars. Initially modelled after American cars of the period, including Chrysler's forward-thinking disaster, the Airflow, Kiichiro's work eventually became innovative and unique. As with the other Japanese car companies, World War II put a commercial and military priority on production. During the war Toyota produced a variety of 4x2 vehicles, the KCY 4x4 truck and a 4x4 amphibious truck based on the KCY. In 1942, captured U.S. jeeps were given close scrutiny and Toyota produced at least five AK-10 1/4-ton 4x4s that were, in concept at least, based largely on a captured Bantam jeep. The AK-10 development came too late in the war for mass production and the tiny Kurogane Type 95 "Black Medal" remained Japan's light-duty 4x4 for World War II.

Toyota jumped into the utility 4x4 market in 1951 with a 1/4-ton 4x4 that resembled, you guessed it, the American Jeep. The impetus for that development came both from the occupying Americans and the newly formed Japanese Defense Forces. Hoping to score a big American contract, development on the new vehicle started in August of 1950 and just five months later, the first prototype had been completed.

Called the BJ, it was built upon the chassis of the postwar 1-ton model SB truck and featured a 3,386-cc six-cylinder model B gas engine that made 85 horsepower at 2,400 rpm and 159 pound-feet of torque at 1,600 rpm. This engine dated back to 1938 and had originally been designed for Toyota's 1 1/2-ton Model GB truck. The GB, just like the Toyota six-cylinder engine, was modelled after a Chevrolet design of the 1930s. At first, this engine seemed like a bit of overkill compared to the smaller engines of the American and British competition, but Toyota President Eiji Toyota's decision to go with the big mill was later applauded as a masterful decision.

Resembling more than anything the original Willys Quad, the BJ was built as a commercial vehicle as well as for the military. The BJ earned some early points by being the first wheeled vehicle to climb to Mount Fuji's sixth station. Unfortunately, the stunt didn't bring a contract with the Americans, although the Toyotas sold well to the Japanese home guard and the police. Reputedly, a few found their way over here in the hands of returning American servicemen. The BJ design stayed in production through 1955, produced the last year alongside the FJ-25 models that replaced it. Other variants of the BJ design were built and sold in Japan and around the world.

The earliest brochures and advertising for the Toyota BJ used the name "Jeep." The use of that jealously guarded trademark ended soon after Willys heard about it, but it illustrates the influence that American-made 4x4s had on the world and the minds of postwar designers.

In mid-1954, the new FJ-25 was introduced with the now familiar moniker, "Land Cruiser." This name was carefully chosen by Managing Director Hanji Umehara to place the FJ in direct competition with the Jeep and the Land Rover, both doing well in various third world markets. The FJ-25 had a look all its own and a whole list of upgrades, including the bigger 95-horsepower, 236-cid six-cylinder model F gas engine that was still a very close approximation of Chevrolet's famous "Stovebolt" six. This engine beat the four-cylinder Jeeps and Land Rovers for power by a considerable margin.

The FJ-25 used a four-speed tranny with a nice 5.41-1 first gear but had only a single-speed transfer case. Offered in a soft-top, the 90-inch wheelbase bobtail had

This was Toyota's first postwar 4x4. The BJ was obviously very heavily influenced by the American Jeep. So much so that the initial models were called "Jeep." Though this trademark infringement was soon discontinued, the BJ was aimed right at the postwar markets dominated by Jeep and Land Rover. The BJ was powered by a 3,386-cc, 82-horsepower six-cylinder gas engine that was later upgraded to 85-horsepower. A four-speed truck transmission was mated to a single-speed transfer case. Axle ratios were 4.11-1. A wide variety of variations were built upon this basic design. The BJ lasted into 1955 before being replaced by the FJ-20 series of vehicles (FJ-20-29 depending on model). The early BJ should not be confused with the 1954 BJ-25 models, which were the new FJ-25 style body with the older B-series engine fitted. There were also 1974 and later BJ models. *Toyota Motor Sales USA*

The first Toyota to see the U.S. market, albeit in very small numbers, was the FJ-25. More distinctive and less jeeplike, the FJ-25 can be readily identified by its rounded rear wheel openings and unique grille. The FJ-25 was introduced in Japan in 1954 but wasn't brought to the United States until 1958. A total of 63 FJ-25s were imported in 1958 and 1959. The records show only one being sold in 1958. The 1958 and 1959 models were virtually identical. It's very likely the rigs sold in 1959 were imported in 1958. *Toyota Motor Sales USA*

If Roy Rogers likes it, it must be good! For several years in the mid-1960s, America's favorite cowboy, Roy Rogers, was the Nissan spokesperson.

a long list of practical options. As the years went by, Toyota was very accommodating to special requests, and a wide variety of body styles developed on two wheelbases.

The left-hand drive FJ-25 hit the U.S. market in 1958, just a year after Toyota Motor Sales, USA, started business in California. U.S. 4x4 sales were a marginal 63 units in 1958 and 1959 but Toyota was in it for the long haul. A total of 15,427 1/4-ton 4x4s had been produced by Toyota between 1951 and the end of 1959, but a mere handful had found their way to the United States.

In 1960, the FJ-40 was introduced worldwide with a variety of improvements over the FJ-25, and this year marked Toyota's commitment to make the Land Cruiser a force to be reckoned with on the byways of America. The Land Cruiser featured a 125-horsepower version of the 236, a three-speed, column-shift transmission and a two-speed transfer case. The odd retrograde to a "three-on-the-tree" was a decision based partly on the fact that many 4x4 manufacturers were offering three-speed boxes and the thought that the American buying public wanted the column shift three-speed. The high-torque capacity of the Toyota six was also reckoned to alleviate much of the need for a low "crawler" gear. The dash-mounted transfer case control and vacuum operated four-wheel drive engagement were two more unique features of the early 'Cruiser.

While generally similar in appearance to the FJ-25, there were a number of cosmetic differences that included the grille and the squared rear fender openings (the FJ-25s had round rear fender openings). The FJ-40 was longer and wider than the FJ-25 but on the same 90-inch wheelbase. The FJ-40 was available here in hard- or soft-top versions.

Initially, only the bobtail FJ-40 was available here but by 1963, the FJ-45 pickup version of the Land Cruiser was offered. Built upon a long-wheelbase chassis, the little 1/2 tons were sold in small numbers through the 1967 model year. Mechanically, the FJ-45 was nearly identical to the FJ-40. The front half of the body was also identical to the FJ-40 but two versions of the FJ-45 pickup bed were offered. The "L" model had a boxy, slab-sided box taken from the 4x2 Stout pickup and a 116-inch wheelbase. The "S" used a box with rounded corners with a beveled edge similar to the FJ-40 rear body and had a 104-inch wheelbase. Some of the pickups used a removable half-cab top and most had bench seats. Both pickup models are rare and very collectable but body parts can be difficult to obtain.

Another variant on the 104-inch wheelbase chassis was the four-door station wagon model FJ-45V. Again, the basic Land Cruiser was enhanced—this time with the addition of a slab-sided four-door body with upper and lower tailgates. This body was built under contract by Yamaha. The FJ-45V offered seating for six with room left over for luggage. It made a capable family rig that *Four Wheeler* rated as "one of the better back country station wag-

The early Land Cruiser interior was a mixture of the eminently practical and the unusual. As with many 4x4s of the period, a front bench seat was regarded as a necessary feature.

The unusual tailgate arrangement featured an accordion-style upper tailgate and a pair of lower side swinging "Dutch" style doors. Even with many miles of hard trails behind it, the rear doors of this early 1965 FJ still operate as they did when new.

The early FJ-40s were all pretty similar in appearance to this 1965 FJ-40 belonging to Fritz McOllough. The small windows, corrugated sides, and split rear windows are trademarks of the earlier TLCs. Though suffering the ravages of time, this old FJ is still very original and has been in the family since new.

ons available today." Today the FJ-45V is very uncommon and few examples remain. While availability of mechanical parts is on par with the FJ-40 of that era, body parts (beyond those that it shares with the FJ-40) are very difficult to obtain. The FJ-45 Wagon Registry was recently organized to locate the remaining station wagons and to open an information sharing exchange with their owners. Their collectability appears to be on the upswing.

Getting back to the FJ-40, there are only a few exterior changes to note on its 23-year run in the United States. Visually, it's very difficult to tell them apart. The 1960–1961 models had "Land Cruiser" on the bar just above the grille. They also had round marker lights on the lower edge of the nose just below the headlights, round turn signal lamps on the headlights, and bumpers with curved ends. In 1962, the Land Cruiser name left the front end and was replaced by a "Toyota" in the grille.

In 1964, the vent under the windshield was eliminated. In late 1965 the hardtop was fitted with much larger side windows and corner windows were added. At the same time, the accordion style upper rear tailgate was replaced by a more conventional one-piece unit. They called the new top the "Skytop" because of all the extra visibility. A padded dash was added in 1968.

In 1969, the small marker lamps were removed from the nose and rectangular combination marker/turn signal lamps replaced the round signal lamps on the fenders. Also the "Toyota" in the grille grew in size and the bumper became a flat channel instead of curved on the ends. As of 1974, the round taillights were replaced by rectangular units. In 1975, larger, two-color front marker/turn signal lamps appeared and the windshield wipers were moved from above, to below the windshield. Also, side-swinging "ambulance" style rear doors replaced the upper and lower tailgate. Late 1976 brought rear vent windows and from there to 1983, it's *really* tough to tell them apart without looking at titles or VIN numbers.

Mechanical Upgrades

The Land Cruiser was upgraded many times in its long run. Here are some of the major mechanical ones. The later units are most desirable from the refinement point of view but the old ones are nicely quirky.

1963- *A three-speed floor shift was optional in place of the column shift.

1968- *The 10-spline axle shafts were replaced by much stronger 30-spline units.
*The front axle ball joints are replaced by Birfield-type CV joints.
*The Siamesed center exhaust ports on the cylinder head are replaced by two ports.
Power increased to 145 horsepower.
*The rod-type throttle linkage is replaced by a cable.
*On-dash transfer case lever replaced by underdash lever.

1969- *Steering linkage improved.
*Cartridge oil filter is replaced by canister type.

1970- *Dual master cylinder installed.

1971- *As of 7/70, power brakes are standard.

1972- *Three-speed floor shift becomes standard along with a floor-mounted transfer case lever.
*Air injection pump installed on engine.

1973- *Steering box improved.
*EGR valve added to engine.
Steering column ignition key/lock installed.

1974- *H42 four-speed replaces J30 three-speed. Transfer case low-range ratio changes from 2.313-1 to 1.992-1.
*236-cid F engine replaced by 258-cid 2F engine.
*Larger universal joints installed on driveshafts.
*Clutch upgraded from spring to diaphragm type.

1975- *Transfer case low-range ratio changes to 1.959-1.

1976- *Front disc brakes installed.

1979- *3.73-1 axle ratios standard, 4.11-1 optional.
*Fuel tank size increased from 18.5 to 22 gallons.
*Power steering added.
*Air conditioning optional.
*Catalytic convertor added.

1981 *Split-case transfer case introduced, 2.276-1 low-range ratio. Parking brake moves from transfer case to rear wheels.
*Rear brakes increased in size from 11.4 to 11.8 inches.
*Spring shackles, hangers, and frame gussets improved.
*Compression ratio increase to 8.3-1.

This 1966 Land Cruiser found on Jim Lytle's used car lot in Hotchkiss, Colorado, has a good looking rust-free body. Though it has been repowered with a 327-cid Chevy, this is still a very original unit. Toward the end of 1965, the top was modified to carry much larger side windows, rear corner windows, and a pair of one piece, side-swinging rear doors with bigger glass panels. The effect was a 100 percent improvement in visibility.

The FJ-45 pickups are among the rarest of the Land Cruisers. This is shorter FJ-45S model with a 104.5-inch wheelbase and rounded bed corners. This nicely restored 1965 model belongs to Alan Case, of DePere, Wisconsin. It's one of the less common models with a removable top. As with most Land Cruisers, this one has had a number of major upgrades, including a stroked Chevy 383-cid smallblock. A 1975 Toyota 4-speed replaces the original 3-speed unit. The axles are stock Toyota but have been upgraded to later units.

Another variation of the Land Cruiser appeared in 1968 and was called the FJ-55. While mechanically very similar to the short Land Cruiser, the FJ-55 four-door station wagon used a new front wrap. The rear body was similar in appearance to the previous FJ-45V station wagon but more refined. It was slightly shorter than the older wagon (much less rear overhang) but built upon a longer 106-inch wheelbase. The FJ-55 continued through 1979 and was replaced by the sleeker FJ-60 in 1980. FJ-55 body parts are extremely difficult to obtain but the vehicles are a popular alternative to standard FJ-40 fanatics needing more room.

After a peak in 1972, the "TLC" continued with declining sales in the United States and finally, in 1983, Toyota ceased importing them. Low sales was more of a marketing blunder than anything to do with the vehicle. Quite frankly, the later units were grossly overpriced for the U.S. market. Just a year later, the old style 'Cruiser went out of production altogether, to be replaced with a more modern FJ-70 short-wheelbase model. The FJ-70 never went on sale in the United States but was marketed in Canada for several years. Just a few years after leaving our shores, the FJ-40's popularity started an upswing and today there is a thriving community of Land Cruiser lovers all over America.

The Land Cruiser was described by *Four Wheeler* testers as a "Battleship." It continues to live up to that reputation with its large following of enthusiasts. The 'Cruiser is one of the most popular trail rigs in America and the potential buyer will find a huge support network available. Most of this network, however, is devoted to modifications that make the LC an even better off-roader. Few Land Cruisers are restored to bone stock, OE condition at the current time. This may change as they get harder to find and the classic 4x4 movement grows.

Parts are readily available for later models but many items for the early rigs are more difficult to obtain. The old 'Cruisers are generally upgraded to the more easily available later parts. This is within the realm of authenticity. Rust is the Land Cruiser's No. 1 enemy, making a good body the major requirement for a premium price. As many Land Cruisers have been heavily modified, you will need to determine the quality and safety of these modifications.

Common major mods include the addition of V-8 engines, usually a Chevy smallblock, and the conversion to a variety of American four-speed truck transmissions (commonly the NP-420 or 435) with an extra-low first gear. The stock drivetrain is up to a hard workout and can usually handle the extra power. Overheating is the common V-8 conversion complaint but there is a great deal of expertise in the aftermarket to deal with this and other retrofit problems.

The Land Cruiser makes a great four-wheeler and current interest is high. The later models are the most popular. The variations on the theme, like pickups and station wagons, are universally liked by 'Cruiser buffs but are not always as easily salable. Whether you want a Land Cruiser as the ultimate trail brawler or a restored classic, the market is alive and flourishing.

Alan Case's FJ-45S interior is preserved much as it was but the transmission and transfer case shifters have been moved to the floor, as in later Land Cruisers. Many of the early and late pieces interchange readily in the Land Cruiser, so an owner can build his unit to suit personal taste or a particular need.

The FJ-55 station wagon debuted in 1968 with a much sleeker body. It was a considerable improvement in comfort over the older FJ-45. An FJ-55 could make a very useful addition to the family as well as being an interesting collectable. The body parts, however, are getting increasingly difficult to obtain. Rust-free examples are difficult to find. *Four Wheeler* magazine

The FJ-45L long-wheelbase pickup offers the collector utility as well as exclusivity. The "L" pickup used a box taken directly from the Stout pickup line. Built on a 116-inch wheelbase, it offered an 8-foot bed. Mechanically, it was identical to the Land Cruiser but had a full floating rear axle instead of the FJ-40's semifloating unit. *Toyota Motor Sales USA*

The old Toyota F series engine is a derivative of the Chevy six, but the bloodlines go back to the days before World War II. In the early 1960s, this 135-horsepower six was the most powerful engine offered in an SWB utility. Shown here is a 1965 era engine.

The FJ-45V station wagon is a fairly ugly brute and somewhat hampered on the trail by its prodigious rear overhang. It has attracted some interest by collectors recently. Some owners have reported removing a plate on the lower tailgate and finding the word "Toyopet" underneath. This is the name that was formerly used by Toyota in different markets, including its first car introduction here in the early 1950s. *Toyota Motor Sales USA*

The later FJ-40s grew to be increasingly more plush, though it's hard to tell by the looks of this Tim Jonet's 1977 model. Many of the later models have been modified by the addition of performance pieces that enhance them in the dirt. There are few purists in the Toyota game but the number is growing.

1958	1959	1960	1961	1962	1963	1964	1965	1966
1	61	162	246	598	1,056	1,681	2,595	3,072

1967	1968	1969	1970	1971	1972	1973	1974	1975
2,782	3,775	5,216	8,000	9,559	11,982	11,082	8,204	9,050

1976	1977	1978	1979	1980	1981	1982	1983
9,236	9,924	8,858	5,716	3,058	2,027	3,088	4,805

DIMENSIONS & CAPACITIES

	LxWxH	Wheelbase	Curb Weight	Fuel Capacity	GVW
FJ-40	152.4.x65.6x76in	90in	3,600lbs	18.5/22gal	4,500lbs
FJ-45S	183.1x65.6x74.4in	104.3in	3,682lbs	18.5gal	4,785lbs
FJ-45V	183.4x67.7x?in	104.3in	4,010lbs	18.5gal	4,113lbs
FJ-45L	187.4x65.6x74.4in	116in	3,700	NA	NA
FJ-55	184x68.3x73.4in	106.3in	4,020gal	23.8gal	NA

SPECIFICATIONS

Toyota FJ-25
Engine:

Type	6-cyl, OHV
Displacement	236cid
Power	105hp @ 3,200
Torque	189 @ 2,000
B&S	3.54 x 4in
CR	6.8-1

Transmission:

Type	4-speed manual
Ratios	1=5.53, 2=3.48, 3=1.71, 4=1-1, R=5.6

Transfer Case:

Type	Single speed
Ratios	1-1

Axles:

Rear type	Semi-floating
Front type	Full-floating
Ratios	4.11-1

Tires:

Type	Non-directional
Size	6.00-16, 6-ply

Dimensions & Capacities

LxWxH	149.3x62x74.8in
Wheelbase	90in
Curb weight	3,135lbs
Fuel capacity	14gal
GVW	3,883lbs

TOYOTA FJ-40, 45L, 45S, 45V AND 55

Engine:

Type	6-cyl, OHV

Displacement	F: 236cid
	2F: 258cid
Power	F: 135hp @ 3,800 (later rated at 145 @ 4,000)
	2F: 145 @ 3,600
Torque	F: 217lbs-ft @ 2,000
	2F: 217lbs-ft @ 1,800
B&S	F: 3.35 x 4in
	2F: 3.70x4in
	CRF: 7.5-1 (early)
	F: 7.8-1 late
	2F: 7.8-1
	2F: 8.3-1 (late)

Transmission:

Type	60-73 - 3-speed manual (J30)
	74-82 - 4-speed manual (H42)
Ratios	J30: 1=2.757, 2=1.691, 3=1.0, R=3.676
	H41: 1= 3.55, 2=2.29, 3=1.41, 4= 1.0, R=
4.271	

Transfer Case:

Type	Two-speed
Ratios	High: 1-1 (all models)
	Low:
	J30 Trans= 2.313-1
	'74 H42 Trans= 1.992-1
	'75 H42 Trans= 1.959-1
	'81–83 Splt Cse= 2.276-1

Axles:

Rear type:	Semi-floating
Front type	Full-floating
Ratios	4.11-1 (3.73 & 3.36 available some years)

Tires:

Size	6.00-16 (early typical)
	7.60-15 (late typical)

Chapter 10

The Odd, Uncommon, and Obscure

In this chapter, we'll round up "everything else." Some of these are vehicles that were imported in very small numbers, for only a short time or by importers that were independent of the vehicle manufacturer. Most are seldom seen military vehicles. If you happen to be a fan of something here, don't regard this classification as a detriment.

AM General M-422 Mighty Mite

This 4x4 military rig started out in 1953, when the Mid-America Research Corporation (MARCO) responded to a USMC request for a more compact version of the 1/4-ton utility vehicle. The Marines were looking for a vehicle that could be easily transported by helicopter and dropped into remote locations. Compact size would enable them to operate in tighter quarters, such as in jungles, more easily than the standard 1/4-ton.

The first prototypes were powered by 44-horsepower (net), air-cooled, horizontally opposed Porsche engines and had a MARCO three-speed transmission and two-speed transfer case. They were tiny, with a total length of 96 inches, a 64.5-inch wheelbase and a weight of only 1,486 pounds. The Mighty Mite design used a fully independent suspension with inboard drum brakes and cast aluminum control arms. Springs were quarter-elliptic leaf types at all four corners. The chassis was tubular steel while the body was aluminum. All in all, it proved to be a good performing vehicle with few bad habits.

American Motors took over the project and produced some similar prototypes around 1957. The new versions were somewhat bigger and heavier and powered by an air-cooled V4 engine that churned out 55 horsepower. They used a four-speed transmission and a single-speed transfer case. After serious testing all through the 1950s, the design was approved and production started on the M-422 in mid 1960.

Almost immediately a variant appeared. The M-422A1 was a slightly longer unit that stretched the wheelbase from 64.5 to 71 inches. In all other respects, it was identical to the shorter version. Production of Mighty Mites continued to about 1963. Records show 1,250 M-422s were built and 2,672 M-422A1s. That would be a total of 3,922 units but later, some M-422s were modified into A1s, and it isn't known if the numbers count the modified rigs twice or not.

The Mighty Mite came aboard just in time to see the Vietnam War and served well there. The A1 models were generally preferred because their slightly larger size made them more useful. As helicopters grew in size and capacity, these lightweight specialty vehicles proved to no longer be necessary. They were gradually phased out and began to appear on the surplus market in the mid and late 1970s.

A Mighty Mite makes a unique military collectable that offers great off-highway performance and fuel economy. Most parts are available and with their aluminum bodies, rust is not a problem with a Mite. In the late 1970s, there was a glut of cheap Mighty Mites on the market but now they are getting scarce and more expensive. They have little potential as a hot collectable but they have retained a moderate interest level among military collectors and people who like something very different.

Austin Champ

This is getting deep into the obscure realm but these British-built rigs were imported to the United States in small numbers during the 1960s. The Austin Champ was a military vehicle whose basic development program began in 1947. The goal was to build a purely tactical 1/4-ton military vehicle to replace the World War II American Jeep and other rigs then in British service. The first direct link in the chain was a vehicle called the "Gutty," built by the Nuffield Organization. Two or three prototypes were built.

The next incarnation was built in about 1948 by Wolseley and was called the "Mudlark." This vehicle was built in a small quantity and the design was very similar to the Austin-built Champ that came later. A Mudlark was tested by the U.S. Army in 1951 and may have provided some inspiration for the M-151 program that was just getting under way. The Champ went into production after a 15,000 vehicle contract was approved in March of 1952.

The Champ used a steel body and frame and featured an independent suspension that used trailing arms and torsion bars. The engine was a waterproofed 171-cid four-cylinder that was built by Rolls-Royce and made 71

SPECIFICATIONS
M-422 AND M-422A1 MIGHTY MITE

Engine:
Type	V4, OHV aluminum construction
Displacement	108cid
Power	55hp @ 3,600rpm
Torque	NA
B&S	3.25x3.25in
CR	7.5:1

Transmission:
Type	4-speed, New Process 4300
Ratios	1=5.24, 2=3.44,3=1.86, 4=1:1,R=NA

Transfer Case:
Type	Single-speed, New Process
Ratio	1.085:1

Axles:
Type	Center mounted, with half-shafts & CV joints
Ratios	5.38:1

Dimensions & Capacities:
LxWxH	107x64.5x60in (M-422)
	113x64.5x60in (M-422A1)
Wheelbase	67.25in (M-422)
	71in (M-422A1)
Curb weight	1,700lbs (M-422)
	1,780lbs (M-422A1)
Fuel capacity	12.5gal
GVW	2,700 (M-422)
	2,780 (M-422A1)

On the left is a very original M-422 in U.S. Marine Corps livery. These days, they are not often found in such complete and good condition. On the right is an M-422A1 in average to good condition. Note the extra wheelbase length of the A1. You can tell an A1 model right away by the extra rib on the body, just in front of the rear wheel arch. *J&L Densinger*

The V4 in the Mighty Mite was aluminum and, by all reports, a very robust powerplant. The shroud at the front contains the engine cooling fan, on which the air-cooled engine depended entirely for staying alive. On top, a Holley single-barrel carb mixed air and fuel for the 108-cubic inch engine. *J&L Densinger*

This Austin Champ has seen better days. It was photographed in the early 1970s for *Four Wheeler* magazine. It represents one of at least 100 that were imported by European Sports, Inc., from Holland in 1965 and 1966. At least three are currently known to be in private hands in the United States, and several more have been seen in wrecking yards. *Four Wheeler* magazine

The Austin Gipsy was imported to the United States in very small numbers. Initially, the Gipsies came with fully independent suspension. Later, they changed to a leaf setup. This SWB unit is a late version using leaf springs all around. *Land Rover Owner Magazine*

horsepower. Some of the Champs also used an Austin A-40 engine but these are rare. The drivetrain was unique. It used a five-speed gearbox that had no reverse gear. The transmission was connected to a single-speed gearbox that not only incorporated the rear differential but reverse gear as well. A long driveshaft ran from the rear up to the front differential. As weird as this sounds, having reverse in the "transfer case" (what else do you call it?) allowed the vehicle to have all the gearing choices in reverse as well as forward. Retreating in reverse at 60 miles per hour. Hmmm?

According to historical reputation, the Champ proved to be a maintenance and repair nightmare. Its performance was reputed to be no better that the more conventional Land Rover then in service but it was almost double the cost. The British Army's requirements also changed and the need for purely tactical vehicles was less important. Champ production stopped in 1956 before the 15,000-vehicle contract was completed and approximately 11,700 were built. During production, an effort was made to bring the Champ into the civilian markets, but only small numbers were marketed and those mostly for export.

Which is which? On the left is a Land Rover and on the right a Gipsy. The resemblance is startling. Though they shared many concepts, they were quite different in overall mechanical design. *Land Rover Owner Magazine*

A small number of Champs were imported to the United States in 1964, as evidenced by a February 1965 issue of *Four Wheeler* magazine that reported 100 surplus units being shipped here from a Holland surplus dealer. How many were brought in beyond these and how many remain is unknown. Parts are difficult to get, even back in Jolly Old England, where they were born.

Austin Gipsy

The Austin Gipsy was another ill-fated British 4x4, but it went more than a few paces into the real world. Built from the ashes of the Champ, the Gipsy was designed to go head to head with the Land Rover, on both the civilian and military markets. This was an audacious move but the fatal flaw was that Austin's effort was based on beating the rather dated Land Rover Series I. When the Land Rover Series II debuted in 1958, at nearly the same time the Gipsy was announced, it put the vehicles on very level footing. Land Rover was also the established manufacturer of British 4x4s and tough to beat.

The short-wheelbase Gipsy (90 inches) went on sale in 1959 to mixed reviews. Under the skin, the Austin was quite different than the Land Rover and it was these differences that Austin hoped would sell the vehicle. The first of these was an independent suspension system, but this setup was considerably different than the earlier Austin Champ. Instead of torsion bars, the Gipsy featured trailing arms that used rubber "Flexitor" springs. So equipped, the Gipsy rode well but had a tendency to drop the differentials onto rocks. Unlike a live axle, when one wheel of an independent suspension encounters a rock, only that wheel lifts. This effectively lowers the rest of the undercarriage into harm's way, and the Gipsy was known for tearing up differentials in rough ground. The Gipsy's suspension design also gave it some unusual handling characteristics. The long-wheelbase models (111 inches) that debuted in 1960 used a more standard live axle/leaf spring setup in the rear.

Power came from either a 62-horsepower 134-cid four-cylinder gas engine or a 133-cid diesel that made 55 horsepower. Both these engines were available in other applications within the Austin/BMC lines. The gearbox assembly consisted of a four-speed manual and a two-speed transfer case.

Unlike the Land Rover, the Gipsy's body was built of steel, and here is the strange part. All of Austin's purported desires to be different apparently were ignored when it came to looks. The Gipsy was a Land Rover clone, especially when viewed from the front. Why Austin built such a decidedly different vehicle mechanically and then to have it take two glances from the average Joe to tell it from a Land Rover—who knows. Perhaps it was designed to capitalize on the famous Rover "look."

As the Gipsy evolved in the 1960s, the Flexitor independent suspension was quietly dropped as standard fare for 1962, but it remained an option for the front to 1965. After then it was dropped completely. It made small but steady sale progress against the Land Rover and eventually it got a chance to compete for a big military contract. It actually made it into the "finals" but fate was to deal the Gipsy a death blow. In 1968, much of the financially ailing British motor industry was nationalized into the British Leyand Corporation. With all the formerly competing models brought together under one umbrella, some were dropped in favor of others. The Gipsy was one of these that was dropped.

The Mercedes Benz Unimog 404S is a more common sight in the United States than you might think. This ambulance-bodied version is an ex-NATO rig that was recently imported for sale. *Seth Kurzner*

In case you wondered how the Unimog performs in the dirt, you should see Kai Serrano wheel his 1970s era U-model around. This rig has conquered nearly all the four-wheeling hot spots around the country. From 1977 into the late 1980s, Unimogs were imported by Case and used as the basis for a variety of special equipment. The Holstein paint job has inspired the nickname, "Unimoog."

The Gipsy's history in the United States is sketchy. According to owners and former owners, they could be obtained through British car dealerships in the early 1960s, though there appears to be no recorded organized effort to market them here. How many were imported remains a mystery. It appears that some came through Canada and as a result the remaining handful seem to be congregated in the Northern states. They have no collector value here but make an interesting rig. Some parts are available but you have to go overseas to get them.

Ford M-151 M.U.T.T.

M.U.T.T. is an acronym for Mobile Utility Tactical Truck; a high-falutin name for a rig that was designed to replace the ordinary military Jeep. The project came about from a perceived need for a faster, more high-tech light utility vehicle. In March of 1951, Ford was given a contract to develop a replacement for the 1/4-ton Jeep. The first prototypes of the new vehicle, called the XM-151, were produced from 1952 to 1954. From the outset, the M-151 was designed to "out-tech" everybody. The MUTT, as it became known, was small and light and featured independent suspension on all four corners. Built with a unitized body, it weighed just under 2,400 pounds. Ford's first concept was built to be a "throw-away" machine that could be cheaply replaced when damaged or worn out. The production designs were built as more repairable units. One prototype, the XM-151E2 of 1957, was built of aluminum and weighed only 2,000 pounds. By late 1959, the M-151 was approved for production.

The M-151 was powered by 141-cid Continental OHV four-cylinder that pumped out 71 horsepower and a generous 128 pound-feet of torque at 1,800 rpm. A four-speed transmission was used with a single-speed, "in-or-out" transfer case. Axle ratios were 4.89:1. The MUTT was sprightly, nimble, fuel efficient (about 18–20 miles per gallon), and had an easy 66-mile per hour top speed.

Due to its coil spring suspension, it rode better than any tactical rig the army had ever owned. As mentioned before, the suspension was fully independent, and therein lies the Achilles heel. The M-151s had a dangerous tendency to roll over when driven carelessly. This was due to the rear suspension allowing the wheels to change camber in turns. This generally occurred when the vehicle was driven fast on pavement. In a fast turn, the lower ends of the wheels would "tuck-in" towards each other. Once this occurred, you had to be a quick thinker to recover. Some people blame the design for these tendencies and others blame the drivers for too much speed, but the end effect was to kill and maim a lot of GIs. Experience showed the M-151 was docile as long as you didn't subject it to sports-car-like driving.

The M-151 was built in three main variants; the original M-151, the M-151A1 from about 1965 that featured a few minor improvements, and the M-

SPECIFICATIONS	
1959–1968 AUSTIN GIPSY (TYPICAL)	
Engine :	
Type	4-cyl, OHV
Displacement	134cid (gas)
	133cid (diesel)
Power	62hp @ 4,100rpm (diesel)
	55hp @ 3,000rpm (diesel)
Torque	110lbs-ft @ 1,500rpm (gas)
B&S	3.125x4.38in (gas)
	3.25x4.0in (diesel)
CR	6.8:1 (gas)
	22:1 (diesel)
Transmission:	
Type	4-speed manual
Ratios	1=4.05,2=2.35,3=1.37,
	4=1.0,R=5.17
Transfer Case:	
Type	2-speed
Ratios	Low=2.02, High=1.0
Axles:	
Type	Bevel gears, center-mounted
	with half shafts & CV joints
Ratios	5.12:1
Dimensions & Capacities:	
LxWxH	139x66.75x73.5in (SWB)
	160x66.75x73.5in (LWB)
Wheelbase	90in (SWB)
	111in (LWB)
Curb weight	3,379lb (SWB)
Fuel capacity	15.5gal
GVW	4,479 (SWB)

151A2 that had lot of revisions. Some efforts were made to correct the suspension problems later in the run. The M-151A2 of about 1972 featured a totally new rear suspension that made the units more predictable.

MUTTs were used in Vietnam and many other conflicts around the globe. They proved themselves the equal of the Jeep when the going got tough. The M-151 design remained in production until about 1978. Initially, they were built by Ford but some were built by Willys Motors (Kaiser Jeep) and later by AM General (a subsidiary of AMC). At least 150,000 units were built in the approximately 18 years of manufacture. The M-151 line was gradually phased out of tactical service by the introduction of the Humvee beginning in 1984. M-151s remained in service with National Guard units until at least the early 1990s. A few may still be in use with the U.S. Armed Forces. Many thousands are still in service with foreign armies around the world. They are popular in Israel, several African countries, and Turkey.

Besides the rear suspension and data tags, the early M151 can be visually differentiated from the M-151A1 or A2. The A1 had small turn signal lamps on the front fenders, but some earlier units were retrofitted. The A2s have large combination turn signal and blackout lights on the fenders, the end of which is dipped to accommodate them. Two variants of the M-151 were built, the M-718 frontline ambulance, fitted with extensions on the rear body to accommodate three litters, and the M-825 weapons carrier that mounted a 106-mm recoilless rifle.

Up to about 1970, early M-151s were released and sold surplus fully operational. The government soon realized the potential liabilities of offering a "tricky" vehicle for public consumption and made buying an M-151 very difficult. At first, they were torched in half before sale. When enterprising buyers began welding them back together, they started quartering them. This still didn't stop the determined folks. Later they added legal roadblocks to M-151 ownership. About all you could buy surplus at that point were the engine, transmissions and t-case, the hood, windshield, and some small parts. The basic body structure and suspension were crushed.

Intact M-151s are very few in number. Some estimates run about 2,000–3,000 units in private hands in North America. Uncut versions are particularly rare. There is some M-151 interest in military circles but they are not yet a hot number in general circles and are likely never to be. Their growing interest seems to be with Vietnam era veterans.

Because of the discouraging attitude the government took over selling the vehicles, some M-151s have forged or semilegal paperwork. Take care when buying one—especially a late model unit. Since most of the existing specimens have been cut and welded back together, pay particular attention to how they were repaired. Parts are moderately easy to obtain, as are the accessories like gun mounts, snorkels, and hardtops. The A2s were retrofitted with a roll cage and this could be a confidence-inspiring accessory.

An M-151A1 was nearly identical to the earlier M-151 models. The turn signal on the front fender is the giveaway, though earlier models were sometimes retrofitted with them also. The front of an A2 model and its characteristic dipped fender can just be seen beyond this unit to the right. This shot shows the typical top arrangement but without the side curtains. *Four Wheeler* magazine

An M-151A1 in topless configuration. This is a Willys-built unit from the early 1960s. Some of the earliest M-151s were fitted with magnesium wheels. The small round holes as seen here indicate steel wheels. Larger oval holes indicate mags. *Jeep House Museum*

This M-151A2 (note dipped fender and larger light) is equipped with a fairly rare hardtop. This is an uncut M-151A2, making it a rare item. With a hardtop and a heater, the M-151 is almost civilized.

SPECIFICATIONS
M-151 MUTT

Engine:

Type	4-cyl, OHV
Displacement	141cid
Power	71hp @ 4,000rpm
Torque	128lbs-ft @ 1,800rpm
B&S	3.875x3.00in
CR	7.5:1

Transmission:

Type	4-speed

Transfer Case:

Type	Single speed
Ratio	1:1

Axles:

Type	Center-mounted with halfshafts and CV joints
Ratios	4.89

Dimensions & Capacities:

LxWxH	133x64x71in
Wheelbase	85in
Curb weight	2,350lbs
Fuel capacity	17gal
GVW	3,290lbs

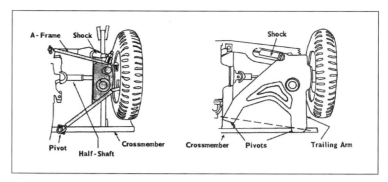

A rear suspension change in the M-151A2 models upgraded the old style setup (left) to a more forgiving design (right). The older units tended to change camber in hard turns, allowing the rear wheels to tuck in.

Mercedes Benz Unimog

While the Unimog is famous nearly all over the world, it has had limited exposure in the United States. It somewhat exceeds our 1-ton limit, being available in capacities from about 1 1/2 tons. They have been imported to the the United States and Canada in small numbers since the early 1950s and used in a variety of commercial and agricultural roles. They are now enjoying a growing popularity in general four-wheel circles and with folks looking for all-wheel drive rigs for use as campers. Surplus European military Unimogs are being imported in steady numbers and most are sold to recreational users.

The Unimog idea started in a postwar Germany that was ravaged on every level. The need for a "universal" tractor/utility truck was acute. The idea went from a brainstorm by engineer Albert Friedrich in December 1945 to a prototype in just seven months and was in production by 1949. Though the Unimog was first produced in another factory due to manufacturing restrictions, by 1951 the vehicles were being built in Mercedes Benz's Heavy Truck Works at Gaggenau, Germany. The name Unimog comes from an acronym, *UNIversal-MOtorGerät*, German for "universal power unit."

While a huge variety of specialty adaptations and models have been built over the years, the most commonly seen model in the United States is the 404S. This truck was in production almost unchanged from 1955 to 1972. With an engine change, they lasted into the 1980s with only a few adaptations. Many of them were built in military configuration for use with NATO forces in Europe.

Two body styles are commonly seen; a troop carrier/cargo truck and an enclosed ambulance body. There are variations on top of variations. The 404 has a canvas top, the 404.1 has a metal roof. Both are identical with a 134-cid overhead cam, six-cylinder gasoline engine of 82 horsepower. A diesel was available on some models. The gearbox has six forward speeds and two reverse, giving the Unimog plenty of torque multiplication for the small engine. The transfer case is integral with the transmission and has no low range, the very deep gearing of the main transmission being adequate. The axles are of the portal type, meaning that the main differential is up high and the output at the wheels is lower. It offers more clearance and the portal contains a gear reduction device.

The Unimogs are nearly bulletproof—literally and figuratively. They may be too big for many tastes but you can't get much better in terms of quality. The ex-military rigs imported are plain-Jane rigs but they are reasonable and parts are easily obtained. While there is little collectable value at present, as interest grows that may change. Nothing that wears the Mercedes Benz star stays cheap for long.

M-274 Mechanical Mule

Probably the smallest load-capable collectable 4x4 you'll see out there is the Mechanical Mule. Essentially the Mule is a platform with an engine, four-wheel drive, and a seat. The only concession to comfort is the meager padding on the canvas-covered seat cushions. This lightweight rig was designed for use with airborne and recon units and was built to carry a 1/2 ton.

The concept went back to 1944 and the Willys WAC (Willys Air Cooled) project. This series of prototypes was designed to supply the military with light, air-portable, low-silhouette vehicles. This idea coalesced into the JBC (Jungle Burden Carrier) of 1945. By 1951, this had developed into the XM-274 "Mechanical Mule" that was accepted for production in 1956.

The M-274 was a rear-engined platform truck that could carry more than its own weight. Rated as a 1/2 ton, it weighed well under 1,000 pounds itself. The early models were powered by a 52-cid 15–17-horse-power four-cylinder Willys-Continental A0-52 air-cooled engine but later was replaced by a similar 13-horsepower two-cylinder A0-42. The downgrade simplified the parts system, since the AO-42 was used in several other military roles. A three-speed transmission, a two-speed transfer case, and 4.11:1 axle gearing with reduction gears at the axle ends completed the transmission of power to the ground. Top speed was 25 miles per hour.

The Mule's suspension was interesting in that it didn't have one! Actually, the low-pressure 7.50-10 nondirectional tires served as the suspension system. Ride quality and load capacity were adjusted by varying the tire pressure. The steering was driver selectable, either four- or two-wheel, and the the steering column could be pivoted to allow the unit to be used as a loader and controlled by a person walking. The wheels, platform, and some drivetrain parts were made of magnesium in the early models, but the M-274A5s were primarily built of aluminum. The latest models could be fitted with electric start kits, alternators and even a capacitive discharge ignition system. Some used an extra-wide terra style tire with an add-on fender.

The Mule served with Army Special Forces units as well as Marine Corps Recon and other units. It served extensively in Vietnam and other conflicts around the world. They were used by several foreign governments as well, most notably Italy. They were used to transport cargo and personnel, and mounted with a 106-mm recoilless rifle as well as a variety of small missile and rocket launchers, including the vaunted TOW missile.

The M-274 was used into the early 1970s and gradually phased out. Surplus models became available in the early 1970s and some are still trick-

This ad appeared in *Four Wheeler* magazine in 1973 and shows both the soft top and hardtop versions of the Brute. *Four Wheeler* was a national magazine at the time, but circulation was heaviest in the west, the Brute's intended market.

Mule Models

All in all, the Mules had six incarnations. Two were rebuild/upgrades of the early models. Besides Willys Motors, there were four other manufacturers, or remanufacturers of the Mule. Baifield Industries, Bowen-McLaughlin-York, Automatic Sprinkler Corporation, and Brunswick Corporation all had a hand in the Mule game from about 1965 on. Here are the five upgrades on the Mule that took place from 1959–1970:

M-274A1 - Built under the Willys Motors nameplate, except for a few later units that were built after Willys changed to Kaiser-Jeep in March 1963. Improvements included having the band-type brake on the front axle replaced by a dual shoe type. Engine modifications included dual fan belts, chrome oil rings, a vented magneto, the oil bath air cleaner replaced by a paper element, and extra carburetor protection. On the outside, the cargo tie-downs were made removable and extra grab handles were added. There was also extra mesh for the driver's feet and the driver's seat adjusted to two positions.

M-274A2 - Built by Bowen-McLaughlin-York. The four-cylinder Willys-Continental AO-53 was replaced with an AO-42 Continental-Hercules two-cylinder, a standard military powerplant used with other equipment. Lifting eyes were cast into the wheel hubs (this feature was retrofitted onto older models). The drop-gear housings were redesigned for more strength. The transmission had some minor internal improvements.

M-274A3 - These units were converted older M-274 models upgraded to the latest M-274A5 spec. These conversions were done in the mid-1960s. The upgrades included an engine swap to the AO-42 two-cylinder The drivetrain was upgraded to the new transmission and drop gear housings. The gear ratios were slightly higher. The work was done at U.S. Army Depot maintenance facilities.

M-274A4- Converted M-274A1s. The work was the same as with the older M-274s, change the engine with the AO-42 and a drivetrain upgrade to the latest style.

M-274A5- These rigs were built by Baifield Industries in about 1965. Brunswick or Automatic Sprinkler built them from about 1970. The magnesium platform was replaced by an aluminum version. Ditto the wheels. Electric start was added to some, as well as an alternator and electronic ignition. Some were fitted with wide terra-style tires and fenders.

ling through Defense Marketing and Reutilization (DRMS) outlets. They were cheap to buy so some folks bought three or four. Most parts are readily found. Some Mule owners have reported getting them licensed for the street, though this may be a difficult process in certain areas of the United States. Beyond the military collector, there is a small circle of owner/enthusiasts but essentially there is no collector market for these unique vehicles. They are still reasonably priced and available through surplus outlets. If your "quad-runner" isn't doing the job on your farm or ranch, consider a Mule!

Suzuki Brute

This pint-sized powerhouse was offered for sale in the United States from 1971 to late 1973 and possibly into 1974. The Brute is a direct ancestor of the Samurai that is now undergoing a popular revival after U.S. sales stopped in 1995. The Brute was offered for sale by the Intercontinental Equipment Corporation, a private distributor in San Diego, California. Distribution was described as "West Coast" and the dealer "network" concentrated in California, Nevada, and Arizona but there is no doubt that some have found their way east.

The Brute was known elsewhere in the world as the Jimney 360 and debuted in 1970 with the Suzuki model designation of LJ-10. The design dated back to 1965 and the Hope Star ON360. The Hope Star Company had delusions of mini-grandeur but went belly-up rather quickly. Suzuki, known best for motorcycles, was in the midst of an expansion into the car market and bought the designs and tooling. By late 1969, they had repowered the unit with one of their own engines and added the Jimney to their car lineup.

The Brute was powered by a 360-cc (22-cid), two-cylinder, two-stroke

32-horsepower engine. The air-cooled "two-banger" could drive the 1,350-pound Brute to speeds slightly in excess of 55 miles per hour. It was reputed to have excellent cross-country abilities but struggled on the highway.

Late in 1972, a water-cooled version of the same 360-cc engine was offered. The air-cooled engine had suffered from reliability problems when driven hard. With all of 32 horsepower, who wouldn't run it hard! The new engine resulted in more reliability and better fuel economy. Both the air- and water-cooled engine were oil-injected, meaning no mixing of gas and oil—à la outboard motors. The engines were quiet, lacking that annoying "ringingingining" sound, especially the water-cooled unit. Suzuki had acquired quite a reputation in the motorcycle arena with powerful two-stroke 380, 550 and 750-cc engines, and this technology went into the Brute.

In addition to the soft top, Suzuki built a hardtop and a pickup version. In 1973, the hardtop sold for $2,800 and the soft top for $2,400. As far as the records show, only the softtop and later the hardtops were imported by IEC. A few pickups have been seen in the United States but these came from Hawaii where the full line was imported.

By the end of 1973, IEC had stopped importing the Brute. It's possible that the ever-more stringent EPA emissions regulations finally caught up with them. Perhaps sales were not what was expected. Who knows. It would be interesting to learn whether sales stopped before or after the Arab oil embargo of 1973.

The Brute is an oddball orphan that may have few prospects. Oddly, many parts are still available through Suzuki dealership sources. The upswing in Samurai popularity in the hardcore off-road crowd may trickle down to the old Brute. For now, the Brute must live in relative obscurity.

A Mule that doesn't need to rest. The M-274, used extensively by the U.S. Marine Corps, is shown here in use during the early 1960s. This is probably a late M-274 or early M-274A1, because it is missing the lifting rings on the wheel hubs. *Jeep House Museum*

The Willys WAC-3 or "Jungle Burden Carrier" of 1944 was a direct ancestor to the 1951 XM-274 Mechanical Mule. It was powered by a 49-cid, horizontally opposed two-cylinder engine made by Harley Davidson. With 24 horsepower on tap and a three-speed transmission, this rig was capable of hauling a 500-pound load. It could barely tow a 1,000-pound load, but was capable of approximately 45 miles per hour. *Jeep House Museum*

MULE PRODUCTION (BY MODEL)

Model	Production
M-274-	2,452
M-274A1-	1,905
M-274A2-	3,609
M-274A3-	(rebuilt M-274)
M-274A4-	(rebuilt M-274A1)
M-274A5-	3,274

Specifications
M-274A5 Mechanical Mule

Engine:

Type	2-cylinder, horizontally opposed Continental-Hercules AO-42
Displacement	42cid
Power	13hp @ 3,000rpm
Torque	NA
B&S	3.0x3.0in
CR	6.8:1

Transmission:

Type	3-speed manual

Transfer Case:

Type	2-speed

Axles:

Type	Solid
Ratios	4.11:1

Dimension & Capacities:

LxWxH	119x49x49in
Wheelbase	57in
Curb weight	900lbs
Fuel capacity	8gal
GVW	2,075lbs

	Day-to-Day	Off-Highway	Investment Potential	Parts Availability
★★★★★	Wonderful to live with. As carlike as you can get.	A real trail brawler! Capable of any terrain	A serious collectable. May already be valuable.	Excellent availability.
★★★★☆	Excellent but showing a few trucklike manners.	Excellent, but with a few limitations.	Very good potential. May already have value.	Still very good.
★★★☆☆	As much truck as car, Has some potential in the future. but a truck with good manners.	Limited to moderate trails.	About average.	Starting to get scarce or pricey.
★★☆☆☆	This is a truck and make no bones about it!	Very limited. Ok for mild situations.	Limited potential now and later.	Parts are scarce or expensive compared to other models.
★☆☆☆☆	Driving this vehicle on the street is like being mugged! OK for inclement weather only.	This is a fair weather rig only, a 4x4 in name only. or unpopularity makes this a bad bet.	No potential. Large production numbers	Parts are extremely difficult to get due to age or small production numbers. Will be pricey.

APPENDIX ONE

CHAPTER 1

	Day-to-Day	Off-Highway	Investment Potential	Parts Availability
FWD Touring Car	★★☆☆☆	★★☆☆☆	★★★★★	★☆☆☆☆
FWD Model B	★☆☆☆☆	★★☆☆☆	★★★★☆	★☆☆☆☆
FWD Model LD	★★☆☆☆	★★★★☆	★★★☆☆	★☆☆☆☆
Jefferey/Nash Quad	★☆☆☆☆	★★☆☆☆	★★★☆☆	★☆☆☆☆
Duplex (Under 2-ton)	★☆☆☆☆	★★☆☆☆	★★★☆☆	★☆☆☆☆
Oshkosh (under 2-ton)	★☆☆☆☆	★★☆☆☆	★★★☆☆	★☆☆☆☆
Other Antique 4x4s	★☆☆☆☆	★★☆☆☆	★★☆☆☆	★☆☆☆☆

CHAPTER 2

	Day-to-Day	Off-Highway	Investment Potential	Parts Availability
Coleman				
1946–1956 Trucks	★★☆☆☆	★★★★☆	★★☆☆☆	★☆☆☆☆
Marmon-Herrington				
1936–1942 Trucks	★★☆☆☆	★★★★☆	★★★☆☆	★★☆☆☆
1937–1942 Cars	★★★☆☆	★★★☆☆	★★★★★	★★☆☆☆
1945–1958 Trucks	★★☆☆☆	★★★★☆	★★★☆☆	★★☆☆☆
1950–1956 Ranger	★★★☆☆	★★★★☆	★★★★★	★★☆☆☆
NAPCO				
1950–1955 Chevy Truck	★★☆☆☆	★★★★☆	★★★★☆	★★★☆☆
(1st & 2nd Series)	★☆☆☆☆	★★☆☆☆	★★★★☆	★☆☆☆☆
1950–1955 Chevy Suburban	★★★☆☆	★★★★☆	★★★★★	★★★☆☆
1955–1959 GMC/Chevy Truck (conversions)	★★☆☆☆	★★★★☆	★★★★☆	★★★☆☆
1956–1959 GMC/Chevy Truck (factory)	★★☆☆☆	★★★★☆	★★★★☆	★★★☆☆
1956–1959 GMC/Chevy Suburban (factory)	★★★☆☆	★★★★☆	★★★★★	★★★☆☆
1958–1964 Studebaker	★★☆☆☆	★★★★☆	★★★★★	★★☆☆☆

	Day-to-Day	Off-Highway	Investment Potential	Parts Availability
CHAPTER 3- DODGE				
1940 VC Series	★★☆☆☆	★★★★☆	★★★★★	★★★☆☆
1941–1942 WC 1/2 ton	★★☆☆☆	★★★★☆	★★★★☆	★★★☆☆
1942–1945 WC 3/4 ton (all except)	★★☆☆☆	★★★★☆	★★★☆☆	★★★★☆
1942–1945 carryall & command car	★★☆☆☆	★★★★☆	★★★★☆	★★★★☆
1946–1968 Power Wagon	★★☆☆☆	★★★★☆	★★★★☆	★★★★☆
1950–1968 M-37	★★☆☆☆	★★★★☆	★★★☆☆	★★★★☆
1957–1960 Power Wagon	★★★☆☆	★★★★☆	★★★★☆	★★★☆☆
1961–1971 Power Wagon	★★★☆☆	★★★★☆	★★★☆☆	★★★★☆
CHAPTER 4- JEEP				
1940–1941 Bantam MkII	★☆☆☆☆	★★★★☆	★★★★★	★☆☆☆☆
1941 Bantam BRC-40	★☆☆☆☆	★★★★☆	★★★★★	★★☆☆☆
1941 Ford GP	★☆☆☆☆	★★★★☆	★★★★★	★★☆☆☆
1941 Willys MA	★☆☆☆☆	★★★★☆	★★★★★	★★☆☆☆
1942 Willys MB Slat-Grille	★☆☆☆☆	★★★★☆	★★★★★	★★★☆☆
1942–1945 Willys MB	★☆☆☆☆	★★★★☆	★★★★★	★★★★☆
1942–1945 Ford GPW	★☆☆☆☆	★★★★☆	★★★★★	★★★★☆
1942–1943 Ford GPA	★☆☆☆☆	★★☆☆☆	★★★★☆	★★☆☆☆
1942–1945 Jeep-based special models	★☆☆☆☆	★★★☆☆	★★★☆☆	★★☆☆☆
1944–1945 CJ-2	★☆☆☆☆	★★★★☆	★★★★★	★★☆☆☆
1945–1946 CJ-2A early	★☆☆☆☆	★★★★☆	★★★★★	★★★☆☆
1946–1949 CJ-2A late	★☆☆☆☆	★★★★☆	★★★★☆	★★★★☆
1949–1953 CJ-3A	★☆☆☆☆	★★★★☆	★★★★☆	★★★★☆
1950–1952 M-38	★☆☆☆☆	★★★★☆	★★★★☆	★★★★☆
1953–1968 CJ-3B	★☆☆☆☆	★★★★☆	★★★★☆	★★★★☆
1952–1957 M-38A1	★☆☆☆☆	★★★★☆	★★★★☆	★★★★☆
1954–1979 CJ-5 (except specials below)	★☆☆☆☆	★★★★☆	★★★☆☆	★★★★☆
1964–1968 Tuxedo Park	★★☆☆☆	★★★★☆	★★★★☆	★★★★☆
1969 "462" Special	★☆☆☆☆	★★★★☆	★★★★☆	★★★★☆
1970 Renegade I	★☆☆☆☆	★★★★☆	★★★★☆	★★★★☆
1971 Renegade II	★☆☆☆☆	★★★★☆	★★★★☆	★★★★☆
1973 Super Jeep	★☆☆☆☆	★★★★☆	★★★★☆	★★★★☆
1972–1975 Renegade	★☆☆☆☆	★★★★☆	★★★★☆	★★★★☆
1973–1979 Renegade	★☆☆☆☆	★★★★☆	★★★☆☆	★★★★☆
1955–1975 CJ-6	★☆☆☆☆	★★★☆☆	★★★☆☆	★★★★☆
1976–1979 CJ-7	★★★☆☆	★★★★☆	★★★☆☆	★★★★☆
1976–1978 CJ7 (V8)	★★★☆☆	★★★★☆	★★★★☆	★★★★☆

	Day-to-Day	Off-Highway	Investment Potential	Parts Availability
1957–1959 FC-150 (narrow track)	★☆☆☆☆	★★★☆☆	★★☆☆☆	★★★☆☆
1959–1965 FC-150 (wide track)	★☆☆☆☆	★★★☆☆	★★★☆☆	★★★☆☆
1957–1965 FC-170	★☆☆☆☆	★★★☆☆	★★★☆☆	★★★☆☆
FC Military Models	★☆☆☆☆	★★★☆☆	★★★☆☆	★★☆☆☆
1947–1963 Pickups	★☆☆☆☆	★★★☆☆	★★☆☆☆	★★★☆☆
1946–1963 Station Wagon	★★☆☆☆	★★★☆☆	★★☆☆☆	★★★☆☆
1967–1971 Jeepster Commando	★★★☆☆	★★★☆☆	★★☆☆☆	★★☆☆☆
1971–1973 Commando	★★★☆☆	★★★☆☆	★★☆☆☆	★★☆☆☆
1962–1969 Gladiator PU	★★☆☆☆	★★★☆☆	★★☆☆☆	★★☆☆☆
1962–1969 Wagoneer	★★★★☆	★★★☆☆	★★☆☆☆	★★☆☆☆
1965–1969 Super Wagoneer	★★★★★	★★★☆☆	★★★☆☆	★★☆☆☆

CHAPTER 5- IHC

	Day-to-Day	Off-Highway	Investment Potential	Parts Availability
1942–1945 M-1-4	★☆☆☆☆	★★★☆☆	★★☆☆☆	★★☆☆☆
1942–1945 M-2-4	★☆☆☆☆	★★★☆☆	★★☆☆☆	★★☆☆☆
1953–1955 R-series PU	★★☆☆☆	★★★☆☆	★★★☆☆	★★★☆☆
1955–1956 S-series PU	★★☆☆☆	★★★☆☆	★★☆☆☆	★★★☆☆
1955–1956 S-series Travelall	★★★☆☆	★★★☆☆	★★★☆☆	★★☆☆☆
1957–1958 A-series PU	★★☆☆☆	★★★☆☆	★★☆☆☆	★★★☆☆
1957–1958 A-series Travelette PU	★★☆☆☆	★★★☆☆	★★★☆☆	★★★☆☆
1957–1958 A-series Travelall	★★★☆☆	★★★☆☆	★★★☆☆	★★★☆☆
1959–1960 B-series PU	★★☆☆☆	★★★☆☆	★★☆☆☆	★★★☆☆
1959–1960 B-series Travelette PU	★★☆☆☆	★★★☆☆	★★★☆☆	★★★☆☆
1959–1960 B-series Travelall	★★★☆☆	★★★☆☆	★★★☆☆	★★★☆☆
1961–1968 C-series PU	★★☆☆☆	★★★☆☆	★★☆☆☆	★★★☆☆
1961–1968 C-series Travelette PU	★★☆☆☆	★★★☆☆	★★★☆☆	★★★☆☆
1961–1968 C-series Travelall	★★★☆☆	★★★☆☆	★★★☆☆	★★★☆☆
1969–1975 D-series PU	★★☆☆☆	★★★☆☆	★★☆☆☆	★★★☆☆
1969–1975 D-series Travelette PU	★★☆☆☆	★★★☆☆	★★★☆☆	★★★☆☆
1969–1975 D-series Travelall	★★★☆☆	★★★☆☆	★★★☆☆	★★★☆☆

	Day-to-Day	Off-Highway	Investment Potential	Parts Availability
1961–1964 Scout 80	★★☆☆☆	★★★★☆	★★★☆☆	★★★☆☆
1965–1968 Scout 800	★★☆☆☆	★★★★☆	★★★☆☆	★★★☆☆
1965–1968 Scout 800 Turbo	★★☆☆☆	★★★★☆	★★★★☆	★★★☆☆
1966–1968 Scout 800 V8	★★☆☆☆	★★★★☆	★★★★☆	★★★☆☆
1969 Scout 800A Aristocrat	★★☆☆☆	★★★★☆	★★★★★	★★★☆☆
1969–1971 Scout 800A&B 4 and 6cyl	★★☆☆☆	★★★★☆	★★★☆☆	★★★☆☆
1969–71 Scout 800A&B V8	★★☆☆☆	★★★★☆	★★★★☆	★★★☆☆
1970–71 Scout 800A SR-2	★★☆☆☆	★★★★☆	★★★★★	★★★☆☆
1972–1980 Scout II (except specials below)	★★★☆☆	★★★★☆	★★★★☆	★★★★☆
1977–1980 Scout II SSII	★★☆☆☆	★★★★☆	★★★★☆	★★★★☆
Scout II w/CVI package	★★★★☆	★★★★☆	★★★★★	★★★★☆
Scout II Midnight Star	★★★☆☆	★★★☆☆	★★☆☆☆	★★☆☆☆
Scout II w/Midas Interior	★★★★☆	★★★★☆	★★★★☆	★★★★☆

CHAPTER 6- LAND ROVER

	Day-to-Day	Off-Highway	Investment Potential	Parts Availability
1948–1953 Series I 80	★★☆☆☆	★★★★☆	★★★★☆	★★★☆☆
1954–1956 Series I 86	★★☆☆☆	★★★★☆	★★★★☆	★★★☆☆
1954–1956 Series I 107PU	★★☆☆☆	★★★☆☆	★★★★☆	★★★☆☆
1955–1958 Series I 107SW	★★☆☆☆	★★★☆☆	★★★★★	★★★☆☆
1957–1958 Series I 88	★★☆☆☆	★★★★☆	★★★★☆	★★★☆☆
1957–1958 Series I 109PU	★★☆☆☆	★★★☆☆	★★★★☆	★★★☆☆
1958–1961 Series II 88	★★★☆☆	★★★★☆	★★★★☆	★★★★☆
1958–1961 Series II 109PU	★☆☆☆☆	★★★★☆	★★★★☆	★★★★☆
1958–1961 Series II 109SW	★★★☆☆	★★★☆☆	★★★★☆	★★★★☆
1962–1967 Series IIA 88	★★★☆☆	★★★★☆	★★★★★	★★★★☆
1962–1967 Series IIA 109 (SW w/ 4-cylinder)	★★★☆☆	★★★☆☆	★★★★★	★★★★☆
1962–1967 Series IIA 109 (SW w/orig 6-cyl)	★★★☆☆	★★★☆☆	★★★★★	★★★☆☆
1962–1967 Series IIA 109 (PU w/4-cyl)	★★★☆☆	★★★☆☆	★★★★★	★★★★☆
1968–1971 Series IIA 88	★★★☆☆	★★★★☆	★★★★☆	★★★★☆
1968–1971 Series IIA 109	★★★☆☆	★★★☆☆	★★★★☆	★★★★☆
1972–1974 Series III 88	★★★☆☆	★★★★☆	★★★★☆	★★★★☆
Forward Control (109 & 110)	★★☆☆☆	★★☆☆☆	★★★☆☆	★★★☆☆
Forward Control 101	★★☆☆☆	★★★☆☆	★★★☆☆	★★★☆☆
All Lightweight	★★☆☆☆	★★★★☆	★★★★☆	★★★☆☆
All Ambulance	★★☆☆☆	★★☆☆☆	★★☆☆☆	★★★☆☆

	Day-to-Day	Off-Highway	Investment Potential	Parts Availability
CHAPTER 7- CHEVROLET & GMC				
1960–1966 Chevy & GMC Pickups	★★☆☆☆	★★★☆☆	★★☆☆☆	★★★☆☆
1960–1966 Chevy & GMC Suburbans	★★★☆☆	★★★☆☆	★★★☆☆	★★★☆☆
1967–1972 Chevy & GMC Pickups	★★★☆☆	★★★☆☆	★★★★★	★★★★☆
1967–1972 Chevy & GMC Suburbans	★★★☆☆	★★★☆☆	★★★☆☆	★★★★☆
1969–1972 Blazer & Jimmy	★★★★☆	★★★★☆	★★★★☆	★★★★☆
CHAPTER 8- FORD				
1942–1944 GTB	★☆☆☆☆	★★★☆☆	★★★☆☆	★★☆☆☆
1959–1960 Pickups	★★☆☆☆	★★★☆☆	★★★☆☆	★★★☆☆
1961–1966 Pickups	★★☆☆☆	★★★☆☆	★★★☆☆	★★★★☆
1967–1972 Pickups	★★★☆☆	★★★☆☆	★★★☆☆	★★★★☆
1966–1977 Bronco	★★★☆☆	★★★★★	★★★★★	★★★★☆
Stroppe Bronco	★★★☆☆	★★★★★	★★★★★	★★★★☆
CHAPTER 9 -				
TOYOTA & NISSAN				
Nissan Patrol L-60	★★☆☆☆	★★★★★	★☆☆☆☆	★☆☆☆☆
Nissan Patrol KL-60	★★★☆☆	★★★★★	★☆☆☆☆	★☆☆☆☆
Toyota FJ-25	★★☆☆☆	★★★★★	★★★★☆	★☆☆☆☆
Toyota FJ-40 (1960–1965)	★★☆☆☆	★★★★★	★★★★☆	★★★☆☆
Toyota FJ-45L&S PU (1963–1967)	★★☆☆☆	★★★★☆	★★★☆☆	★★★☆☆
Toyota FJ-45V SW (1963–1967)	★★★☆☆	★★★★☆	★★★☆☆	★★★☆☆
Toyota FJ-40 (1966–1973)	★★☆☆☆	★★★★★	★★★★☆	★★★★☆
Toyota FJ-40 (1974–1984)	★★☆☆☆	★★★★★	★★★★★	★★★★☆
Toyota FJ-55 SW (1968–1980)	★★★☆☆	★★★★☆	★★★★☆	★★★☆☆
CHAPTER 10 - MISC				
Austin Champ	★★☆☆☆	★★★★☆	★☆☆☆☆	★☆☆☆☆
Austin Gypsy	★★☆☆☆	★★★★☆	★☆☆☆☆	★☆☆☆☆
Mercedes Unimog	★★☆☆☆	★★★★★	★★★☆☆	★★☆☆☆
M-151 MUTT	★☆☆☆☆	★★★★☆	★★☆☆☆	★★☆☆☆
M-422 Mighty-Mite	★☆☆☆☆	★★★★☆	★★☆☆☆	★★☆☆☆
M-274 Mule	★☆☆☆☆	★★★★☆	★★☆☆☆	★★☆☆☆
Suzuki Brute	★★☆☆☆	★★★★☆	★☆☆☆☆	★★☆☆☆

APPENDIX TWO

BIBLIOGRAPHY

Any author in a particular genre owes a debt to those who paved the way before him. Whether it be via inspiration or facts, either directly or indirectly, authors aid each other in perfecting knowledge. Here is a list of a few authors and books to whom the writer of this book is indebted.

All-American Wonder, Volume 1
1993 Ray Cowdery
USM Incorporated
ISBN: 0-910667-10-1

Boss: The Bill Stroppe Story
1984 Tom Madigan
Darwin Publications
ISBN: 0-933506-13-9

Chevy & GMC Light Truck Owners Bible
1995 Moses Ludel
Robert Bentley Publishers
ISBN: 0-8376-0157-6

Chevrolet Pickups 1946-1972
1988 John Gunnell
Motorbooks International
ISBN: 0-87938-282-1

Chevrolet Pickup Red Book
1993 Peter C. Sessler
Motorbooks International
ISBN: 0-87938-771-8

Dodge Military Vehicles, Collection 1
T. Richards
Brooklands Books
ISBN: 0-946489-27-0

Dodge Pickup Buyers Guide
1994 Don Bunn
Motorbooks International
ISBN: 0-87938-847-1

Dodge Pickups History and Restoration Guide 1918–1971
1991 Don Bunn & Tom Brownell
Motorbooks International
ISBN: 87938-491-3

Ford Bronco 1966–1977
R. M. Clark
Brooklands Books
ISBN: 1-85520-0384

Ford F-Series Pickup Owners Bible
1994 Moses Ludel
Robert Bentley Publishers
ISBN: 0-8376-0152-5

Ford Pickup Red Book
1993 Peter C. Sessler
Motorbooks International

ISBN: 0-87938-789-0
Ford Trucks Since 1905
1994 James K. Wagner
Motorbooks International
ISBN: 0-87938-906-0

The Four Wheel Drive Story
1954 Howard William Troyer
McGraw Hill Book Company
LCCCN: 54-7361

The Heavyweight Book of American Light Trucks
1988 Tom Brownell and Don Bunn
Motorbooks International
ISBN 087938-289-9

Indestructible Jeep
1973 D. Denfield, M. Fry
Ballantine Books

The Illustrated Encyclopedia of American Trucks
1996 Albert Mroz
Krause Publications
ISBN: 0-87341-368-7

International Pickup and Scout Buyers Guide
1993 Tom Brownell
Motorbooks International
ISBN: 0-87938-777-7

International Scout Gold Portfolio 1961–1980
R. M. Clark
Brooklands Books
ISBN: 1-85520-305-7

Jeep
1982 Michael Clayton
David & Charles Inc.
ISBN: 0-7153-8066-4

Jeep Owners Bible
1992 Moses Ludel
Robert Bentley Publishers
ISBN: 0-8376-0154-1

Land Rover — The Unbeatable 4x4 (Third Edition)
1989 K&J Slavin & G. N. Mackie
Haynes Publishing Company
ISBN: 0-85429-721-9

Maintenance Manual for Willys Truck
1942 TM-10-1513
Willys-Overland Motors, Inc.

The Marmon Heritage
1990 George & Stacey Hanley
Doyle Hyk Publishing
ISBN: 0-9615817-0-0

Military Vehicles of the World
1976 Christopher F. Foss
Charles Scribner's Sons
ISBN: 0-684-14678-9

Observers Fighting Vehicles Directory
1969 Bart Vanderveen
Frederick Warne & Co
ISBN: 0-7232-1034-9

Observers Army Vehicles Directory to 1940
1974 Bart Vanderveen
Frederick Warne & Co.
ISBN: 0-7232-1540-5

A Source Book of Military Wheeled Vehicles
1976 Bart Vanderveen
Ward Lock Limited
ISBN: 0-7063-1285-6

Standard Catalog of 4x4s
1993 Robert C. Ackerson
Krause Publications
ISBN: 0-87341-203-1

Selling the All-American Wonder
1997 Frederic L. Caldwell
USM Incorporated
ISBN: 0-910667-25-X

The Standard Catalog of American Light-duty Trucks
1993 John A. Gunnell
Krause Publications
ISBN: 0-87341-238-9

Standard Catalog of Military Vehicles
1995 Thomas Berndt
Krause Publications
ISBN: 0-87341-223-0

This Was Trucking
1966 Robert F. Karolevitz
Bonanza Books
LCCN 66-25421

The Story of Land Cruiser
1985 Yuichi Ishikawa
4x4 Magazine Co. Ltd.

3/4-Ton 4x4 M37/M37B1, M37CDN Canadian Vehicles:
The Production Story 1949-1968
1987 John Zentmeyer
Industrial Products Company

U.S. Military Vehicles of World War II
1970 E. J. Hoffshmidt, W. H. Tantum IV
WE Incorporated

U.S. Wheeled Military Vehicles
1994 Fred W. Crismon
Motorbooks International
ISBN: 0-87938-907-9

World Directory of Modern Military Vehicles
1983 Bart Vanderveen
Arco Publishing
ISBN: 0-668-06022-0

APPENDIX THREE

Classic and Collectable 4x4 Price Guide

This price guide is just that, a guide. It isn't intended as an engraved-in-stone "Bible," but the author did have the chance to talk to a number of acknowledged experts and recent buyers or sellers, and he consulted a variety of publications in making this guide. Many of the vehicles discussed in this book have never been priced in print.

It all boils down to this in the end—the more you pay, the more it's worth. Whether you are a buyer or seller, remember that rare doesn't necessarily equate to valuable. Value seems to have more to do with popularity than anything else. You may find that the really popular but relatively common rigs may bring a higher dollar price than the very rarest 4x4s.

Price Guide Classifications

General-The range of prices reflects the minor differences in trim or condition that one might find in a vehicle. They also reflect the pricing differences noted during sales research that may be indicative of popularity.

Class 1-A restorable vehicle but in rough condition. Could also be a fairly complete parts vehicle. Figure that a vehicle in this class could be missing a few nonvital parts or have some significant, but repairable, problems and it may or may not be a running vehicle. It is assumed that most of the major and important (read expensive) parts are still on the vehicle.

Class 2-Generally a running vehicle in good overall condition and fairly complete but still needing some work. Vehicles in this class are generally good runners and probably capable of being a daily driver. May be a good original vehicle or an old restoration showing its age.

Class 3-Either a stored-in-the-barn outstanding original or a restoration. For the purposes of defining the term, a restoration is *not* a concours style, 95-point show job that lives on a trailer. For this guide, a restored truck is a vehicle put back to factory specifications—no better no worse—and then driven sensibly and maintained in an excellent state. The minor wear and tear of an owner enjoying his vehicle is not counted against it here. Concours style restorations are not uncommon and if that standard is worth more to you, that difference in price is something to be worked out between you and your pocketbook.

Vehicle	Class 1	Class 2	Class 3
Chapter 1- Pioneers			
FWD Touring Car	3–5,000	8–12,000	18–30,000
FWD Model B	200–1,000	3–6,000	7–15,000
FWD Model LD	2–800	1–3,000	5–8,000
Jefferey Quad, 1913–1916	200–1,000	3–7,000	9–18,000
Nash Quad,1916–1919	2–800	2–4,000	7–10,000
Nash Quad, 1920–1928	500–1,500	4–7,000	10–18,000
Duplex (under 2 ton)	500–1,000	3–5,000	7–10,000
Oshkosh (under 2 ton)	500–1,000	3–5,000	7–10,000
Other Antique 4x4s	200–1,000	1–6,000	8–15,000
Chapter 2- Conversions			
Coleman Light Truck Conversions			
Chevy, 1946–1953	400–1,000	1–2500	4–6,500
Chevy, 1954–1956	400–1,500	2–2,500	5–8,000
Dodge, 1946–1947	300–1,000	1–1,800	3–5,500
Dodge, 1948–1953	100–800	1–1,500	2–5,000
Dodge, 1954–1956	300–1,000	1–1,800	3–6,000
Ford, 1948–1952	300–1,000	1–1,500	3–5,500
Ford, 1953–1956	300–1,000	1–2,000	3–6,000
Notes: Add 5 percent for V8 when applicable.			
Marmon-Herrington Light Truck Conversions			
Ford PU, 1937–1939	400–1,000	15–2,000	3–5,500
Ford Sedan, Coupe, all yrs.	800–1,500	4–6,000	10–15,000
Ford Woody, all yrs.	25–3,800	6–8,500	12–19,000
Ford PU, 1940–1945	300–800	2–3,000	5–7,000
Ford PU, 1946–1952	350–850	22–3,200	55–7,500
Ford PU, 1953–1956	400–900	25–3,500	6–8,000
Ford PU, 1957–1958	250–600	15–2,500	4–6,000
Ford Panel (MH Ranger) 1950	500–900	25–3,500	5–7,000
Ford Panel (MH Ranger) 1951–1956	750–1,250	35–4,500	6–8,000
Notes: Add 5 percent for V8 when applicable.			

NAPCO Light Truck Conversions (Kits & GM factory insto)

Vehicle	Class 1	Class 2	Class 3
Chevy PU (First Series) 1950–1955	450–1500	2–3,000	5–7,000
Suburban (First Series) 1950–1955	500–1,600	25–3,500	55–7,500
GMC PU, 1950–1955	400–1,000	18–2,500	45–6,500
GMC Suburban 1950–1955	450–1,500	2–3,000	5–7,000
Chevy PU, 1955–1956	550–1,500	2–3,000	55–8,000
Chevy PU, 1957–1959	550–1,500	2–3000	55–8,000
Chevy Suburban, 1957–1959	600–1800	25–3,500	66–10,000
GMC PU, 1956–1959	500–1,000	15–2,500	45–7,000
GMC Suburban, 1956–1959	550–1,500	2–3,000	55–8,000
Studebaker PU, 1958–1964	650–1,800	4–6,500	7–10,000
Notes: Add 10 percent for V8 when applicable.			
Chapter 3- Dodge			
1940 VC Command & Radio	15–2,500	4–6,000	8–12,000
1940 VC PU	500–1,000	2–4,000	6–8,000
1940 VC Panel	15–3,500	5–7,000	9–15,000
1941–1942 WC 1/2 ton, PU Closed	600–1,500	3–5,000	7–10,000
1941–1942 WC 1/2 ton, PU Open	400–1,000	25–4,500	6–9,000
1941–1942 WC 1/2 ton, command car	1–2,000	4–6,000	8–12,000
1941–1942 WC 1/2 ton, all others	500–1,200	27–4,800	65–9,500
1942–1945 WC 3/4 ton, command car	15–2,500	4–6,000	9–12,000
1942–1945 WC 3/4 ton, carryall	900–1,800	3–5,000	75–10,500
1942–1945 WC 3/4 ton, all others	400–1,000	2–4,000	6–8,000
1946–1947 WDX Power Wagon	1–2,000	3–5,000	75–10,000
1948–1956 B & C Power Wagon	500–1,000	15–3,000	55–8,000
1957–1960 W300M Power Wagon	400–800	1–2,500	4–6,000

1961–1968 WM-300 Power Wagon	700–1,500	25–4,500	65–8,500
1950–1964 M-37, all types	300–800	12–2,500	4–5,000
1957–1960 W-100, W200	400–900	15–3,000	45–6,000
1958–1960 W-300	300–700	12–2,500	35–4,500
1957–1960 Town Wagon	500–1,000	18–3,000	4–5,500
1961–1971 W-100, W-200 Sweptline	300–500	900–2,000	3–4,500
1961–1971 W-100, W-200 Utiline	400–600	1–2,200	32–4,600
1961–1971 W-300	500–800	1–2,000	3–4,000
1961–1971 Town Wagon	400–800	15–2,500	4–5,500

Notes: Add $300 for winch. Add 8 percent for V8 on 1957-71. Add $150 for 4-speed or auto 1957–1971. Add $150 for PS 1957–1960.

Chapter 4- Jeep

1941 Bantam BRC-40	3–5,000	7–9,000	11–20,000
1941 Ford GP	15–3,000	4–6,000	8–15,000
1941 Willys MA	7–10,000	12–18,000	22–30,000
1942 Willys MB Slat-Grille	900–1,500	3–5,000	7–10,000
1942–1945 Willys MB	700–1,200	25–4,500	6–9,000
1942–1945 Ford GPW	700–1,200	25–4,500	6–9,000
1942–1943 Ford GPA	15–2,500	4–6,000	9–12,000
1944–1945 CJ-2	2–3,000	5–7,000	9–15,000
1945–1946 CJ-2a early	800–1,500	22–4,000	6–9,000
1946–1949 CJ-2A late	400–900	18–3,000	5–7,500
1949–1953 CJ-3A	400–900	18–3,000	5–7,500
1950–1952 M-38	600–1,000	2–4,000	55–8,500
1953–1968 CJ-3B	400–900	18–3,000	5–7,500
1952–1957 M-38A1	300–800	15–3,500	5–7,000
1954–1979 CJ-5 (except specials)	400–1000	15–5,500	3–7,000
1964–1968 Tuxedo Park	500–900	25–3,500	45–6,500
1969 "462" Special	400–700	15–2,500	35–5,000
1970 Renegade I	400–700	18–2,800	37–5,200
1971 Renegade II	400–700	18–2,800	37–5,200
1973 Super Jeep	400–1,000	25–3,500	4–7,000
1972–1975 Renegade V8	500–1,000	25–3,500	55–7,500
1976–1979 Renegade	600–1,000	2–3,000	5–6,500
1955–1975 CJ-6	400–1,000	15–3,500	4–6,000
1976–1979 CJ-7	600–1,000	2–3,000	5–6,500
1976–1978 CJ7 (V8)	600–1,000	28–3,800	58–7,800
1957–1959 FC-150, narrow track	400–600	15–2,500	3–5,000
1959–1965 FC-150, wide track	500–700	18–2,800	35–5,500
1957–1965 FC-170	500–700	18–2,800	35–5,500
FC M-series Military Models	900–1,500	25–3,500	4–6,500
1947–1963 Pickups	400–900	15–2,500	35–5,000
1946–1963 Station Wagon	450–950	16–2,600	38–5,800
1967–1971 Jeepster	500–1,000	2–3,000	3–5,000
1967–1971 Commando SW	300–800	15–2,500	3–4,000
1967–1971 Commando Roadster	300–800	15–2,500	3–4,000
1971–1973 Commando	300–800	15–2,500	3–4,000
1962–1969 Gladiator PU	200–600	1–2,000	25–3,500
1962–1969 Wagoneer, 2dr	300–700	12–2,200	28–3,800
1962–1969 Wagoneer, 4dr	350–750	13–2,300	29–3,900
1965–1969 Super Wagoneer	450–900	15–2,500	32–4,000

Notes: Add 10 percent for V8 on models where applicable. Add 10 percent for V6 on models where it was optional. Add $150 for automatic trans or 4-speed on models where it was optional. Add $150 for winch.

Chapter 5- IHC

1942–1945 M-1-4	600–1,000	25–3,500	45–7,500
1942–1945 M-2-4	500–900	22–3,200	42–7,200
1953–1955 R-series PU	500–900	2–3,000	4–6,000
1955–1956 S-series PU	300–600	15–2,500	3–4,500
1955–1956 S-series Travelall	600–1,000	22–3,500	4–5,500
1957–1958 A-series PU	250–500	1–1,800	2–4,000
1957–1958 A-series Travelette PU	550–900	25–3,500	4–4,500
1957–1958 A-series Travelall	600–1,000	25–3,500	4–5,500
1959–1960 B-series PU	250–500	1–1,500	2–4,000
1959–1960 B-series Travelette PU	500–850	2–3,000	35–5,000
1959–1960 B-series Travelall	600–1,000	25–3,500	4–5,500
1961–1968 C-series PU	350–550	12–1,800	22–4,500
1961–1968 C-series Travelette PU	350–550	12–1,800	22–4,500
1961–1968 C-series Travelall	450–950	16–2,500	35–4,500
1969–1975 D-series PU	500–900	2–2,500	3–4,200
1969–1975 D-series Travelette PU	450–950	15–2,500	3–4,000
1969–1975 D-series Travelall	600–1,000	18–2,500	35–4,500
1961–1964 Scout 80	400–800	15–2,500	3–4,000
1965–1968 Scout 800	500–900	18–2,800	32–4,200
1965–1968 Scout 800 Turbo	500–900	19–2,900	32–4,400
1966–1968 Scout 800 V8	700–1,200	22–3,200	35–4,500
1969 Scout 800A Aristocrat	700–1,300	26–3,600	4–5,500
1969–1971 Scout 800A&B 4&6cyl	500–900	15–2,500	3–4,000
1969–1971 Scout 800A&B V8	600–1,000	22–3,500	35–4,500
1970–1971 Scout 800A SR-2	700–1,300	25–3,500	4–5,200
1972–1980 Scout II, 4 & 6cyl (except specials below)	600–900	15–2,200	3–4,000
1972–1980 Scout II, V8 (except specials below)	700–1,000	18–2,500	32–4,500
1977–1980 Scout II SSII	600–900	2–2,800	35–4,700
Scout II w/CVI package	1–1,500	25–3,500	45–6,000
Scout II Midnight Star	1–1,500	25–3,500	45–6,500
Scout Terra PU	600–900	18–2,500	3–4,000
Scout Traveler	600–900	19–2,600	32–4,200

Notes: Deduct 5 percent for normally aspirated diesel engine. Add 3 percent for Rallye Package. Add 2 percent for 392 V8 in trucks. Add $150 for 4-speed or automatic transmission. Add $150 for 345 V8 in Scout II.

Chapter 6- Land Rover

1948–1953 Series I 80	500–1,000	25–3,500	4,500–6,500
1954–1956 Series I 86	400–900	2–3,000	4–6,000
1954–1956 Series I 107PU	800–1,200	35–4,500	45–7,000
1955–1958 Series I 107SW	1–1,500	4–5,500	65–8,000
1957–1958 Series I 88	400–900	2–3,000	4–6,000
1957–1958 Series I 109PU	400–900	2–3,000	4–6,000
1958–1961 Series II 88	600–1,000	35–4,800	55–7,500
1958–1961 Series II 109PU	600–1,000	35–4,800	55–7,500
1958–1961 Series II 109SW	600–1,000	4–5,000	6–8,000
1962–1967 Series IIA 88	700–1,200	42–5,200	65–8,500
1962–1967 Series IIA 109 (SW w/4-cylinder)	700–1,200	4–5,000	55–7,500
1962–1967 Series IIA 109 (SW w/orig 6-cyl)	800–1,300	5–6,000	75–8,500
1962–1967 Series IIA 109 (PU w/4–cyl)	1–1,600	4–5,000	55–7,500
1968–1971 Series IIA 88	1–1,800	4–5,000	6–8,000

1968–1971 Series IIA 109	1–1,600	5–6,000	7–8,000
1972–1974 Series III 88	800–1,300	4–5,000	6–7,500
Forward Control 109 &110	700–1,000	35–4,500	6–7,000
Forward Control 101	15–2,500	6–7,000	8–9,000
All Lightweight	8–1,200	55–6,500	75–8,500
All Ambulance	600–900	25–4,500	6–7,000

Notes: Add $300 for winch. Add $350 for tropical roof where applicable. Add 2 percent for Deluxe interior.

Chapter 7- Chevrolet & GMC

1960–1966 Chevy & GMC PU	500–1,100	15–2,500	4–5,500
1960–1966 Chevy & GMC Suburbans	400–1,000	12–2,000	35–5,000
1967–1972 Chevy & GMC PU	800–1,500	25–3,500	45–6,500
1967–1972 Chevy & GMC Suburbans	600–1,200	2–3,000	4–5,500
1969–1972 Blazer & Jimmy	800–1,500	25–3,500	45–6,500

Notes: Add 5 percent for V8 in 1960-64. Add $150 for 4-speed or automatic. Add 5 percent for CST or Cheyenne Package where applicable. Add $150 for A/C. Add $150 for winch.

Chapter 8- Ford

1942–1944 GTB	800–1,500	3–4,500	55–7,000
1959–1960 PU, Styleside	400–900	15–2,500	35–5,000
1959–1960 PU, Flareside	550–1,000	18–2,800	4–6,000
1961–1966 PU, Styleside	400–900	15–2,500	35–5,000
1961–1966 PU, Flareside	550–1,000	18–2,800	4–6,000

1966 PU, SWB Flareside	550–1,000	18–2,800	4–6,000
1967–1972 Pickups	500–900	15–2,500	35–4,500
1966–1973 Bronco	700–1,200	25–4,500	55–7,500
1974–1977 Bronco	800–1,300	28–4,800	6–8,000
Stroppe Bronco	15–2,500	55–7,500	95–15,000

Notes: Add 5 percent for V8 in PU. Add 10 percent for V8 in Bronco where applicable. Add $150 for automatic or 4-speed in PU. Add $250 for automatic in Bronco.

Chapter 9 - Toyota & Nissan

Nissan Patrol L-60 & KL-60	100–400	800–1,250	2–3,000
Toyota FJ-25, 1958–1959	600–900	15–2,500	4–6,000
Toyota FJ-40, 1960–1965	750–1,050	25–3,500	45–6,500
Toyota FJ-45L&S PU	700–1,000	2–3,000	45–6,500
Toyota FJ-45V SW	500–900	15–2,500	35–5,500
Toyota FJ-40, 1967–1973	800–1,100	28–3,800	5–7,500
Toyota FJ-40, 1974–1983	800–1,500	3–4,000	55–8,000
Toyota FJ-55 SW	600–950	15–2,500	35–5,500

Chapter 10 - Odd, Uncommon & Obscure

Austin Champ	100–250	800–1,200	2–3,000
Austin Gypsy	150–350	900–1,500	25–3,500
Mercedes Unimog	15–2,500	4–5,500	65–9,000
M-151 MUTT	500–900	2–3,500	45–6,500
M-422 Mighty-Mite	650–1,000	25–4,000	5–7,000
M-274 Mule	400–800	12–1,800	2–3,500
Suzuki Brute	250–550	900–1,500	2–3,000

APPENDIX FOUR
COLLECTOR RESOURCES

Enthusiast Organizations
General-
American Truck Historical Society
PO Box 531168
Birmingham, AL 35253-1168

Antique Truck Club of America
PO Box 291
Hershey, PA 17033

Military-
Military Vehicle Preservation Association
PO Box 520378
Independence, MO 64052
(816) 737-5111
(816) 737-5423 fax
http://users.aol.com/supplyline/mvpa/mvpa.html

Brand Specific-
International Harvester
Scout and IH Light Truck Association
4026 Senour Road
Indianapolis, IN 46239
(217) 582-2689

Binder Bunch
7371 South Eudora Way
Littleton, CO 80122
(303) 779-8353

East Coast Binders
20 Charles Street
Williston Park, NY 11596
(516) 248-8922

Northwest Binders
29525 38th Place South
Auburn, WA 98001
(206) 475-5232

Sonora Desert Scouts
PO Box 62421
Phoenix, AZ 85082-2421
(602) 970-0541

Scout Owners of Texas
1910 Quail Green Street
Missouri City, TX 77489-3041
(713) 499-7498

Scouts West
1925 W. Orange
Orange, CA 92667
(714) 992-5345

Sierra Nevada Scouts
14549-B Oak Leaf Lane
Grass Valley, CA 95945

Southern Scouts
PO Box 29372
Greensboro, NC 27429

West Texas IH Club
5720 66th St. #249
Lubbock, TX 79424

Jeep-
Forward Control Willys Jeep Association
PO Box 343
Stevensville, MT 59870

Jeep Registry
172 Long Hill Road
Oakland, NJ 07436-3113
(201) 405-0480

The Willys Club
Willys World
PO Box 5466
Plainfield, NJ 07060

West Coast Willys
4000 Green Valley Road
Suisun, CA 94585

Land Rover-
Bay State Rover Association
PO Box 342
North Scituate, MA 02060

Blue Ridge Land Rover Club
PO Box 507
Parkersburg, WV 26102-0507

Flatland Rover Society
16007 W. 82nd Place
Lenexa, KS 66219

Land Rover Owners Association
PO Box 130
Walnut Creek, CA 94597

Ottawa Valley Land Rovers
1016 Normandy Crescent
Ottawa, Ontario
Canada, K2C 0L4

Rover Owner's Association Of Virginia
1633 Melrose Parkway
Norfolk, VA 23508-1730

Solihull Society
Box 916
Monument, CO 80132

Studebaker-
Studebaker Drivers Club (Many Regional Chapters)
PO Box 28788
Dallas, TX 75228
(800) 527-3452

Toyota-
FJ-45 Wagon Registry
4741 Montgomery Avenue
Downers Grove, IL 60515
(630) 968-7820

Toyota Land Cruiser Association
1495 Gunview Road
Windsor, CA 95492
(707) 837-7353

Parts & Service
General-
Beechwood Canvas Works
PO Box 137
Island Heights, NJ 08732
(908) 929-3168
Reproduction canvas tops, seat covers, straps and welting.

Classic Carburetors
3116 E. Shea Blvd
Phoenix, AZ 85034
(602) 971-3300
Carburetors, kits, & rebuilding of early carbs 1916–1960.

Coker Tires
1317 Chestnut Street
Chattanooga, TN 37402
(800) 251-6336
Vintage truck tires, including solid rubber.

Eastwood Company
580 Lancaster Avenue, Box 3014
Malvern, PA 19355
(800) 345-1178
Restoration products and supplies.

Egge Machine
11707 Slauson Avenue
Santa Fe Springs, CA 90670
(800) 866-3443
Manufactures or remanufactures vintage engine hard parts from "Day One" to about 1970, including pistons, valves, cams, etc.

Idaho Engine Welding
2600 Shoshone Road
Idaho Falls, ID 83401
(800) 255-6743
Block, head, and cast iron repairs, major to minor.

George Pounden
1520 High School Road
Sebastapol, CA 95472
(707) 823-3824
Magneto repair and rewinding.

Kohnke Machine
60615 330th Avenue
Clare, IA 50524
(515) 546-4551
Re-babbitt bearings, poured and insert types.

Olson's Gasket
3059 Opdall Road
Port Orchard, WA 98366
(360) 871-1207
Antique and vintage gaskets.

Paul Weaver's Garage
680 Sylvan Way
Bremerton, WA 98310
(360) 373-7870
Obscure, obsolete piston rings from day one, all makes.

Precision Wiring Service
4 Leavenworth Road
Eldred, NY 12732
(914) 557-6156
Reproduction wiring harnesses for trucks from 1920–1960.

Brand Specific-
Chevrolet, GMC & NAPCO
Jim Carter Antique Truck Parts
1508 East Alton
Independence, MO 64055
(816) 833-1913
(800) 262-3749 fax
New, used and reproduction 1934–1972 Chevy, GMC and NAPCO Parts.

Pickups Northwest
7136 Dickford Avenue
Snohomish, WA 95290
(360) 568-9166
Chevy & GMC trucks, 1932-1972.

The Truck Shop
PO Box 5035
Nashville, GA 31639
(800) 245-0556
Chevy & GMC truck parts, 1927–1987.

Coleman
Howe Brothers Inc.
16 Sweetmilk Creek Road
Troy, NY 12180
(518) 279-3421
(518) 279-1907 fax
Many new Coleman front axle parts in stock.

Dodge Power Wagon
Adirondack Dodge Parts
803 State Street, Box 99
Prospect, NY 13435
(800) 932-8020
New and used parts for 1950-68 M-37 Dodge Power Wagon.

Kanter Auto Products
76 Monroe Street
Boonton, NJ 07005
(800) 526-1096
Hard to find Dodge engine parts, 1934–1980.

Roberts Motor Parts
17 Prospect Street
West Newbury, MA 01985
(508) 363-5881
Early Dodge truck and Power Wagon parts.

Sultan Dodge Truck Parts
4753 S. Pacific Hwy.
Phoenix, OR 97535-9602
(541) 535-3522
sultan@opendoor.com e-mail

Vintage Power Wagons
302 S. 7th Street
Fairfield, IA 52556
(515) 472-4665
New, used, reproduction 1940–1972 civilian and military Dodge Power Wagon parts and vehicles.

Ford/Marmon-Herrington
Chuck's Trucks
1521 Shepard Avenue
Hamden, CT 06518
(203) 287-9830
chuck4850@aol.com
1932–1979 Ford and Marmon-Herrington NOS, new, used parts and vehicles.

James Duff Enterprises
PO Box 696
Sequim, WA 98382-0696
(206) 683-2160
Everything for early Bronco.

K Bar S
3753 Scripps Way
Las Vegas, NV 89133
(800) 266-1941
Everything for early Bronco.

Tom's Bronco Parts
2294 Sage Road
Medford, OR 97501
(503) 779-1339
New and used early Bronco parts.

Vintage Broncos
8925 E. Florian Avenue
Mesa, AZ 85208
(602) 986-6689
Everything for early Bronco.

IHC Scouts and Trucks
Coonrods
49352 Hwy 285, PO Box 146
Grant, CO 80448
(800) 276-8505
Acres of used IHC Scout and truck parts.

Giddem' Up Scout
3625 N. Stone Avenue
Colorado Springs, CO 80907
(719) 632-8294
New & used Scout parts and accessories.

Scout Connection
5908 Avenue O
Fort Madison, IA 52627
(319) 372-3272
New and used Scout parts.

Scout M.A.D.ness
5403 89th St.
Lubbock, TX 79424
(806) 745-7475
http://www.maroon.com/madness
New, used and reproduction Scout parts and restorations.
Jeep (Incl Willys, Kaiser & AMC)
Army Jeep Parts
PO Box 1006
Bristol, PA 19007
(215) 788-6012
Military Jeep parts and supplies.

Border Parts
PO Box 501
La Mesa, CA 92041
(800) 533-0171
Jeep parts, 1942–1995.

Brent Mullins Jeep Parts
Po Box 9599
College Station, TX 77842
(409) 690-0203
Military and early Jeep parts.

D&L Bensinger
2442 Main Street
Narvon, PA 17555
(610) 286-9545
Miliary vehicle parts and restorations. Mighty Mites a specialty.

The FC Connection
PO Box 237
New Melle, MO 63365
(314) 828-4290
Jeep Forward Control parts.

Ken Hake's Jeep Parts
607 N. Main, Box 126
Tipton, KS 67485
(913) 373-4145
(9130 373-5295 fax
Restoration of Jeeps, specializing in prototype Willys MA, Ford GP, and Bantam BRC-40. Also has a wide selection of impossible to find NOS and reproduction parts for these vehicles.

The Jeepsterman
238 Ramtown Greenville Road
Howell, NJ 07731
(732) 458-3966
Jeep parts from 1942 to the present, including rubber parts, and literature.

Mepco 4x4 Warehouse
7520 S. 620 W.
Midvale, UT 84047
(800) 388-5337
New Jeep parts from 1942 up.

S&J Salvage
2931 Hwy 92
Hotchkiss, CO 81419
(800) 598-3666
Used Jeep parts, all years and types

Willys Jeep Parts
PO Box 11468
Yuma, AZ 85366
(602) 343-9216
1941-63 Willys Jeep parts.

Land Rover
Atlantic British
PO Box 110
Mechanicville, NY 12118
(800) 533-2210
(518) 664-6641
New & used Land Rover parts, 1948 to present.

British Pacific
3317 Burton Avenue
Burbank, CA 91504
(800) 554-4133
New and used Land Rover parts, 1948 to present.

Campart Distributors Ltd.
221 41st Ave. N.E.
Calgary, Alberta
Canada, T2E 2N4
(403) 276-2211
New parts, 1948 to present.

Rovers North
1319 Vt Rte 128
Westford, VT 05494-9601
(802) 879-0032
rovers@together.net
New and used Land Rover parts, 1948 to present, restorations.

Mercedes Benz Unimog
Michael's Classics
954 Montauk Hwy.
Bayport, NY 11705
(516) 363-4200
Used Unimogs and parts.

Seth Kuzner
PO Box 22500
Telluride, CO 81535
(970) 728-6869
Used Unimogs for sale.

United Parts Service
Unimog Erzatsteile
PO Box 827
Palo Alto, CA 94302
(415) 364-9184
(415) 365-7384 fax
Unimog parts, literature and vehicle sales.

M-151 MUTT
Riv-Rad Inc.
1181 East Main Street
Riverhead, NY 11901
(516) 727-2792
New and used M-151 parts.

Nissan Patrol
Advance Adaptors
U.S. Agent for Mark's Adaptors, Australia
PO Box 247
Paso Robles, CA 93446
(805) 238-7000
Five-speed transmission
Ford six-cylinder Engine adaptor kit

Four Wheel Drives
304 Middleborough Road
Blackburn South, Victoria 3130 Australia
011-61-613-9890-0500
011-61-613-9898-6374 fax
Nissan Patrol parts, new and used.

Specter Off-Road
21600 Nordhoff Street
Chatsworth, CA 91311
(818) 882-1238
(818) 882-7144 fax
New and used parts.

Studebaker
Newman & Altman
PO Box 4276
South Bend, IN 46634
(800) 722-4295
(219) 287-3386fax
New, used and reproduction parts. Can research vehicle history via their extensive record collection.

Suzuki Brute
Victory Engineering
4117 West 159th Street
Lawndale, CA 90260
(310) 793-8585
New & used Suzuki parts.

American Suzuki Motor Company
Call 1(800) 650-4445 for the dealer nearest you, or 1(800) 934-0934 for help from customer relations.

Toyota
Con Fer
123 South Front Street
Burbank, CA 91502-1983
(213) 849-1800
New Land Cruiser parts and more.

Downey Off Road Manufacturing
10001 S. Pioneer Blvd.
Santa Fe Springs, CA 90670
(310) 949-9494
New and aftermarket parts for Toyota trucks and Land Cruiser.

Man-A-Fre
5076 Chesebro Road
Agoura, CA 91301
(818) 991-6689
New, OE and performance parts for Land Cruiser.

Ozone Off-Road Center
4623 Canyon Ridge Road
Reno, NV 89503
(702) 747-5445
New, used, reproduction parts and vehicles.

Specter Off-Road
21600 Nordhoff Street
Chatsworth, CA 91311
(818) 882-1238
(818) 882-7144 fax
New, used, reproduction parts and vehicles.

TLC
14743 Oxnard Street
Van Nuys, CA 91411
(818) 785-2200
(818) 785-2209 fax
Restoration of Toyota Land Cruiser.

Specialist Publications & Literature
Binder Books
PO Box 230269
Tigard, OR 97281-0269
(503) 684-2024
Books, information, and literature on International Harvester.

Bob Johnson Auto Literature
21 Blanden Avenue
Framingham, MA 01702
(800) 334-0688
(508) 626-0991 FAX
102433.100@compuserve.com E-MAIL
Original and reproduction service and owners manuals, sale literature. Hours 1 A.M. *to 6* P.M. *EDT.*

Land Rover Owner Magazine
Anglian House, Chapel Lane
Botesdale, Diss, Norfolk IP221DT England
011-441-370-890056 (from U.S.)

Military Vehicles Magazine
12-N4 Indianhead
Morristown, NJ 07960
Bimonthly magazine covering military vehicles from 1935–1975.

Portrayal Press
Box 1190
Andover, NJ 07821
(201) 579-5781
Reproduction Jeep and Dodge manuals, plus a variety of military truck manuals.

This Old Truck
PO Box 562
Yellow Springs, OH 45387
(800) 767-5828
Bimonthly magazine on restored old trucks.

Walter Miller
6710 Brooklawn
Syracuse, NY 13211
(315) 432-8282
Original sales literature and manuals.

INDEX